PICASSO

Pascal Bonafoux

PICASSO

The Self-Portraits

T&H

Translated from the French by Bethany Wright

First published in the United Kingdom in 2022 by
Thames & Hudson Ltd, 181A High Holborn,
London WC1V 7QX

First published in the United States of America in 2023 by
Thames & Hudson Inc., 500 Fifth Avenue, New York, New York 10110

First published in France under the title
Picasso par Picasso by Pascal Bonafoux

Edited and typeset by Andrew Brown at Art Books Publishing Ltd

British Library Cataloguing-in-Publication Data
A catalogue record for this book is available from the British Library

Library of Congress Control Number 2022938460

ISBN 978-0-500-02583-3

Printed and bound in China by C&C Offset Printing Co. Ltd

FSC
www.fsc.org
MIX
Paper | Supporting responsible forestry
FSC® C008047

Contents

9 Over to you!

95 The Self-Portraits

206 List of illustrations
214 Prologue by Cervantes
217 Bibliography
221 Postscript
223 Picture credits

I am me again, exactly as I am not.

Fernando Pessoa,
The Book of Disquiet

This 'I' is that of my 'work'.

Paul Valéry, *Cahiers I*, 'Ego'

A work of art is just a beautiful lie.

Stendhal, *A Roman Journal*

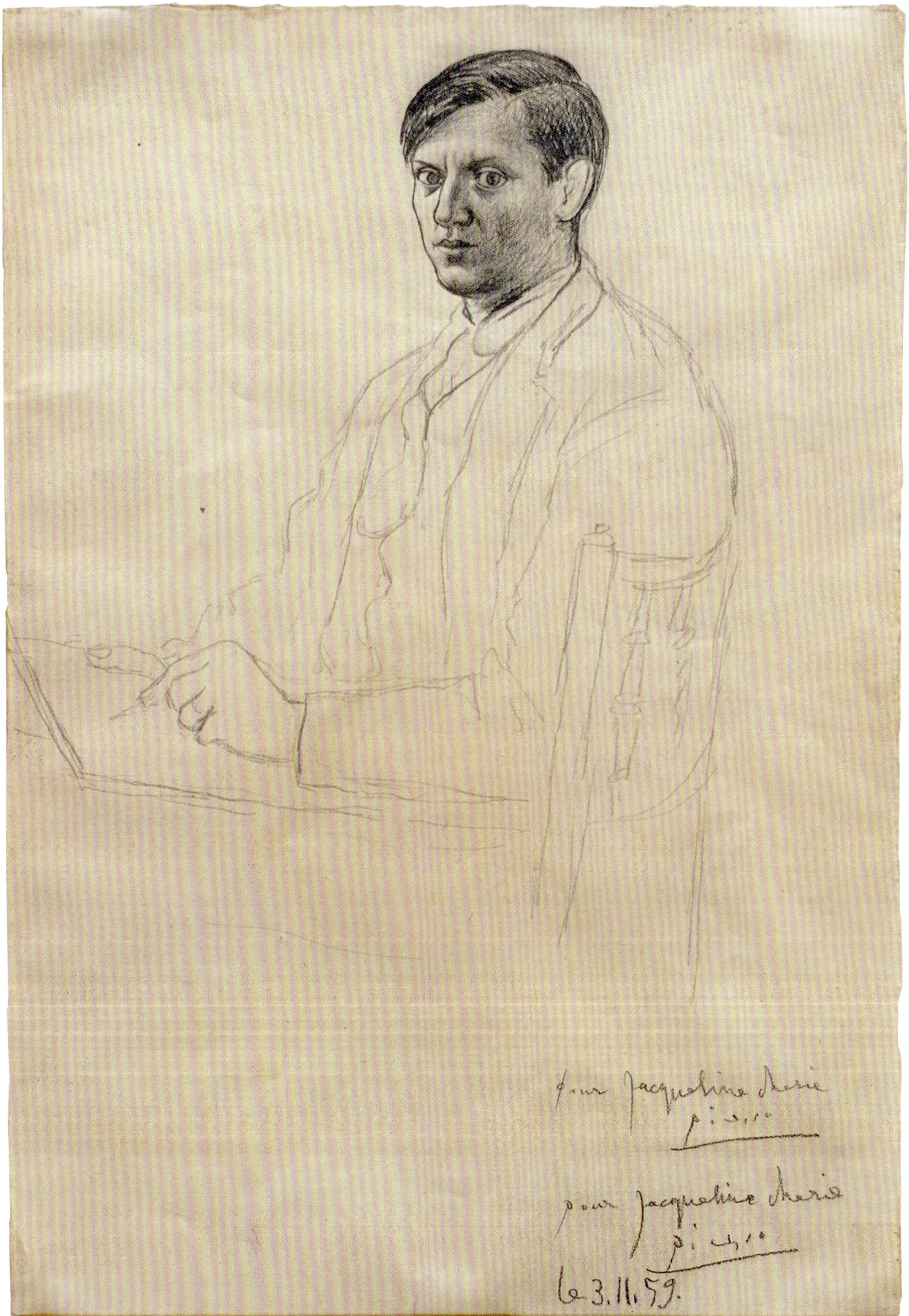
pour Jacqueline Marie
Picasso
pour Jacqueline Marie
Picasso
le 3.11.59.

Over to you!

One evening during dinner, Jacqueline Picasso asked me how I came to spend two years at the Villa Medici, as a fellow at the French Academy in Rome (perhaps she was afraid that I would tell her that I had earned my place as a painter or a sculptor). The thesis that I had defended a few months before the selection competition was on the subject of self-portraits in Western painting, at the time an underexplored area of research. That, along with my desire to work with the collections held at the Accademia di San Luca in Rome and that of the Grand Dukes of Tuscany at the Uffizi Gallery in Florence, which dates back to the seventeenth century and boasts hundreds of examples, convinced the jury that, as an art historian, I would not be stealing a place from someone more deserving.

Jacqueline asked if I had referred to Pablo's self-portraits in my research. I had limited myself to quoting Brassaï's story about Picasso learning of Guillaume Apollinaire's death in November 1918 while shaving in front of a mirror at the Hôtel Lutetia; afterwards, Brassaï asserted, he could not bear to look in mirrors and had stopped drawing and painting himself. I had never questioned the veracity of this claim.

I should have done ... because, Jacqueline told me, Brassaï was wrong. Pablo never gave up making drawings, paintings, or even etchings of himself – as I would easily discover. It should not be too difficult, with her help, to collect all of his self-portraits for the book I should write. I would simply need to do what I had never dared, she said: to ignore what others had written about Picasso (the surname by which she rarely referred to him) when they claimed to be quoting the painter's own words accurately. I would also need to avoid accepting at face value and repeating the claims that he had depicted himself as a Harlequin, as a Minotaur.... Although he had never been the same, he had always been himself. That includes the occasion when, at not yet twenty years old, he playfully donned a wig to paint a self-portrait (29). This was the first indication (considered by some to date to 1896 and by others to 1897 or 1900) of the metamorphoses to follow.

A few days later, while I was putting together the exhibition *Picasso: The Music Room in Mougins*, which opened at the Centre culturel du Marais in 1982, Jacqueline Picasso came to show me the self-portrait that he had dedicated to her, *For dear Jacqueline, Picasso. 3.11.59*. (In the exhibition catalogue, published in spring of that year, it appears on page 11.) It is a self-portrait in pencil drawn in 1917 (1). In it, Picasso is seated and drawing with his left hand – because he was looking at himself in the mirror. His chair, jacket, waistcoat, and shirt, as well as the paper resting on his knees, are roughly sketched in, and the artist's face at thirty-six – perhaps thirty-seven, if the drawing was finished after his birthday on 25 October – is the only part that is shaded. I ventured to remark that in 1959, the year of the dedication, Picasso no longer resembled this young man. I was not wrong. Jacqueline told me that the artist had kept many of the self-portraits that he had drawn and painted years earlier, stored in boxes or hung on the walls of his house in the Californie neighbourhood of Cannes and at Notre-Dame-de-Vie, his villa in Mougins. In 1971, Arlette Perrenoud photographed one of those painted in 1906 that was hanging on a wall in Notre-Dame-de-Vie (106, 107). Why? Jacqueline assured me that if he had needed one or other of the portraits, he would have been able to find it quickly. When I asked if she could say how many of his self-portraits we would need to track down, she replied that I seemed to be confusing her with Christian Zervos, the famous art historian and cataloguer of Picasso's work. Shamefaced, I nodded. 'Over to you!' she challenged me.

After Jacqueline Picasso's tragic death by suicide at Notre-Dame-de-Vie on 15 October 1986, I was determined to keep the promise that I had made to her. 'Over to you', she had said, and I had replied, 'Challenge accepted.' I promised to write the book, although I said that I would need time. 'Take your time.' I did.

Over the years that followed, month after month, I read everything that I could find about Picasso, almost at random. Books and catalogues. And I took every opportunity to visit museums where

I could find his self-portraits. I took my notebook with me, as it is only when standing in front of the work itself, taking in its size and physical presence, that you can (perhaps) understand something of it. And, month after month, these 'encounters' with Picasso's works, and with the biographies, essays, and prefaces that I read and annotated, awoke in me a strange sense of unease – muted at first, creeping, but inescapable. I put off the task at hand.... And time slipped by.

For years, I found all sorts of excuses to ignore the project. But, for better or worse, through my museum visits and my reading, I was slowly putting together a catalogue of Picasso's self-portraits, one that it seemed would always be hopelessly incomplete. Because – and this was the most worrying aspect for me – some of them undeniably challenged the very concept of the self-portrait. It was not simply about likeness: Picasso by Picasso sometimes does not *look like* Picasso.

Sometimes the title of a work could hide the fact that the sitter was Picasso himself. In 1945, a journalist spoke to Picasso about his painting *The Sailor*, which he had seen at the Salon de la Libération and immediately interpreted as a self-portrait. Picasso replied, 'Yes, it's me.' The journalist asked why he had painted himself as a sailor. 'Because I always wear a sailor's jumper. Look.' He unbuttoned his shirt to reveal a blue-and-white-striped jumper. Irrefutable proof. He denied that the butterfly placed between the net and the figure's nose had 'the slightest political significance', saying that just because it is red, that did not mean it symbolized the flag of the proletarian revolution. However, he had no hesitation in admitting that the sailor, on whose beret he had written his name in capital letters, was him: 'Yes, it's me.' (In 1459 or 1460, Benozzo Gozzoli wrote 'OPUSBENOTII' on the red hat that he is wearing in one of the frescoes in the Magi Chapel in the Palazzo Medici in Florence. Was Picasso's inclusion of his own name inspired by that signature? As far as we know, he had never seen Benozzo Gozzoli's work.)

The book *Picasso: Propos sur l'art* features a black-and-white photograph of the painting captioned 'Pablo Picasso, *The Sailor*, 23 January 1938, New York, Museum of Modern Art, donated by Jacqueline Picasso'. On page 180, it says the work is an oil on canvas, measuring 121.6 by 86.3 centimetres (148). The two authors, Marie-Laure Bernadac and Androula Michael, no doubt carried out rigorous research when writing the book. *The Sailor* ... who gave the work this title? Writing in 1957 – more than half a century after he had painted the picture known as *La Vie*, in 1903 – Picasso declared, 'It wasn't me who gave it this title.' But did he ever give his works titles? Matters get even more complicated when we read the 'Warning' with which Pierre Daix opens his *Dictionnaire Picasso* (Robert Laffont, 1995). He writes, 'With Picasso, the main difficulty is the fact that, aside from a handful of paintings, such as *La Vie* and *Guernica*, Picasso never named his works, or only gave them what we might call workshop titles, which he used when discussing them with friends or collaborators, titles that are not used elsewhere, either in Christian Zervos's *Picasso Catalogue* or in exhibitions.' Might Daix be wrong about who gave *La Vie* its title, just as Brassaï was wrong? Or did Picasso deliberately mislead people about it to perpetuate a sense of mystery?

The Sailor ... Elsewhere, the same painting is called *Maya in a Sailor Suit*. Maya is Picasso's daughter with Marie-Thérèse Walter, born on 5 September 1935. When this portrait was painted, on 23 January 1938, she would have been less than three years old. The fashion for dressing children in sailor suits had been around for some decades. But, in his diary entry for 8 January 1967, Michel Leiris remembers seeing 'among the paintings exhibited shortly after the Liberation ... [a] young boy wearing a sailor's hat on which was written PICASSO in capital letters'.

What trap is Picasso setting when he replies, 'Yes, it's me'? Is it a malicious joke? Or is he simply putting in their place those who have the audacity to attempt to impose interpretations on his work? As early as 1935, he was well aware of the dangers of such complacency. He told Zervos, 'People who try to explain pictures are usually barking up the wrong tree. Gertrude Stein joyfully announced to me the other day that she had at last understood what my picture of the three musicians was meant to be. It was a still life!'

Does this mean we must accept uncertainty? And that we should never forget what Picasso said when presenting one of his etchings: 'You see this truculent character here, with the curly hair and moustache? That's Rembrandt, or maybe it's Balzac, I'm not sure. It's a compromise, I suppose.'

What kind of 'compromise' are Picasso's self-portraits?

I cannot stop thinking about Jacques Prévert's question: 'And isn't Picasso real when he is painting his own self-portrait in disguise, here and there, throughout the whole world?' Can we identify these disguises?

In his 1930 text 'Bonjour Monsieur Picasso', Robert Desnos wrote, 'We have said everything about Picasso, including what shouldn't be said. Therefore, from now on, I refuse to contribute to the farcical interpretations of his work.' Twenty years later, in September 1950, Claude Roy gave this piece of advice: 'We must talk about Picasso in simple terms, forget the extraordinary flood of commentary, exegesis, and hyperbole that his work has inspired and cast aside the mystifying arguments over language that have grown around his paintings, like mildew of the spirit.' Finally, in the issue of *Les Lettres françaises* dated 18 November–17 December 1954, in a text entitled 'La Verve de Picasso', Louis Aragon feels moved to remind us: 'Painting is a strange thing, in the way it charms us and the stupid things that it makes us say.'

After reading these words by men who were close to Picasso – each of them knew him, some as friends, some as brief acquaintances – how could I not worry that I would deliver only a gloss that would be at best 'burlesque', a 'mystifying argument over language', or, if I proved to be incapable of either of those, would simply say stupid things? These warnings seemed to me sufficient excuse to put off writing the book.

Jacqueline Picasso said I could take my time, and I took it. Almost forty years ...

Perhaps I should have examined the self-portraits of Rembrandt, Vincent van Gogh, Paul Cézanne, the Impressionists. Or turned to any of the 285 artists whose works appear in my study of the self-portrait in the twentieth-century *Moi: Je par soi-même*, or the 150 self-portraits from that same century that I brought together in the exhibition *Me* (at the Musée du Luxembourg in Paris and the Uffizi Gallery). Or perhaps I should have studied those painters from the fourteenth century to the twentieth who inserted themselves surreptitiously into their altarpieces, their frescoes, their paintings. Maybe I should have considered all of that before I could claim to know anything about self-portraits, the challenges that they pose and the misunderstandings that they spark.

I came to wonder if I necessarily *had to* study self-portraits by other artists before tackling Picasso's works. This excuse deserves another. Because in the end, it is blindingly obvious that Picasso's self-portraits are unlike any others. They change the stakes, embrace all the challenges of the self-portrait, a genre that fuses together myth and anecdote. A genre that consistently confounds, one that we must approach with humility.

'Now comes maybe the age of another experience: that of unlearning, of allowing the unpredictable reshuffling that forgetfulness imposes onto the layering of knowledges, of cultures and beliefs that one has passed through. This experience has, I believe, the illustrious and obsolete name that I will dare uphold, at the crossroads of its etymology: *Sapientia* – no power, a little knowledge, a little wisdom and as much flavour as possible.' These were the closing words of Roland Barthes's inaugural lecture at the Collège de France on Friday, 7 January 1977. It is this *Sapientia* that I shall come to encounter.

Over to you!

It is now finally my turn to play. That does not necessarily mean playing by the rules. But it does mean running the risk of losing.

A puzzle

In 1985, a few weeks before the Musée National Picasso opened its doors at the restored Hôtel Salé, Yvonne Baby, who was then culture editor at *Le Monde*, set up an interview for me with Jean Cassou. Shortly after the Second World War, he had been a poet, essayist, and novelist, recognized as an important figure in the French Resistance and liberation. He was also the first director of the Musée National d'Art Moderne in Paris: '[It was a] revolutionary creation. We exhibited contemporary work for the general public to see. It spelled the end for the Musée du Luxembourg, which people began to forget about. They cast it aside.'

He told me that over the course of almost thirty years he had 'met Picasso many times. In the early days when he was living in poverty and later when he was celebrated. Our meetings are impossible to describe. They were emotional. We were almost always overjoyed. We embraced, we grasped each other's hands.' Picasso donated paintings to the museum when it had no collection yet to speak of. He called Cassou and invited him to come to his studio on the Rue des Grands-Augustins one morning at eleven: 'There were canvases propped against the walls, against the furniture, lying on the floor. They were paintings from all periods of his work. Like *The Blue Coffee Pot* – that was there. Paintings that were important to him, that he had kept for himself, that he had refused to sell. "I'll give you these." He counted. There were eleven. "Is that all right? It's not too many?"'

Cassou told me that Picasso came regularly to the museum to see where he had placed his works. 'He moved them around. He uncovered new relationships between them. He discussed them with me and with the museum attendant. And, every time, he found new ways to talk about them.' Cassou's reflections, published in *Le Monde* on 26 September 1985, closed with these words: 'His comments on his works could not be used for guided tours. They were ambiguity itself. Everything he said hinted at something else, something other than what we heard. And that something became something else. It was a kind of magic.'

Listening to Cassou was also a kind of magic. I could have listened to him for hours. But I did not want to take advantage, to tire him out, so I packed up my things. Just before I left, I ventured to tell him – with all the misplaced confidence of a young man – that I had promised Jacqueline Picasso that I would write about Picasso's self-portraits. The 'advice' that he gave me sounded uncannily like a warning: 'Do you know those wooden games, those Chinese puzzle boxes? Choose one of the most complex ones. Solving that will be easier than deciphering the self-portraits that he left behind.' Ever since then, I have known what to expect, and now I take it for granted. And I know it all the more today because, even if Cassou rightly said that Picasso's comments on his own work 'were ambiguity itself', the artist also made it clear that when people asked him about his work, his words should not be trusted: 'You shouldn't always believe what I say. Questions are an invitation to lie, especially when there is no response.' What responses, if any, should we expect when it comes to his self-portraits?

Scoundrel!

In 1937, Picasso set up his studio on the top floor of the Hôtel de Savoie at 7 Rue des Grands-Augustins. This was also the studio of Balzac's fictional painter Frenhofer in *The Unknown Masterpiece*. In the story, when Frenhofer presents a canvas to Poussin, who sees in it nothing but a confused mass of colour, he cries out,

'You see nothing? Clown, infidel, scoundrel, dolt!' Perhaps these are the same insults that I would merit, standing perplexed before one of Picasso's self-portraits.

Depictions and distortions

Self-portraits have been my obsession for years. I was around fifteen or sixteen when I came across one by Filippino Lippi at the Uffizi Gallery and found myself surprised, mesmerized by some strange presence. That encounter sparked a passion that has endured for forty years.

All the self-portraits that I have seen in museums, whether paintings or drawings, dating from the fifteenth century or the twentieth, from the Trecento or the start of the new millennium, have continually challenged everything that I thought I was beginning to understand about the genre. The one thing of which I came to be fairly certain was that the self-portrait is a unique genre in itself, not simply a specific kind of portrait, even if, throughout the centuries, self-portraits have been referred to as 'portrait of the painter, or the artist, by himself'. Did I say certain? It is futile to aspire to certainty given that art and its history have little use for it.

For some time now I have been disorientated, baffled, confused by the irreconcilable differences between Picasso's self-portraits – between, to confine ourselves to the best known, the 1901 self-portrait from his Blue Period that is in the collection of the Musée National Picasso at the Hôtel Salé (53), the 1907 portrait at the National Gallery in Prague (116) and the 1972 portrait acquired by the Fuji Television Gallery (166). They seem to have nothing in common, other than a passing resemblance to Picasso's face. A strange kind of resemblance ...

Taken together, these self-portraits have nothing in common with the series of drawings, etchings, and paintings that Rembrandt made of himself, which offer us (some) insight into his approach to creating his incomparable body of work. Similarly, the series of self-portraits by van Gogh and Cézanne reveal how they rose to the particular challenges of painting and how they, dare I say it, 'came to be' Vincent and Cézanne.

However, the sheer diversity of Picasso's self-portraits means that they do not have that same coherence. Picasso is constantly changing; he never looks like Picasso and yet he is always undeniably Picasso.

Looking at these self-portraits, you cannot help but notice how often they defy the centuries-old conventions of what self-portraits were allowed or supposed to be. It is no coincidence that none of Picasso's self-portraits was ever acquired by the Uffizi Gallery, whose unparalleled collection boasts almost two thousand examples of the genre, including those that Cardinal Leopoldo de' Medici left to his nephew, the Grand Duke of Tuscany. It was in 1870 that Couder 's self-portrait entered the collection. In the gallery's 1979 *General Catalogue*, it is referred to by the reference A261, a number assigned to it the previous year. The artist signed it 'L. C. Aug' – that is, Louis-Charles-Auguste – '*Pictor Gallus Aetatis SUAE LXXXI SEIPS. PINGEBAT ANNO DOM. MDCCCLXX.*' With this work, Couder claimed a place for himself in – as he called it – the 'Pantheon of Painting'. Born in London in 1789, Couder was a student of Jacques-Louis David and made his name with a painting that featured at the Salon of 1817. He contributed paintings to the Gallery of Great Battles in the Palace of Versailles and was elected to the Institute in 1832. His self-portrait entered the 'Pantheon of Painting' three years before his death, in Paris in 1873.

Even if Picasso had been invited to take his place in this prestigious collection, alongside Rembrandt, Velázquez, Delacroix, and Ingres, among many others, would he have accepted? Perhaps not. Because no single example from among Picasso's self-portraits conveys the sheer number of metamorphoses that marked his artistic career.

Definition

One day Picasso asked Brassaï, 'What is sculpture? What is painting? Everyone's still clinging to outdated ideas, obsolete definitions, as if the artist's role was not precisely to offer new ones.' In 2015, Madonna made a similar declaration, saying, 'That's our job as artists, to turn the world upside down and make everyone feel bewildered and have to rethink everything.' The Queen of Pop is perhaps not so different from Picasso, with her reputation for revelling in provocation. And their view of the role of the artist has been shared by many over the centuries. As Vasari wrote, 'He who follows others can never surpass them.' It is true. There are those rare artists who break new ground and those who follow in their footsteps, digging ruts in the road.

What is a self-portrait? Who can say? Perhaps I can offer only an outdated answer to this question, and the definitions I can think of are obsolete. These definitions might apply to the drawings, paintings, and photographs that Picasso made of himself up until the 1950s, but after that, his self-portraits become something else together. Although ...

When looking at Picasso's self-portraits, we must always keep in mind his words: 'Naming, well ... In painting, we should never name objects.' Are we then to understand that Picasso's self-portraits cannot be named, that they are unqualifiable, and that they flout every definition of the self-portrait?

Without these familiar points of reference, how are we to understand his self-portraits? How can we uncover what they seek to express? It is futile to hope that Picasso's own words might offer the key. Which of his statements should we trust? On the one hand, he claimed that 'the work we create is like keeping a diary', while on the other, he said that 'the artist must know how to convince others of the truth of his lies'.

How should we reconcile the idea of his work as a diary with the fact that for months, years even, he did not paint any self-portraits? Does this tally with the idea (or perhaps the hope) that a self-portrait 'says' more about the artist himself than a painting with any other subject? And if his work was designed to convince us of the 'truth of his lies', what lies are present in his self-portraits? Any attempt to 'decipher' these works presents us with a dilemma. Diary or lie? Or a diary made up of lies?

Picasso's own question – 'For me, a painting speaks for itself; what is the point of adding explanations after the fact?' – contains within it a note of warning. And we must also remember Mircea Eliade's words: 'Translating an image into concrete terminology, reducing it to a single plane of reference, is worse than mutilating it, destroying it as an instrument of knowledge.'

'So why bother?' It seems easier to give up. The entire undertaking seems highly risky, as confirmed by Gaëtan Picon's claim (which I am not sure whether to take as disillusioned, malicious, or sardonic) that 'those who seek to explain a painting usually head down the wrong path'. For 'usually', perhaps we should read an implacable 'always'.

According to Picasso, there is a simple explanation as to why paintings are inevitably misunderstood: 'The public does not always understand modern art, it's true, but that is because they haven't been taught anything about painting. They are taught to read and write, to draw or sing, but no one has ever thought to teach them how to look at a painting.' As he also said, 'People *always* misunderstand at first. Afterwards, it only seems as if they understand. But that's great. Because I have no idea what they understand.' Perhaps this misunderstanding does not matter. Because, as he said to Claude Roy, 'When I read a book about Einstein's theories of physics, even though I understand nothing, that allows me to understand *something else*.'

We must therefore acknowledge that failing to understand one of Picasso's self-portraits could lead us to understand *something else*. And perhaps it is Albert Einstein who offers the solution, writing in a letter about Picasso, 'Given that our way of experiencing each of his paintings depends on our personal subjectivity, we should seek many different points of view in order to understand the work as a whole.'

Or perhaps Picasso was deliberately choosing to follow in the proud, even arrogant footsteps of Fernando Pessoa, who said that he 'always rejected being understood. To be understood is to prostitute oneself.'

Talent! Genius?

Between 1894 and 1900, Pablo Ruiz Picasso made more than twenty drawings and paintings of himself. He was still only twelve years old when he drew a seated portrait of himself as a young boy, if it was before his birthday on 25 October, or thirteen if it dates to the later months of 1894 (2). In 1895, he worked on an unfinished painting of himself in three-quarter profile behind a man believed to be a relative. The following year, he produced three pencil drawings of just his face (3) and covered two pages of a sketchbook with drawings in pencil and ink (4, 5), including one of himself standing with his foot on a chair or stool, working. He also produced three oil paintings (6, 7, 8), one of which remained unfinished (7). He did another three drawings in 1897. One showed his own face above sketches of cats (9). Another depicted him sitting on a chair, one leg crossed over the other, working (10); at the bottom of the page is written 'P. Ruiz Picasso'. The third is a pencil drawing in which he seems to be turning towards a canvas that rests on an easel – indicated only by a few dark lines – the signature reads simply 'P. R. Picasso' (11). There are also two pages of studies where he appears with his torso bared, which perhaps also date to 1897: one where he stands with his arms crossed over his chest (12) and another that shows him working (13). Others, however, believe that these pages (both of which have the same dimensions, 23.5 by 33 centimetres), date to 1899. There is also some uncertainty around the date of a drawing that shows him in three-quarter profile, with two paintings or drawings hanging on the wall behind him (16): could it be 1899? It is more likely to be 1897, according to Jaime Sabartés. Over the course of 1899 and 1900, he drew himself twelve times: sometimes just his face (17, 22, 28, 30, 31); sometimes among studies in his sketchbook (18, 20, 21) . He signed these early drawings only occasionally (10, 11, 15, 25, 27). Then, suddenly, on the blue watercolour background behind his head and hair, which are half-obscured by shadow, there is the word '*YO*', or 'me' (23).

The centre parting that he usually sports in this series of self-portraits produced between the ages of thirteen or fourteen and nineteen, and which can still be found in a drawing of 1901 (35), is replaced by a lock of hair around the same time as he stops signing his paintings 'Pablo Ruiz Picasso' and switches to simply 'Picasso'.

These sketches, drawings, and paintings show Picasso as a child, a teenager, and a young man who is fully aware of his own talent and whose ambition may well lead him to the heights of genius. But, growing up in Spain – Madrid and Barcelona – he knew that this would be possible only if he took the brave step of moving to Paris, the art capital of the world.

'Heaven sometimes shows itself in showering upon one single person the infinite riches of its treasures, and all those graces and rarest gifts that it is wont to distribute among many individuals, over a long space of time, could be clearly seen in the no less excellent than gracious Raffaello Sanzio da Urbino.... Wherefore it may be surely said that those who are the possessors of such rare and numerous gifts as were seen in Raffaello da Urbino, are not merely men, but, if it be not a sin to say it, mortal gods.' Thus begins Giorgio Vasari's biography of Raphael, in his *Lives of the Most Excellent Painters, Sculptors, and Architects*. A biography of Picasso could open with the same words, including when Vasari writes, '[Raphael's] father Giovanni de' Santi [was] a painter of no great excellence, and yet a man of good intelligence, well able to direct his children on that good path which he himself had not been fortunate enough to have shown to him in his boyhood.' All we need to do is replace the name Giovanni Santi with José Ruiz Blasco.

In 1821, Ingres wrote, 'Raphael set the eternal and incontestable bounds of the sublime in art.' As Nicolas Mignard proclaimed on 3 September 1667 in an address to the French Royal Academy of Painting, 'It is impossible to overstate the great genius of this incomparable painter when we consider how far he surpassed his masters in so little time and how he suddenly elevated the art of painting to a point so far above where it had been before that even today no one has been able to usurp him as the greatest master of all painters.'

In 1917, on a visit to Rome to work on the costumes and set for the ballet *Parade*, Picasso went to see Raphael's frescoes. When a friend who was with him expressed his admiration for them, Picasso replied, 'Yes, very good, but we can do likewise, don't you think?'

Picasso never did 'likewise'...

The painter Gérard Garouste claimed, 'As for Picasso ... he devoured heritage, he was one of those geniuses who kill the father and the son. He pushed painting as far as it could go, right to its glorious breaking point. He consumed painting, shattered it, along with its models and landscapes, and created a unique body of work. Looking at *The Weeping Woman*, I know that sadness is not the subject, but the pretext. The subject is the fact that Picasso, the iconoclast, can paint a woman's tears. The subject is the artist himself. It is always like that when painting sparks a scandal. Picasso explored as far as he could go, to the limits of style. He made everything that came after him look conventional. He is painting and its outcome.'

Raphael. Picasso. Two bodies of work that point to the sacred dimension in painting, but by very different means. Raphael because he is a 'mortal god', as Vasari writes. And, as Paul Claudel argues, 'Picasso is so angered by the human form, he abuses it in a way that we can only compare to the blasphemy of a tortured soul. Surely this can only be because he sees the image of God. What could be more sacred than sacrilege?'

Partners in crime

In 1900, when he was living in Barcelona, Picasso produced an ink drawing of himself with a friend, Manuel Pallarès. It is in a cartoon-like style and looks like a draft poster for an art '*ESPosicion*' (exhibition) – the word appears in both upper and lower case, the letters split up on either side of the two men in hats and long coats (24). The artist signed his name as *RUIZ Picasso*. That same year, but this time in Paris, he drew himself pointing out the Eiffel Tower to Pallarès (33). He also drew himself in a similar pose with another friend, Carles Casagemas, walking behind two women who are enclosed in a frame (26) – perhaps because they are unattainable? For the second issue of the journal *Arte Joven*, dated 15 April 1901, he sketched a group of Bohemian artists in Madrid (37). According to Sabartés, the man on the left is unknown, while the others are S. Cornuti, Francisco de Asis Soler, Alberto Lozano, and Picasso himself. In *Madrid: Notas de Arte*, Picasso drew himself alone with Francisco de Asis Soler (40). It may have been him who took the photograph of Pere Mañach and Torres Fuster in the studio that Picasso shared at 130 Boulevard de Clichy (41). And another sketch shows the Eiffel Tower, this time in the distance, with himself and Jaume Andreu Bonsons walking along by the river in the foreground (45). During this first trip to Paris, he wrote a letter to his friend Miquel Utrillo (42). On the front of the page, under the word PARIS written in capitals, the letter begins with the words, 'My dear Utrillo, it seems you don't want to reply to me. How is the exhibition going? I'm sending you a newspaper cutting from *Le Journal* about me.' On the same page there are three drawings. To the right of the text are three people, from left to right: 'Manolo', a woman called 'Germaine', and Picasso. He is seated in front of an easel that displays his painting *Bedizened Old Woman*. In an article published on 17 June 1901 in *Le Journal*, the newspaper that advertised Picasso's exhibition (in fact a joint exhibition with Francisco Iturrino, although his name is not mentioned) at Ambroise Vollard's, Gustave Coquiot was no doubt referring to that painting when he wrote, 'The focus is on women decked out in jewelry, fresh-faced girls or haggard old women.' He continued, 'This very young Spanish painter, recently arrived in Paris, is a passionate lover of modern life.' He did not mention that Picasso was a lover of more than just modern life.... He concludes by writing, 'Tomorrow we will celebrate the works of Pablo Ruiz Picasso.' Picasso's affair with Manolo's lover Germaine was (possibly) the cause of the fight between Bonsons and Mañach, whom he drew on the same page next to a conversation between his friends and Spanish relatives in Paris, a city where he still knew hardly a soul.

On his return to Spain, to Barcelona, in 1902, he drew a group seated at a table at the Els Quatre Gats café, with the words '*ES-SERVEIX-BEURE-Y-MENJAR-A-TOTES-HORES*' ('Food and drink served at all hours'). He is in the foreground, with the others behind the table: the proprietor Pere Romeu sitting on a chair, Josep Rocarol, Emili Fontbona, Àngel Fernández de Soto, and, stanl ding, Sabartés. Underneath he wrote the address of the Els Quatre Gats, Carrer Montesion (58). Another drawing shows him wearing a wide-brimmed black hat, sitting at a table with Àngel Fernández de Soto and Sebastiá Junyer-Vidal (59). They also accompany him on a visit to the city's brothels (55, 66). In 1903 or 1904, he drew himself one last time sitting on the terrace of a café in Barcelona, accompanied by Junyer-Vidal (78).

The last of these drawings that show the bonds between Picasso and his Spanish friends appear in 1904, a series of five colour drawings in pencil (80–4). In one (80), he is sitting in a third-class train carriage with Junyer-Vidal, on a visit to Paul Durand-Ruel, who is shown in another drawing handing over a bag with the figure of $1,000 scribbled on it (84). One can dream....

The last hint of a friendship with a Spanish artist in Paris is a photograph taken in 1904, showing the painter Ricard Canals sitting in an armchair by a fireplace with a photograph of his model Benedetta Bianco, whom he was soon to marry, on the mantelpiece. And, behind this portrait, reflected in the mirror, is Picasso himself. He took the photograph with a camera borrowed from Canals (89). On the back of the print, he felt it necessary to write 'in the mirror, me, Picasso', underlined to leave no doubt that he is the creator of this rigorous composition. This is Picasso's first photographic self-portrait.

Did he know that a few years earlier, on 16 December 1895, Edgar Degas had taken a photograph and offered a print to Paul Valéry, who described it thus: 'This photograph was given to me by Degas, whose camera and ghost can be seen in the mirror. Mallarmé is standing next to Renoir, who is sitting on the sofa. Degas made them hold the pose for 15 minutes, with the scene lit by nine gas lamps. It was taken on the fourth floor of no. 40 Rue de Villejust.'

The year 1904 ... the time of friendships in Madrid and Barcelona was over. Let us both go to Paris!

Enigma

For centuries, because mirrors were the only way for people to see themselves, artists turned to them when painting self-portraits. Whether they chose to place them on their left or right did not change much about the overall process. (Although, for example, always placing the mirror on his right allowed van Gogh to avoid painting the left side of his face, where he had lost an ear.) Because the artist had to turn towards the mirror, it was easiest to depict themselves in three-quarter profile. However, some decided to face the mirror front on, while others chose to show themselves only in profile. Picasso explored all three of these possibilities, depicting himself in three-quarter profile, in full face, and in profile.

Two of those portraits where he faces the viewer straight on are a drawing of 1901/2 (57) and another of 1908 (117). They are separated by six years, and although both figures look like Picasso, those six years have revolutionized his style and craftsmanship, meaning the two drawings have almost nothing in common with each other – or with the self-portraits of June and July 1972 (166–9).

Now to three-quarter profile. In 1901, Picasso drew himself with a beard and moustache, his hair swept back to show his forehead, half-turning towards the viewer (52). In 1903, he drew himself with a centre parting and moustache, looking over his shoulder (70). Two drawings, the first in sepia ink, the second in Indian ink. But the precision of his lines has nothing in common with that of a pencil-and-charcoal drawing of 1917 (133). These drawings are all variations on the theme of the self-portrait, and none of them is a study for a painting.

Neither are those – more numerous – in which Picasso depicts himself in profile. He drew the first for an article that was published in the newspaper *La Tribuna* on 24 March 1904 (86). Although this was by no means the first article about him, it is (perhaps) no coincidence that he provided the newspaper with this portrait. Surely he was aware that these portraits drew on a long and illustrious history. Since ancient times, coins and medals have been embossed with faces in profile. This pose was reserved for famous figures, even up to the Quattrocento portraits that abounded in Florence, Milan, and Ferrara. Painting a portrait in profile was a clear sign that the model was worthy of such an honour. That is why Picasso chose to draw himself in profile in 1901 and 1902–3 (39, 69) and in 1921 (143, 144).

If, as some have suggested, Picasso's self-portraits are to be understood as a diary, a kind of autobiography, the twenty or so that show him standing and in profile are undoubtedly those that 'illustrate' him best. The first can be found on a page of sketches from 1900, where Picasso drew himself with a pipe between his lips and a hat on his head, next to Pallarès (25). Why? What are they doing? Where are they going? Another shows him introducing Rosita to Casagemas (27). Who is Rosita? How did he know her and why was he introducing her to his friend? Every time, it is the same questions that arise. And every time, they remain unanswered.... Why are he and Casagemas following two young women (26)? Why did he draw himself in the middle of a page of sketches, wearing a hat, with his hands in his pockets (32)? Does Manuel Pallarès need Picasso to point out the Eiffel Tower to him? Or is this gesture designed to make him look away from the sirens or nymphs lying at his feet (33)? What prompted him to depict himself wearing a hat and holding a cane (54) in 1902? Or, the following year, wearing a beret and standing with his hands in his pockets between two nude figures (67)? He is wearing the same beret in another self-portrait of 1903, in which he also holds a dog on a lead (72). In 1904, he wears a peaked cap in a sketch of himself next to a male nude (95), and again sitting on a café terrace (87) and standing with a pipe in his hand (96). In the series of drawings that show the stages of his journey from Barcelona to Paris in 1904, he is accompanied by Junyer-Vidal wearing a beret (80–3). What 'event' or emotion led him to draw himself on an envelope in 1915, standing in the street with a basket in each hand (123)? Or to create a line drawing, a caricature of himself in profile, in 1917 or 1918 (130)? Why the apparent mockery? On 26 December 1966, he drew himself again in profile (161). Did this lead to the two etchings of himself in profile in 1968 (163, 164)?

It is impossible to impose a narrative.... And equally impossible to determine what led Picasso to reach for his pen or open a notebook, as he did to draw a sketch in 1901 (38). We must admit that Picasso remains indecipherable. His self-portraits are sphinx-like, mysterious. Where in his autobiography should we place one precisely dated self-portrait: 23.6.55 (159)? For years before that, he had not produced a single self-portrait. And he would not produce another until seven years later.

Doubts

It is a simple pencil-and-charcoal drawing on an ochre background, measuring a little over twenty centimetres by just over fifteen and dating to 1899 or perhaps 1900 (19). A portrait of an elegant young man wearing a shirt with a wing collar, a waistcoat, and an ascot tie. Can we be sure of the model's identity when we compare this drawing from the collection of the Museu Picasso in Barcelona with another that dates to 1900, this time in the collection of the Metropolitan Museum of Art in New York: ink and watercolour on an almost square piece of paper, nine and a half centimetres by a little over eight and half (23)? The word '*Yo*' written on the blue background behind the sitter's hair in this second picture leaves no room for doubt. This face, with three wrinkles on its forehead, can only be that of Picasso. While the sitter for the first of these two portraits sports the same centre parting, his hair is far flatter than in the second. That by no means proves that it is not Picasso. However, the face seems gaunt, even emaciated in comparison. At most, we could say there is a 'family resemblance'. Around the same time, Picasso produced another portrait, a pencil drawing that dates to 1900, in which his hair shows no trace of the centre parting seen elsewhere (31) . This and drawing number 19, too, have only a 'family resemblance' with him.

However, all of them have been classed as self-portraits. Is that a mistake? A simple error? Should we infer that in 1899 and 1900, Picasso was starting to move away from lifelike depictions? Or did he already subscribe to Rimbaud's idea that 'I is an other'? Was it '*I*' who drew the portraits of this *Other* who looks more like a brother, or even a half-brother? Or was he casting off his singular identity as Fernando Pessoa did when he adopted the heteronyms Ricardo Reis, Bernardo Suares, Alberto Caeiro, Alvaro de Campos, and so many others? It seems that Picasso distrusted the official, straightforward identity imposed by the photobooths that first appeared in France in 1928.

Elegance

Throughout the Belle Époque, clothing choices were governed by strict rules of etiquette that did not allow for the slightest deviation. During the daytime, it would have been unthinkable to pay a visit to a friend or attend a ceremony in a three-piece suit. One had to wear a morning coat, or even a frock coat. Fittingly, in 1901, Picasso drew a portrait of himself sporting highly elegant attire. He is standing, wearing a white shirt with a wing collar, a bow tie and a black waistcoat. His hand rests in the pocket of his striped trousers, pushing back what looks like a tailcoat (34). It is the kind of outfit that it was customary to wear to parties.

That same year, he appears in a photograph (48), standing beside two of his paintings, the *Portrait of Gustave Coquiot* and *The Absinthe Drinker*. In the portrait that he likely painted from this photograph (50), he is flanked by prostitutes – perhaps from the brothel in the Rue de Londres? – who stand in the background, the same space occupied by cabaret dancers in the portrait of the critic Coquiot.

He is the picture of elegance, sporting a flower in his buttonhole, a white scarf, and a top hat. When they were first introduced, top hats were a way for men to show their status in society. But since around 1830, they had been referred to in the streets as 'stovepipe hats' and had been worn by everyone from aristocrats and men of independent means to newspaper hacks, all the way down to shopkeepers and pimps. They were no longer a symbol of respectability, as proven by the fact that they could be worn to brothels. But in this portrait of 1901, when Picasso was penniless and living hand to mouth, can his elegant attire be seen as anything other than a disguise? The apprentice painter that he still was at that time would not have been welcome at the salon hosted by Proust's Madame Verdurin ...

Mirror

According to Paul Éluard, 'When they were painting their self-portraits, they were looking at themselves in a mirror, without considering that they themselves were the mirror. But they removed its silvering, as they removed the silvering from the mirror that is the outside world.' A criticism that does not apply to

Picasso's self-portraits. Perhaps because we have long known that it is the duty of a painter to act as a mirror. As Leonardo wrote, 'A painter's mind must be like a mirror, which takes on the colour of whatever it sees and fills itself with as many images as there are objects before it.' Picasso could not have cared less about whether his mind was like a mirror.

However, as painters had done for centuries before him, Picasso turned to the mirror. In a drawing that probably dates to 1897, Picasso uses his right hand to steady the sketchbook that rests on his thigh, while it is his left hand, hidden by the paper, that holds the pencil (13). Two years later, in 1899, he drew himself sitting in front of an easel, his left hand reaching towards the paper that rests there (15). Just behind the nape of his neck he has written his name – still 'P. Ruiz Picasso', underlined. These are the self-portraits of a young man of sixteen and eighteen. A young man who sees no reason not to bow to tradition, because following it does have one advantage: it proves, if there were ever any doubt, that he is a painter. A painter among painters. He would repeat the exercise one last time in 1897, drawing himself sitting on a chair, one leg crossed over the other, his right hand holding the board or canvas that rests on his thigh (10). This means that he appears to be drawing with his left hand, so he must be following the image that he saw reflected in the mirror. Similarly, in a 1917 drawing, he holds the board with his right hand (132). In contrast, a self-portrait from 1938 shows him holding a brush in his right hand (147). Does the difference between this later charcoal drawing and the 1917 self-portrait and the one dedicated to Jacqueline (1), both produced in the same year, suggest that he had now definitively, irrevocably given up drawing himself by looking in a mirror?

Jaime Sabartés remembers hearing Picasso grumbling about mirrors, saying, 'What a stupid invention!' Sabartés wondered, 'Does he want to see himself differently, or does he not like seeing himself as he truly is, every day getting further and further away from the image of himself that he would like to preserve?' Sabartés left the question unanswered. How could anyone claim to know the true reason?

However, Sabartés did claim, 'I heard Picasso say many times that he is afraid of mirrors and cannot bear the sight of his own reflection when he accidentally finds himself before one.' He risked an explanation: 'It is possible that the reason why he had such a distaste for seeing his own reflection was simply because a mirror will always reflect the same thing back at you, while by his very nature Picasso always aspired towards change, transformation, and rebellion. He wanted to be constantly moving forward, never adhering to generally accepted principles or allowing himself to become a slave to preconceived ideas. He abhorred clichés, scorned convention and routine. Put simply, he did not want to grow old, especially in his artistic work.'

Perhaps it would be useful at this point to turn to Brassaï's *Conversations with Picasso*, particularly the entry dated 27 April 1944:

> 'PICASSO: You've come at a good time. Just this morning I was thinking about photography. When I woke up and looked at myself in the mirror with my dishevelled hair, do you know what thought came to me? Well, I was sorry I wasn't a photographer! It's completely different, the way other people see you and the way you see yourself in the mirror at certain moments. Several times in my life, I happened to catch an expression on my face that I've never been able to find in any of my portraits. And they may have been my truest expressions. Someone ought to make a hole in a mirror so that the lens can capture your most intimate face unawares.'

Was Picasso thinking of the stunned expression on his face on that day in November 1918 when he heard the news of Guillaume Apollinaire's death (136)? He was in the middle of shaving at the Hôtel Lutetia. 'From that day onwards', so Brassaï claimed, 'he had an aversion to mirrors, all the mirrors that force us to confront ourselves day after day, the cruel coldness of those reflections, the furrows, the wrinkles, the dark shadows that time paints under our eyes. After seeing the shadow of death pass over his own face on that day, he stopped drawing and painting himself.' (Although we must not forget, as Jacqueline reminded me, that he produced around twenty more self-portraits after this incident.) In two photographs, one from 1904 (89) and the other from 1940 (149), Picasso seems to appear in mirrors 'by accident'. At least, it seems to be an accident.... But both photographs – the first, where his reflection can be seen in the mirror behind Ricard Canals, and the second, which shows the room that served as his studio at the villa Les Voiliers in Royan – were carefully staged.

How are we to interpret Daniel-Henry Kahnweiler's claim that, 'His paintings have always been autobiographical. They have now become even more so than ever. Everything is focused on his own feelings, on his own life.' He went on to write, 'Picasso [...] is constantly confessing. All he does is speak about his life, his inner life.' In 1939, when Brassaï visited the artist in his studio in the Rue des Grands-Augustins, Picasso said, 'Tell me the truth! We haven't seen each other for some time – I've changed a lot, haven't I? Look at the condition of my hair. When I run across old portraits of myself, I get scared.' As we can clearly see from the fear he describes to Brassaï, it is to his 'old portraits' that Picasso turns, more than anything else, as a vital reference.

To quote Sabartés, 'he did not want to grow old'. Could that be because he couldn't bear to see the changes that time wrought on his face? There was no question of following in the footsteps of Rembrandt, whose portraits painted between 1625 and 1669 clearly show the wrinkles around his eyes, the bloating that dulls his features.

So Picasso avoided mirrors ... and thereby also avoided the myths that have haunted painting for centuries, playing on the minds of painters.

One of these myths was more influential than any other. In *On Painting*, published in 1435, the first treatise on painting ever written in Europe, Leon Battista Alberti wrote, 'I used to tell my friends that the inventor of painting, according to poets, was Narcissus, who was turned into a flower; for, as painting is the flower of all arts, so the tale of Narcissus fits our purpose perfectly. What is painting but the act of embracing by means of art the surface of a pool?'

What painter would not want to be the father of painting, like Narcissus? The metaphor is an apt one for Picasso, who drew and painted himself again and again.

However, even if he had never read Alberti, he would not have thought much of his claim that it 'is remarkable how every defect in a picture appears more unsightly in a mirror. So the things that are taken from Nature should be emended with the advice of the mirror.' Advice that Picasso did not hesitate to throw overboard.

Similarly, he had little use for the mirror's potential to invite introspection, as described by Seneca: 'Mirrors were invented in order that man might know himself, destined to attain many benefits from this: first, knowledge of himself; next, in certain directions, wisdom. The handsome man, to avoid infamy. The ugly man, to understand that what he lacks in physical appearance must be compensated for by virtue. The young man, to be reminded by his youth that it is a time of learning and of daring brave deeds. The old man, to set aside actions dishonourable to his grey hair, to think some thoughts about death. That is why Nature made it possible for us to see ourselves.'

Diogenes Laërtius wrote that Socrates 'recommended to the young the constant use of the mirror, to the end that handsome men might acquire a corresponding behaviour, and ugly men conceal their defects by education'. Picasso likely paid no heed to the words of Seneca or Socrates, as recorded by Diogenes Laërtius. It was not to the mirror that he turned in order to recognize himself or change his behaviour. Nor did he turn to the mirror to see how the passage of time had marked his face. Because his 'old portraits' were the only reference that mattered.

It seems more likely that in his approach to painting Picasso subscribed to St Augustine's assertion that, 'Certainly what the eyes see is not called "false" unless it have some similitude of the true.... We call that also ... a false face which is reflected from a mirror.' Augustine goes on to ask, 'Does not your image in the mirror appear to will to be you yourself, but to be therefore false, because it is not?'

The matter of the mirror is settled then. They are of no use to Picasso.

In the preparatory sketch that he drew for *Yo Picasso* in 1901, it is the artist's right hand that holds the pencil, charcoal, or paintbrush (46). In every sketch on a page filled with studies that dates to 1901, and others that date to 1906, he holds the palette in his left hand. The same is true of his self-portrait 'with palette' of 1906. In *The Artist in Front of his Canvas* (147), a charcoal drawing dated 22.3.38, we see only the thumb of his left hand hooked through the hole of an almost circular palette, holding a bunch of paintbrushes. It is his right hand that reaches towards the canvas. This is the last self-portrait in which Picasso depicts himself at work as a painter. The ink-on-paper drawing of 1941 on which he wrote the title 'Portrait de l'auteur' is not a portrait of himself as a painter but of Picasso the writer, author of *Desire Caught by the Tail* (152).

Gósol

Throughout 1906, Picasso produced around ten drawings of himself; a few were quick sketches, while others were studies for paintings. He had not been so prolific in producing self-portraits since 1901. In these drawings (99, 100–5, 108, 110, 113) and the paintings from that year (111, 112), there is no sign of the centre parting or the lock of hair that are present in earlier self-portraits. His hair is cut short. Only one of these drawings shows him full face (99). According to Sabartés, Picasso drew it in Gósol in the province of Lleida in Catalonia. It is possibly the first drawing in this series. Picasso went to the village with Fernande Olivier towards the end of May that year, planning to spend the summer there, although he left in a hurry in mid-August, fleeing a cholera epidemic. What happened that led him to choose predominantly ochre tones for the paintings that he produced in Gósol and on his return to Paris?

On 8 June 1903, the Galerie Durand-Ruel held an extraordinary exhibition of frescoes discovered at Boscoreale on the slopes of Vesuvius, a kilometre north of Pompeii, which were to be sold at auction. Picasso was in Barcelona at the time and could not visit the exhibition. However, it seems likely that on his return to Paris he came across the catalogue and, after examining the reproductions of the Pompeian paintings, went to the Louvre, which had acquired some of them in the auction. He was greatly inspired by the red tones of the paintings. It was also at the Louvre that he first discovered Iberian sculptures; since 1904, the museum had had an entire room dedicated to them, organized around the Lady of Elche, and it put on an exhibition that Picasso visited in 1906. For some years, the sculptures had been classed – for want of a better category – as 'Mediterranean antiquities' and described as examples of a 'Greco-Phoenician Spanish style'.

Picasso was equally inspired by the Roman art that he saw in the 'Art Nacional' exhibition at the Palau de Belles Artes in Barcelona in 1902. This was the art that he searched for on the column heads at the Sant Pau del Camp monastery in Barcelona and found in the twelfth-century *Virgin of Gósol* at the Church of Santa Maria del Castell.

Gósol ... the greys, the earthy browns, the pale ochre of canvases and walls. An ochre that has no use for blue or pink. Reflecting the bleakness of daily life in a village that could be reached only on the back of a mule, where, according to Fernande Olivier, the men were 'almost all bootleggers'. It was there that Picasso cast off his earlier influences – El Greco, Ingres, and others – embracing instead a new purity of form that he achieved through a kind of archaism. And the self-portraits that he painted there are reminiscent of masks.

On his return to Paris, after this formative period, Picasso knew that he had the talent to rival Matisse, the Fauvist artist. The word 'Fauvist' was coined by Louis Vauxcelles in his review of Room 7 of the Salon d'Automne exhibition, published in the supplement of the periodical *Gil Blas* on 17 October. Apollinaire wrote about the 1910 Salon d'Automne, 'Some of the talk was of a bizarre demonstration of cubism [this is his first recorded use of the word]. Ill-informed journalists saw in it a kind of concrete metaphysics. But it is not even that, it is a flat, lifeless imitation of works that have not yet been exhibited, works painted by an artist with a strong personality who has not offered up his secrets to anyone. This great artist is called Pablo Picasso.'

What happened in Gósol was merely the precursor to an important museum visit that Picasso described to Malraux:

> 'When I went to the Trocadéro, it was disgusting. A flea market. The smell. I was all alone. I wanted to leave. I didn't leave. I stayed. I realized that it was very important: something was happening to me, no? The masks, they weren't sculptures like the other works. Not at all. They were magical things. And why not the Egyptians, the Chaldeans? We didn't pay attention to them. We saw them as primitive people, not magical people! The Negroes' sculptures were intercessors – that is when I learned the word in French. Intercessors against everything; against unknown, threatening spirits. I kept on looking at the talismans. I realized that I am also against everything. I also think that everything is unknown, an enemy. Everything! Not details, not women, children, animals, smoking, playing ... but all of it! I understood the purpose of sculpture, for Negroes. Why they made sculptures like that rather than another way. After all, they were not cubists! Because cubism didn't exist! Of course, some people created models and others followed those models – that's what tradition is, isn't it? But all the talismans, they served the same purpose. They were weapons.

> To keep people from being ruled by spirits, to help them free themselves. They were tools. If we give form to these spirits, we become free of them. Spirits, the unconscious (it was not yet much discussed), emotions, they are all the same thing. I understood why I was a painter. All alone in that terrible museum, with masks, Redskin dolls, dusty mannequins. *Les Demoiselles d'Avignon* arrived that day, but not because of the shapes: because it was my first painting that was an exorcism!'

His self-portraits were another kind of exorcism. His only way of grappling with the passage of time.

Proof of reinvention

In 1683, the Grand Duke of Tuscany Cosimo III asked Charles Le Brun to send a self-portrait to him in Florence. He wanted it to become part of the collection of self-portraits created by Cardinal Leopoldo de' Medici, who had begun to be celebrated as the 'most glorious patron of the century' shortly after his death in 1670. Louis XIV's court painter hastened to reply to His Serene Highness with all humility: 'How could I refuse to give your Highness my portrait? I would be honoured to bring it to your Highness in person if my duties to the greatest King of the universe did not oblige me to stay in Paris.' The portrait was not finished until 20 November 1684. On 29 November, Charles Le Brun entrusted it to l'Abbé Charles Antoine de Gondi, secretary of state to the Grand Duchy of Tuscany. He sent a letter with the portrait in which he wrote that, 'I have never taken pleasure in being known by my features.' On 9 April 1944, Picasso said to Brassaï, 'My self-portraits are very rare. Really I haven't spent much time on my own face.' A strange echo of Le Brun's words two hundred and sixty years earlier.

The twentieth century has nothing in common with the reign of Louis XIV. Especially because, in the twentieth century, it was photography that served to spread fame. By 1944, Picasso had already been taking photographs of himself for some years, but now he began to pose for photographers: Brassaï, Cartier-Bresson, Dora Maar, Man Ray, Robert Doisneau, Robert Capa, René Burri, David Douglas, and many more.

He even began to paint details onto photographs that others had taken of him. In 1972, he sent Lucien Clergue a print on which he had drawn a monocle, beard, and hair, this time in ink. He wrote, 'I did that for you, as a way of understanding the difference between how we see ourselves and how we see others, which is often nothing more than a caricature of ourselves or others.'

Picasso, who by that point had resigned himself to being ambushed by paparazzi, knew only too well that he was known and recognized by '[his] features'. For centuries, a painter's only way of being known – and recognized – was to paint himself. Had that now become superfluous? Or, given that Picasso kept many of his self-portraits, did he see them as proof that he never ceased to reinvent himself? And that this reinvention was for himself alone ...

Dedications

In 1902, Picasso wrote to Max Jacob from Barcelona, illustrating his letter with multiple drawings (60, 61). One shows him standing, with a hat on his head and a cane in his hand, an amphitheatre and a church in the background. To ensure that Jacob knew who the figure was, he wrote: 'Picasso en Espagne'. On one side of the paper, he wrote that he was working a lot, while on the reverse, he drew his head again, behind the rump of a horse and next to that of another. The caption reads: 'The bullfights. They are taking the horse away. That is the horse's head that they are taking away.'

Another drawing shows him in profile, with a pipe in his mouth, sitting on a café terrace (87). Sabartés writes, 'On this ink drawing, we can see the following dedication, written in Spanish: "For Sebastiá Junyer, Picasso. December 1904. My portrait."' He continues, 'At that time he liked to wear a peaked leather cap. He was so pleased with it that most likely he wanted to create a record of it for posterity.' At the time that Sabartés wrote these words for his book *Portraits et Souvenirs*, which was published in 1946, he could be fairly certain that Picasso's reputation would endure. However, when Picasso drew the picture in 1904, shortly after arriving in Bateau-Lavoir, could he say the same about his 'peaked leather cap'? It seems unlikely. Why was it this cap that he wanted to record for posterity, rather than the large traditional Andalusian hat – worn by *paveros*, or turkey farmers – that earned him the nickname Little Goya? In 1902, he drew a pen-and-ink portrait of himself wearing a hat, with a cane in his hand (54). A handwritten note makes it clear that the decision to leave his coat open over his waistcoat was a deliberate one; the waistcoat is the same kind that he wore on his walk along La Rambla, a very special velvet waistcoat made for him by Pallarès's mother in Horta during the winter of 1898–9. It seems unlikely, however, that posterity has much use for a cap or a waistcoat.

In 1904, Picasso gave one of his self-portraits to Jacob (88). It is a pen-and-ink drawing that shows him in profile, with a pipe in his mouth. According to Sabartés, Picasso drew it in Barcelona. That same year, in a letter to Suzanne Bloch, Picasso drew a picture of himself with Jacob and a cat (93). He had just finished painting – or was preparing to paint – a portrait of the Belgian opera singer, who was known for her Wagner interpretations. In 1907, above a portrait of himself looking rather portly, wearing a herringbone jacket and holding his hat in his hand, he wrote: 'Bonjour Mlle Cone'. Did he mean Etta or Claribel Cone? The two sisters were friends with Gertrude Stein, who introduced them to the world of the Parisian avant-garde. As heiresses to the Cone Textile Business fortune, they could afford to buy many works by Picasso and Matisse on their visits to Paris. Matisse even began to call them 'my Baltimore ladies'. The sisters bought more than 140 works from Picasso – surely enough to merit him throwing a drawing into the bargain.

On 16 August 1918, Picasso wrote to his friend Apollinaire from Biarritz, where he was staying at the villa La Mimoseraie, on the Route de Bayonne. On one side, he wrote that he was happy to be working, while on the other, he drew a sketch of himself and Apollinaire sitting opposite one another at a table. Picasso is wearing a hat, while Apollinaire has a bandage on his head (134). On 17 March 1916, three days after he learned that his application for French citizenship had been successful, Second Lieutenant Apollinaire of the 96th Regiment was hit by a piece of shrapnel, which pierced through his helmet and left a hole in his skull. Above the drawing, Picasso wrote:

> A TOAST, as in Biarritz
> TO YOUR HEALTH ________AND YOURS
> APPRECIATED__________LIKEWISE

On 28 August, he wrote to Jean Cocteau from La Mimoseraie, illustrating his letter with a remarkably similar drawing to the one he had sent to Apollinaire a few days earlier. However, in this drawing, there are three figures around the table: himself, on the right, Cocteau, and the painter André Lhote (135). Underneath the drawing, he wrote:

> I toast your health as they do in Bordeaux
> TO YOUR HEALTH – AND YOURS
> APPRECIATED – LIKEWISE

Are these self-portraits that show Picasso 'in context' the only ones that we can be confident of interpreting as autobiographical? Picasso also included a drawing with a letter he wrote to Cocteau on 8 November 1962. It is a double portrait of himself and Cocteau (160), with their two faces layered on top of each other. Could we see this drawing as a symbol of a friendship that had endured through thick and thin since they first met in 1915, enjoying the good times but also surviving countless misunderstandings, arguments, and frustrations? Could it be seen as autobiographical?

Interpretations

Who decided to call the self-portrait of 1897, signed 'P. R. Picasso', *Perplexed Picasso* (11)? Who thought that one of those painted in 1906 was a *Childish Self-Portrait* (111)? How could the same self-portrait be interpreted by one critic as 'yet another expression of the artist's ever-changing personality, which is constantly shifting as his work progresses', while another viewed it as 'a first serious interrogation of his future'? Does another self-portrait reveal Picasso's desire to 'depict himself as a romantic artist'? Can we be confident in claiming that, in another self-portrait, his 'disillusioned gaze expresses a deep sense of failure'? Did Picasso ever 'etch the hardships of life onto his own face'? Can one self-portrait, more than any other, be said to be a sign that he 'was searching for a new form of artistic expression'?

In *Portrait of Picasso as a Young Man*, Norman Mailer writes (probably about one of the two drawings from 1902 or 1903 [68] that are both commonly referred to as *Nude with raised arm*): 'One can make too large a case of the nude he did of himself in this period – modest, unadorned, a little seedy, certainly depressed, and taking the vow of allegiance to ... to what? To his continuing heterosexuality? It is tempting to read too much into this drawing.' In the preface, Mailer carefully describes his book as 'an interpretative biography': 'Which is equal to saying that the interpretation of Picasso's life and work as a young man is my individual understanding of him, and I will rest on such a claim.'

Again and again I come back to the sentence: 'It is tempting to read too much into this drawing.' What self-portrait – drawing, painting, or etching – would not tempt the viewer to 'read too much into it'? And what might we read there? Surely our interpretations cannot help but be, inevitably, unavoidably, necessarily – is that clear enough? – the expression of an 'individual understanding'. 'Individual', subjective, perhaps mistaken.... And therefore debatable.

In a letter of 11 January 1917 to the collector Jacques Doucet, who bought *Les Demoiselles d'Avignon*, Max Jacob, who gave the painting its title, wrote: 'I have written nothing about Picasso. He loathes being written about. He loathes having his work misunderstood, loathes careless talk, and I feel such deep respect and gratitude towards him that I would hate to do anything that would displease him. I have seen how much he was upset by the behaviour of our dearest friends, and I will not do as they did. Some friends have used his name to further their own cause, living off rumours, gossip, tall tales. Well ... later ... we'll see ... but much later, actually, never, I think.'

Doesn't offering an interpretation always come with the risk of being wrong? Because we cling to what we believe, to what we think we have understood, perhaps we are always in danger of not considering the various 'disguises' that Picasso adopted throughout his career. And to do so would be to disregard André Breton's words: 'Reflecting oneself in a work of art that is about oneself, not only recognizing that the depiction is different from ourselves, but wanting it to be the opposite of ourselves.'

We must exercise caution when seeking to interpret a work of art. Every interpretation is an act of speculation that can, at best, offer a credible possibility.

I always return to these words of Picasso's: 'How could a viewer possibly experience my painting in the same way as I experienced it? A painting comes to me from far away; who knows how far, I sensed it, I saw it, I made it, but the next day even I cannot see what I have done. How could someone else hope to understand my dreams, my instincts, my desires, my thoughts, which have developed slowly over time, or to go so far as to recognize what I have done without perhaps being aware of it myself?'

A self-portrait *does not mean anything*. It simply is. It is what it is. It is an event.

Has it ever been possible to definitively name the circumstances, the coincidences, the chance occurrences that led to a particular event? Can we truly claim to understand the impact of the alignment of the planets, the workings of fate and determinism, the flap of a butterfly's wings in Barcelona, in the Rue Ravignan in Montmartre, or in the gardens of his house in Cannes, or Notre-Dame-de-Vie in Mougins? We must allow every gaze, every emotion the freedom to perceive – to comprehend? – what they will. As Jean Cassou writes, 'We are most likely on the right track, appreciating Picasso's work as he would like us to, when we do not allow ourselves to be scared or offended by his indifferent manners towards us, his impertinence even, and instead admire his creativity, energy, and inventiveness, the most extraordinary of any artist in history.'

Black and white

A photograph from 1901, taken in the studio on the Boulevard de Clichy, shows Picasso sitting on a stool in front of a portrait of Iturrino. He is looking directly into the camera's lens, as are Mañach, sitting beside him, and Fuster, who is standing (41). Who was the photographer telling them to hold still? Was it Picasso who decided on the poses and set up some sort of folding camera? We have no way of knowing. Just as we do not know who took another photograph that same year, which shows him standing in his studio surrounded by paintings, a shadowy figure wearing a top hat (48).

In 1904, however, there is no doubt. It was definitely Picasso who decided that his reflection should appear in the mirror on the mantelpiece behind Ricard Canals's armchair (89). This is a rare find, the first self-portrait where Picasso's image is only a small detail. He appeared in a similar position – reflected in a mirror – in a photograph taken in 1940, at the villa Les Voiliers in Royan (149). However, for photographs taken in 1909 and 1910, he posed in his studios. Wearing a coat, with a pipe in his hand, at the

Bateau-Lavoir. Sitting in his studio on the Boulevard de Clichy (118–20). In his studio on the Rue Schœlcher.

There are six photographs of Picasso taken in that studio between 1915 and 1916 (121, 122, 124–7), five of which show him standing. In one he wears a suit and tie and stands with his hands clasped behind his back; in another, he is bare-chested, wearing only shorts. Sometimes he wears a hat, sometimes his head is left bare.... It is clear that he and he alone decided where to pose in the studio and what to wear. What does it matter if (perhaps) he asked some photographer to take the photographs? They are, they *declare themselves to be*, self-portraits. What kind of account of Picasso do they offer? When he poses in fine clothing, does he want to imply that his time scraping together a living as a struggling artist is over? When he poses as a boxer, is he sending a message that he is engaged in a fight from which he knows he will emerge victorious? What answer can we venture, except 'perhaps'.

In the photograph taken in the summer of 1921 (142), is it (almost) by accident that he appears reflected in the mirror of a wardrobe door? By contrast, in 1927, does he make a deliberate choice to photograph the shadow cast by his face in profile? Only two of these photographic self-portraits were used as a basis for paintings: the photograph from 1901 (48) served as a 'model' for the drawing that shows him wearing the same top hat, standing in front of a group of prostitutes (50), while the photograph from 1927 inspired three paintings (including 145 and 146).

In his use of photography – a medium that claims to capture the exact likeness of the sitter – Picasso constantly confounded the viewer as he did throughout his artistic career, his work relentlessly challenging the reliability of appearances.

Shock

When and where did Guglielmo Alberto Wladimiro Alessandro Apollinare de Kostrowitzky and Pablo Ruiz Picasso make each other's acquaintance? There is no record at all of the circumstances of their first meeting. For thirteen years, they were close friends, with an unfaltering loyalty to one another. They had occasional fallings-out, brief quarrels during which they abandoned projects on which they had embarked together, but nothing could threaten the bond between the poet and the painter. When they wrote to each other, they addressed their letters to 'My dear Pablo' and 'My dear Guillaume'. During his stay in Gósol in 1906, Picasso added a note at the bottom of Fernande's letter to Apollinaire: 'Hello my dear friend Guillaume, I kiss you, on your belly button.'

On 27 February 1907, after a dinner at Picasso's where the painter showed him some new works, Apollinaire wrote in his diary that they possessed 'a magnificent language that no work of literature could convey because our words come readymade'. Despite the 'readymade' nature of words, he wrote many articles and forewords trying to describe Picasso's painting.

However, according to Apollinaire's first editor, Daniel-Henry Kahnweiler, who published his work *The Rotting Sorcerer*, he 'knew nothing about painting and had a pathological need to say things that were simply not true. One of his favourite sayings was "what is true is never interesting".' A troubling claim that would cast doubt on the apparent certainty of some of the poet's grand statements; his foreword to the catalogue for an exhibition that ran at Paul Guillaume's gallery from 23 January to 15 February 1918 opened with the words: 'Picasso is the heir to all the great artists. Suddenly awakened, he sets off down a path that has not yet been explored. He changes direction, retraces his steps and sets out again more confidently, always growing, becoming stronger through contact with the unknown or through the trial of comparison with his predecessors.'

Apollinaire's admiration of Picasso was mutual. On 29 May 1913, Picasso wrote to Apollinaire from Céret, saying, 'I received your book *Alcools*. You know how I love you and you know what joy I found in it; reading your poems makes me happy.' Kahnweiler remembers Apollinaire telling him, 'Even years ago, when he didn't speak French very well, he had a talent for evaluating, for immediately appreciating the beauty of a poem.'

In July 1918, Picasso signed off two letters to Apollinaire with the words 'Your dear brother', 'Your big brother'. Four months later, while he was staying at the Hôtel Lutetia, the telephone in his bedroom rang. Apollinaire had just died of the Spanish flu, on 9 November, in his apartment at 202 Boulevard Saint-Germain. Picasso was in shock. His brother was dead.

He picked up the first piece of paper that he could find and drew his portrait. In the book *Picasso: Documents iconographiques*, published in 1954, Jaime Sabartés wrote the following note on document number 122, entitled *Picasso, by himself*: 'This is how Picasso saw himself in the bathroom mirror at the Hôtel Lutetia in 1918, when he had just received a phone call informing him that his friend Apollinaire had died. The printmaker G. Aubert used it as the basis for his portrait of Picasso that appears in the edition of the *Nouvelle Revue Française* that was dedicated to the artist, with text by Pierre Reverdy, published in 1924.' That would mean the picture in question is a pencil drawing on paper that measures thirty-four centimetres by twenty-six – with the catalogue number Z.III.75 (137). However, this drawing, its style somewhat reminiscent of Ingres, does not convey any hint of the violent emotion that Picasso must have been feeling at the time. This is much more evident in an earlier sketch hastily scribbled in a notebook measuring fourteen centimetres by nine and a half (136).

Sabartés goes on to write, 'If, in the course of this study, I am led to refute certain claims that have been published elsewhere, it will not be for the simple pleasure of contradicting others, but rather in order to correct the record, basing my analysis on the most reliable documents, the most precise memories, whether personal or otherwise, all without forgetting that memory generally bends to fit the narrator's interpretation of events, even if he is convinced that he has in no way altered the facts.'

Pierre Cabanne, Picasso's biographer, wrote that Sabartés's 'unconditional admiration does not preclude unintentional omissions or deliberate distortions of the truth designed to present a version of events that suits the author'. Is it possible that Sabartés considered the sketch that Picasso drew at a time of heightened emotion unworthy of him? Perhaps. Either Sabartés made a mistake or he deliberately misrepresented events. As did Brassaï some years later, when he wrote without the slightest hesitation, 'After seeing the shadow of death pass over his own face on that day, he stopped drawing and painting himself.'

Teasing interpretations

According to Roland Penrose, 'The image of Harlequin recurs intermittently throughout the work of Picasso. Even during the cubist period, shorn of literary allusions, the diamond pattern of his costume still betrays his presence. This persistence has led Professor Jung to claim that the motive for his haunting reappearances is a subconscious desire in Picasso to portray himself in this disguise. The theory is strengthened by the frequency in early years with which we find Harlequin as Picasso's self-portrait. Let us not assume, however, that this is Picasso's only characterization of himself. His love of disguises prompts him to imagine himself in many different roles. It can be said that the bull, the horse, the minotaur, the owl, the dove, the meditating lover, the bearded artist and even the child holding a candle are also symbolic of Picasso himself.' There are plenty more images that could be added to this list of supposed 'symbols' and 'characterizations': guitars, bull fighters, and why not the palm trees of Cannes that he could see through the windows of his house in the Californie neighbourhood?

It is too late to advise Penrose to read Merleau-Ponty's *Sense and Nonsense*. If he had done so, he would have found the following words: 'Unlike the natural sciences, psychoanalysis was not meant to give us necessary relations of cause and effect but to point to motivational relationships which are in principle simply possible.' It is too late to quote Michel Foucault to him: 'Psychoanalysis has never managed to make images speak.' Those words might have made him take Professor Jung's claims with a pinch of salt.

'Why do you think I date everything I make? Because it's not enough to know an artist's works. One must also know when he made them, why, how, under what circumstances. No doubt there will some day be a science, called "the science of man", perhaps, which will seek above all to get a deeper understanding of man via man-the-creator. I often think of that science, and I want the documentation I leave to posterity to be as complete as possible. That's why I date everything I make.'

But for the moment, at least as far as I can tell, this 'science of man' that Picasso speaks of does not yet exist. At most, the psychoanalytical approaches proposed by Freud, Jung, and Lacan might be said to be the first tentative steps towards it. Just like the centuries-old traditions of palm reading and handwriting analysis.

In 1902, Max Jacob read the twenty-one-year-old Picasso's palm (56), seeing in it a 'fiery temperament' and predicting that he would experience a 'change of fortune before the age of thirty or thirty-five, as well as exceptional artistic success'. And so on. He closed the reading with this 'strange observation. All the lines on this hand seem to originate from the fate line. It is like the first spark of a firework. A sort of living star that we see only rarely, in the palms of individuals destined for greatness. Like a jet of water spraying out towards the mount of inspiration, this line indicates a poetic temperament, as the long shape of the hand has already suggested.' However, Jacob also pointed out that the life line ended at the age of sixty-eight, that the health line was 'broken' and 'weak', a sign of 'poor health', and that 'the thumb is short, indicating a weakness of character'.

Thirty years later, on 21 May 1942, Paul Éluard commissioned a well-known handwriting expert by the name of Raymond Trillat to analyse Picasso's writing in a letter dated 14 September 1936. Rushing to note down the expert's findings – Trillat spoke very quickly – Éluard recorded that Picasso's handwriting showed: 'He is from another time, another world: chivalrous, childlike, and wild'; 'He loves intensely and kills what he loves'; 'His life is marked by tragedies that he creates himself through his flouting of conservatism and his carelessness'; 'He is sad. He seeks a way to escape his sadness through an act of pure creation. Joy and happiness are detrimental for him. Sadness is useful'; 'He is very gentle and yet very tough. He has no use for the middle ground, for moderation'; 'He has an immediate sensuality around certain subjects, which is at first seductive and complicated, then defiant'; 'He is afraid of being taken over by anxiety'; 'The question of money is not important to him.'

Éluard claimed that 'for anyone who knows Picasso, this analysis is impressive'. However, can we use these conclusions as a key to decoding his self-portraits? Should we see these works as signs of the same 'fiery temperament' that Jacob identified? Or as expressions of the 'chivalrous, childlike, and wild' character that the handwriting expert saw in Picasso's letter? Which of the many portraits offered him a way to 'escape his sadness through an act of pure creation'? And which shows that he 'has no use for the middle ground, for moderation'? Palm reading and handwriting analysis have no better claim than psychoanalysis to be '"the science of man", perhaps, which will seek above all to get a deeper understanding of man via man-the-creator' that Picasso hoped for.

And what of art history? Faced with Picasso's self-portraits, if it does not offer a highly conceptual theory – which would be nothing more than a vain trick – it must content itself with stammering out a few tentative, unverifiable hypotheses.

Aristotelian?

Could we perhaps see Picasso as embodying Aristotle's teaching more than many other painters? 'The poet being an imitator, like a painter or any other artist, must of necessity imitate one of three objects: things as they were or are, things as they are said or thought to be, or things as they ought to be.' If we follow this principle, laid out by Aristotle in his *Poetics*, we may say that over the course of seventy years, Picasso painted some things as they were, others as they were said to be, and still others as they ought to be. Which means that he took as his subject many things that had been disregarded by those who understood *mimesis* only in the narrow sense of imitation.

Gaze

It is a drawing (131). Or at least, what is left of it. It seems that Picasso cut up a self-portrait, leaving only his eyes staring out from the paper. As if the rest of his features did not matter in the end. Or, alternatively, because he knew that his gaze was unique.

More than anything else, it was this that fascinated everyone who met him.

Fernande Olivier remembered meeting his gaze at Bateau-Lavoir when she was still living under the name Madame de la Baume with the sculptor Laurent Debienne, whom everyone believed to be called Monsieur de la Baume: 'He stared at me with his big, heavy eyes that were at once lively and pensive, that possessed a constant fire, and he looked at me with such intensity that I could not help looking back at him.' Others, around the same time, could only remark that 'his insistent gaze demanded attention'.

In her book *The Autobiography of Alice B. Toklas*, Gertrude Stein wrote that his eyes had 'a strange faculty of opening wide and drinking in what he wished to see'. For Apollinaire, his eyes were 'watchful, like flowers that always turn towards the sun'. For André Salmon, they were 'eyes like blackcurrants'. Blaise Cendrars claimed that he 'never blinks, because he has the transfigured eyes of faith'. Cocteau was fascinated by his 'snowdrop eyes', his 'terrifying, deep-set gimlet eyes'. In one of his poems, Paul Éluard wrote: 'You opened your eyes, which go their own way / Among natural things of all ages / You harvest natural things / And you sow for all times', concluding that Picasso's eyes 'perhaps never close'. According to Prévert, 'Picasso looks up, looks at us and smiles, but his gaze is ... I don't know how to describe it ... to be honest, we could say that this gaze is like a great surgeon's staple, like a great couturier's label, like the chalk mark drawn by a customs officer, like a murderer's fingerprint.'

In 1932, Brassaï wrote the following description: 'Picasso wore a grey suit with a rather rumpled double-breasted jacket with misshapen pockets and stained lapels over a blue pullover sweater, plus a cardigan. The collar of his shirt was curled, unfolding like a petal. But I could not bother with these details of clothing because I was so fascinated by the eyes trained on me. "Black diamonds", "glowing eyes", "jet-black eyes". I noted at the time that, contrary to what some have said and believed, these eyes are neither abnormally large nor abnormally dark. They appear enormous only because they have the odd ability to open wide, revealing the white sclera – sometimes even above the iris – where light can reflect and sparkle. It is the wide eyelids that render his gaze fixed, mad, hallucinatory. That is also why, with the pupils widely dilated, the iris, normally a dark brown, seems so black. It is the eye of a visually oriented man, and designed for perpetual astonishment.'

When he visited Picasso at Notre-Dame-de-Vie, André Malraux encountered these 'same eyes from beyond the grave that are to be found in the face of a surprised sad clown'. On seeing the self-portrait that Picasso drew on 30 June 1972 (166), René Char wrote, 'Look at the painting: the left eye is the working eye, the right eye is a black circle, filled with darkness. But the figure is not one-eyed, not blind. It is night next to day. It is life. It is the unblinking clarity in the middle of the face.'

Flights of fancy

Often, when critics claim to reveal what Picasso *wanted to say* – as if a work of art should and can have only one meaning – I find that their interpretations unsettle me and cloud my own relationship with the work. I am uncomfortable with such certainties spoken from on high. Worse still, according to Emil Cioran: 'Nowadays we are more and more interested, not in what an author said but in what we think he wanted to say, not in his actions but in his intentions; less in his actual work than in his ideal work.'

These claims about what Picasso *said* or *wanted to say* appear again and again in works that discuss the painterly gaze. Picasso is not spared such scrutiny. Because his gaze is intense, critics are not shy in inferring that he is worried, perhaps even tormented, anxious, who knows what else.... What adjective should we apply to his apparent pout in a drawing of 1900 (28)? It seems that he kept this scrap of paper (measuring only ten and half centimetres by six) until 1970. Similarly, he kept a page from his sketchbook (14) on which he had drawn a dark self-portrait next to a study of an ear, with a study of a hand below, until he donated it to the Museu Picasso in Barcelona. Would he have kept these sketches for seventy years if they had not been important to him? Only Picasso knows why he kept them. Only Picasso knows what they express.

The gaze of a painter meeting the eye of the viewer who stands before his self-portrait is not so different from that of artists looking in the mirror over the centuries. A calm, fixed, confident gaze. It should come as no surprise. It is obvious where the strange intensity of this gaze comes from, although we may prefer not to acknowledge it. If it is unique, that is because it belongs to a man whose whole existence revolved around his way of seeing. Seeing as no one had been able to see before. Or, perhaps, as no one had dared to. Seeing as a way of showing. Seeing as a way of – in the title of a collection of Éluard's writings on painting, *Donner à voir* – making visible.

The Eiffel Tower and the Moulin Rouge

How best to show that one is in Paris? By drawing oneself with the Eiffel Tower in the background. Or – why not? – the Moulin Rouge. Although France had suffered in the aftermath of Napoleon's defeat and the fall of its empire, the Third Republic was keen to present a show of strength in its celebrations to mark the centenary of the Revolution. Therefore, the authorities decided to build a tower on the Champ-de-Mars, on the banks of the Seine. A tower designed by Mr Gustave Eiffel. It was opened on 31 March 1889. By 1900, no one wanted to take down what Paul Verlaine had called a 'belfry skeleton', what Joris-Karl Huysmans had described as a 'funnel-shaped grill', a 'hole-riddled suppository'.

The Eiffel Tower's status as a patriotic symbol of the Republic was not lost on Joseph Oller and Charles-Joseph Zidler. However, they had their eye on the millions of visitors who streamed into Paris for the World's Fair, where the tower was the main attraction. Montmartre was famous for its cabarets and its dancing. The windmill on the Boulevard de Clichy, a stone's throw from the Place Blanche, was never seen with its sails turning in the wind, but it had the potential to turn heads. However, work on the site took longer than expected. On 6 October 1889, some weeks after the World's Fair had closed its doors on 31 March, the Moulin Rouge was finally open for business. It was an immediate success, the raucous atmosphere and cancan dancers proving irresistible.

It is not the Louvre that Picasso is pointing out to his friend Manuel Pallarès in a sketch of 1900 (33). One year later, in a drawing of himself walking along the banks of the Seine with Jaume Andreu Bonsons, it is not the Louvre that appears in the background. It is the Eiffel Tower (45). And, that same year, 1901, when he draws himself wearing a large black hat and carrying an easel, a palette and a box of paints, he places himself in front of the Moulin Rouge (44). The Eiffel Tower appears one more time behind the neck of a carriage horse in a sketch of 1904 that shows him recently arrived in Paris with Sebastià Junyer-Vidal (83). A few days before they set off for Paris, the ever perceptive Junyer-Vidal wrote in the 24 March 1904 edition of the newspaper *El Liberal*: 'Picasso is more, so much more than what people think, even those people who seem to know him. He is the beginning of an end.'

The Eiffel Tower, the Moulin Rouge ... Paris! How could Picasso resist depicting himself against this ultimate bohemian backdrop? Michel Leiris wrote in his *Diary* on Tuesday, 15 August 1961: 'When Picasso came to Paris as a young man, he went to see – and greatly enjoyed – Puccini's *La Bohème*.' After he had lived in Paris for a few years, perhaps he might have nodded knowingly at the words sung by the painter Marcello in the first act: '*Rodolfo, io voglio dirti un mio pensier profondo: ho un freddo cane*' ('Rodolfo, I'll tell you my profound conviction: I'm freezing cold.') The artists' studios in Bateau-Lavoir were known to be very chilly.

A few years after the Moulin Rouge opened its doors, Apollinaire could be confident in his claim, written in an article published in the Berlin bimonthly newspaper *Der Sturm*, that, 'In terms of artistic culture, we can say that today France plays the same role that Italy played for classical painting.' The arrival in Paris of his friend, the Spanish painter Picasso, was the greatest proof of all.

Nudes

Two pages filled with studies that Picasso drew in Barcelona in 1897 include self-portraits that show the artist bare-chested (12, 13). He drew another, again in Barcelona, in 1902, which shows him reclining on a beach, with his back to the viewer and his face in profile, holding a palette in his left hand and a paintbrush in his right (62). He appears bare-chested again in the self-portrait that he drew on a sheet of newspaper (113) in 1906 and one that he painted in the same year. Finally, in 1915 or 1916, there is the photograph of him standing bare-chested, posing as a boxer in his studio on the Rue Schœlcher (127).

From 1903 onwards, Picasso depicted himself nude. As no painter had dared to do for centuries. Four centuries, to be exact. The first known nude self-portrait is a pen-and-brush drawing on blue paper by Albrecht Dürer, which is believed to date to either 1500, 1505, or 1512. It shows him nude against a strip of black background painted onto the page. To dare to depict himself naked as no other painter had ever done, was Picasso sending a message that he was prepared to break all taboos? Nudity was by no means the least of these. It was strict Morality – with a capital M, if you please – and its accomplice hypocrisy that laced women into tight corsets, leaving no space to breathe. Nudity was permitted only when painting gods and goddesses, nymphs and heroes. And the occasional female figure from the Bible. Even then, artists had to take care to conceal their genitalia, with the briefest wisp of fabric draped fortuitously around their stomach. Was Picasso trying to show that he was prepared to face criticism, condemnation, and even scandal? A drawing dated 26 December 1966 is the last time that he depicted himself naked (161). One final act of rebellion?

In 1903, at the age of twenty-two, he drew a series of self-portraits in pen and watercolour. One shows him sitting on a bed with his arms wrapped around his knees, next to a young woman with her head in her hands (65), her face hidden by her long hair, which falls all the way to the bedclothes. In another, he is lying on a bed with a nude woman whose nipples are coloured with ochre, his penis clearly visible (63). Did he show these drawings only to those with whom he visited the brothels of Barcelona, such as Sebastià Junyer-Vidal, who appears in one drawing – a parody of Manet's *Olympia* – bearing a plate of fruit, while Picasso sits nude in the foreground, one hand reaching towards a female nude lying on the bed (66)?

When he was putting together an exhibition, Jean Leymarie asked Picasso what was the difference between art and sexuality. The painter replied that there was none.

Between 1902 and 1904, he drew himself standing in the nude many times. One drawing shows him with his left hand raised and his right on his chest (68), another with his right hand raised but his left hanging by his side (77). These are both pencil drawings, but there is another, this time ink on paper, that is made up of only a few sketched-in lines. Could these drawings have been preparatory studies for his painting *La Vie* ? In one, before he decided against depicting himself in the painting, he is standing, nude, next to a nude woman, who leans on his shoulder with her arm around his neck (75, 76). Serving as his own model would have been a way to save money in this period when he was struggling financially, when blue became the colour of poverty.

Picasso finished *La Vie* in 1903, and he thought it important to set the record straight about the painting: 'It was not me who gave it this title, *La Vie*.... I did not set out to paint symbols. I simply painted the images that appeared before my eyes: it is for others to find in them a hidden meaning.' What should we make of his ultimate decision not to depict himself in the painting, not to be identifiable, recognizable? Does that mean his features and his body did not match the images that appeared before his eyes?

This title, *La Vie*, was not the only one that he objected to: '*Les Demoiselles d'Avignon*, that name is so annoying! It was Salmon who came up with it. You know very well that it was originally called "The Brothel of Avignon". Do you know why? For me, Avignon was always a name that I knew, a name with a close connection to my life. I lived a stone's throw away from the Calle de Avignon. That's where I bought my paper, my watercolours.'

Brothels

A young man lies on a bed, his hands behind his head, watching a young woman with long hair whose head is buried in his lap. This painting is known by the very prudish title *La Douceur*, meaning 'contentment' (73). (Other titles might have been more appropriate, such as the very factual *Fellatio*, or *The Blow Job*, *Sucking Off*, or others from the rich world of slang.) Kahnweiler had no doubt that the male figure was Picasso. The lock of hair that falls over the young man's forehead is a fairly reliable sign of his identity.

In 1960, when shown a photograph of this work, Picasso denied ever having painted it. He said it must have been a dirty joke by his friends. However, some years later, it emerged that in 1912, Daniel-Henry Kahlweiler had bought two paintings from Benet Soler. Around 1903, Soler – a tailor in Barcelona – had made clothes for the impecunious Picasso, who had given him some paintings in lieu of payment. *La Douceur* was among them. Kahnweiler kept it until 1923, when an erotica collector bought it at auction.

This painting is not the only self-portrait that shows Picasso as a frequenter of brothels, whorehouses, and houses of ill repute. In a pen-and-ink drawing from *c.* 1903 (59), meticulously catalogued by Zervos (XXI, 332), Picasso draws himself wearing a wide-brimmed black hat and sitting at a table with his friends Àngel Fernández de Soto and Sebastiá Junyer-Vidal. Junyer-Vidal sports a moustache, and his curly hair forms a kind of halo around his head. His resemblance to the man who appears behind the bed, carrying a plate of fruit, in the parody of Manet's *Olympia* (66) is striking. The same bushy moustache, the same mass of curls on his head. And on the other side of the bed, on the right, there is a nude man whose lock of hair and moustache look uncannily like Picasso's in a drawing in the Museu Picasso in Barcelona, which shows him sitting, fully clothed, beside a nude woman lying on a bed (64). This drawing dates to 1902 or 1903. It is not the first that has a touch of debauchery to it. In 1901, Picasso drew himself sitting on a prostitute's lap on the edge of a bed (55). He is wearing a coat buttoned up over his wing-collared shirt and black tie, one hand fondling the bare breast of the young woman, whose hair is caught up in a chignon. His eyepatch does little to disguise him, while the lock of hair that falls over his forehead leaves no room for doubt. Sitting behind the bed, with a cigarette dangling from his lips, is de Soto. (Picasso did not hold back from drawing his friend's erect penis being masturbated by a young woman whose clitoris he, in turn, is pleasuring.)

Along with Sebastià Junyer-Vidal, as well as Isidre Nonell, the Matteu brothers and Àngel Fernández de Soto, Picasso was a regular client at the brothels of the Barrio Chino in Barcelona. One of the madams, Carlotta Valdivia, posed for him (78, 79). She became famous under the name La Celestina, a crafty businesswoman who appears in Fernando de Rojas's *Tragicomedy of Calisto and Melibea*, published with that title in 1500 in Toledo, a work that was perhaps as well known as *Don Quixote*. The date (March 1904) appears on the back of Picasso's painting, while on the frame he wrote: *Valdivia calle Conde Asalto 12°-4, 1a Escalera interior*. A very precise address. The only thing missing is the price list.

In a song about the Calle Conde Asalto, with lyrics by Rosendo Llurba and music by Rafael Iriarte, one verse compares this perverse, crazy street to a beloved woman that the singer cannot put out of his mind. Perhaps that was the same woman Picasso drew holding a mirror, and beside whom he wrote: '*Cuando tengas ganas de joder, jode*' ('When you feel like fucking, fuck'). Christian Zervos catalogued this pencil-and-watercolour work too: Z., XXI, 343. Similarly, he listed a 1904 drawing as Z., I, 235, a drawing sometimes called (by whom?) *Meditation* and elsewhere (again, by whom?) *Contemplation*. In it, Picasso rests his chin on his hand as he watches a sleeping woman in a nightdress, one arm flung behind her head (90). This is the last time that he draws himself with a woman.

In 1960, Picasso refused to admit that he had painted *La Douceur*, reluctant to resurrect these self-portraits that testify to a time when he was a regular visitor to brothels. He did not want his reputation to be tarnished by accounts of his escapades. These highly erotic drawings led one critic to add another period onto the many that marked the artist's work: 'the dirty period'.

Egon Schiele would not have cared about being considered indecent, even pornographic. He died of Spanish flu in 1918. As early as 1910, when he was twenty years old, he was one of very few painters who dared to depict himself nude. In 1911, he was apparently the only one who depicted himself in the act of masturbation. Could these self-portraits that Schiele drew in Vienna – part of the Austro-Hungarian Empire under the rule of Franz Joseph I – and the ones that Picasso drew in Barcelona, in staunchly Catholic Spain, be seen as signs that the emerging twentieth century would be a period marked by transgression?

Anomalies

Picasso's smallest self-portrait appears on a piece of letterhead paper from the Grand Hôtel Victoria in Naples, dated 20 April 1917. The drawing, which he sent to Apollinaire, shows a bird's eye view of that city (128). To make sure there was no doubt as to its identity, he drew Vesuvius at the top left, complete with a plume of smoke. Sailing boats are dotted around the bay. At the bottom of the page, there is a group of musicians. Finally, at the top right, a horse-drawn carriage travels along the Via Scarlatti – Picasso wrote the street name on the drawing. In this carriage, sitting side by side, with their names written above their heads, are Picasso and Olga. He had only recently met her. Olga Khokhlova was a twenty-six-year-old ballerina with the Ballets Russes, Sergei Diaghilev's company.

Picasso's work on the set of *Parade* – with a scenario by Jean Cocteau, music by Erik Satie, and choreography by Léonide Massine – brought him to Rome, where the company was touring. In a studio on Via Margutta, he worked on the costumes, scenery, and stage curtain that he had designed. They were finished on 10 April, which left him time to visit Naples and Pompeii before he was due to return to Paris. *Parade* premiered on 18 May 1917 at the Châtelet Theatre, sparking an immediate scandal. Erik Satie had included typewriters as part of the orchestra. An insufferable 'collage' not unlike those that Picasso had experimented with a few years earlier during his cubist period. Francis Poulenc wrote: 'This time, art has gone mad.'

When they returned to France, Picasso and Olga moved into a house at 22 Rue Victor-Hugo, in the suburb of Montrouge. Picasso had lived there since 1916, but Olga did not consider it a suitable home. Especially now that Picasso had established his reputation as an artist, she thought it was not in keeping with his standing to invite guests to such a messy house. The couple married on 12 July 1918 in the Russian Orthodox Alexander Nevsky Cathedral in Paris, and Madame Picasso demanded that they find a new home as soon as possible. On 9 December 1917, Picasso drew a pencil drawing of their dining room (129). It shows himself and Olga sitting opposite one another at the table, eating lunch (or dinner). A birdcage appears in the background, near a window, and two dogs sit behind Picasso. A maid – whose presence shows that Picasso's Bohemian lifestyle is no more – stands behind Olga.

Olga is the only one of Picasso's legal wives to appear alongside him in his work. And only one of his mistresses was granted this 'privilege': Geneviève Laporte. What conclusion should we draw from that? Is there only one conclusion to draw?

In 1919, Picasso drew himself again: alone this time, holding a pipe in his hand, sitting by a window in the apartment at 23 Rue La Boétie, where he moved with Olga in 1918. He is talking to a bird that perches in a cage on a side table (141). What should we make of Olga's absence from this drawing?

In profile

In his *Letter on the Blind*, Diderot writes: 'Of all the men we have seen, the one we least remember is our own self. We notice faces to recognize people; and if we do not remember our own, it is because we are never liable to mistake ourselves for another person or another for ourselves.'

The year is 1899. Picasso and Casagemas walk side by side. Both are wearing hats. Picasso's is red. He has a cane tucked under his arm and is wrapped up in a long brown coat, with a splash of colour provided by the blue book he is carrying (26). This was the first time that he drew himself in profile. But it was far from the last.... In 1900, on a page of studies, he drew himself wearing a black hat, standing with his hands in his pockets (32). That same year, he drew himself with Manuel Pallarès, again wearing a hat, pointing out the Eiffel Tower (33).

A drawing of 1901, which appeared in the magazine *Arte Joven*, shows him talking to a group of artists: one unidentified figure, S. Cornuti, Francisco de Asis Soler, and Alberto Soler. It is signed 'P. Ruiz Picasso' (37). On an ink drawing of *c*.1903 that shows him sitting at a table with Àngel Fernández de Soto and Sebastiá Junyer-Vidal, the signature is simply 'Picasso' (59). The previous year, he drew himself lying on a beach, with a palette in his hand, and again signed the drawing 'Picasso' (62). Another drawing – from 1902 or 1903 – again shows him in profile, sitting on the edge of a bed, turning towards a nude young woman who is lying there (64). He is nude in the parody of *Olympia* that he drew in 1902 or 1903 (66). In another drawing, he stands clothed between two female nudes, with his hands in his pockets and a pipe in his mouth, wearing a beret (67). As Sabartés says, 'that does not mean that the beret, the cap or the hat denote a specific period, but rather that the inclusion of one or the other indicates a possible state of mind'.

Between 1902 and 1968, Picasso depicted himself in profile another twenty or so times. Holding a dog on a lead, wearing an ascot tie, and sporting a moustache, often with a pipe in his mouth, his chin resting on his hands, looking rather portly and holding a top hat, and so on. Finally, bald, with a cane in his hand.

They are pencil drawings, ink drawings. Sometimes coloured with pencil or watercolour. They are studies. Sometimes, perhaps, for a painting that he decided not to paint. Sometimes they are caricatures. All of Picasso's self-portraits confirm that he, in Diderot's words, was never liable to mistake himself for another person.... He knows better than anyone else who he is, and what he looks like.

Then, in 1927, a photograph. In it, his face in profile is just a shadow. Nothing more than a shadow. In 1929, this same shadow appears again in the painting *Bust of a Woman and Self-Portrait*. It is in a frame on the wall behind a woman whose mouth hangs open, her snakelike triangular tongue sticking out (146). The composition of the painting is such that this shadow seems at risk of being devoured by the woman's open mouth, her square teeth. The shadow also appears, this time with its mouth open, in the painting *Nude in the Yellow Mirror* that dates to 1927 (or 1928) (145).

How can we not think about this shadow? It is a shadow unlike any other. In his preface to *The Lives of the Most Excellent Painters, Sculptors, and Architects*, Vasari describes the invention of painting, writing with absolute confidence that, 'according to what Pliny writes, this came to Egypt from Gyges the Lydian, who, being by the fire and gazing at his own shadow, suddenly, with some charcoal in his hand, drew his own outline on the wall'. A wonderful story: the first work by the first painter was a 'portrait' of himself. A self-portrait.

In the same preface, Vasari wrote, 'It was the wont of the finest spirits in all their actions, through a burning desire for glory, to spare no labour, however grievous, in order to bring their works to that perfection which might render them impressive and marvellous to the whole world.' Picasso's ambition was no different.

We do not know whether Picasso ever read Vasari's *Lives*; there is certainly no record that he did. However, in this photograph from 1927, in these paintings from 1928 and 1929, was his decision to depict himself as a shadow a way of claiming his place, like Gyges the Lydian before him, as the inventor of painting? After all, this identity, 'the inventor of painting', is the only one that he is certain truly resembles him. And suits him very well.

Yo Picasso

If there is one title that we can be sure Picasso himself gave to a painting, it is this one: *Yo Picasso* (I, Picasso). Painted in Paris in 1901. *Yo Picasso*. Nothing more. (By then, the string of names that he had been given when he was born on 25 October 1881 had long been forgotten: Pablo Diego José Francisco de Paula Juan Nepomuceno María de los Remedios Cipriano de la Santísima Trinidad Ruiz y Picasso.)

A few months earlier, in Madrid, he had drawn a portrait of himself with Francisco de Asis Soler, for the periodical *Notas de Arte*. It appeared on the front cover of the first edition published on 11 March 1901. Underneath the title, he had signed it Pablo Ruiz Picasso (40), the same signature we see underlined with a bold stroke of charcoal on a self-portrait that shows him sitting and drawing (15). In 1897, he signed another self-portrait, showing him with a centre parting, 'P. R. Picasso' (11).

As for the word *Yo* – 'I' or 'Me' – he had already written it on two of his self-portraits. Firstly, on the lost self-portrait in which the words *Yo el Rey* – I, the king – appear three times, forming a kind of halo around his head. Secondly, on a drawing done in ink and watercolour in 1900, he wrote the single word *Yo* behind his dark hair (23).

In his *Conversations with Picasso*, under the entry for 20 October 1943, Brassaï writes that he heard the artist say, 'My friends in Barcelona called me by that name. It was stranger, more resonant than "Ruiz". And those are probably the reasons I adopted it. Do you know what appealed to me about that name? Well, it was undoubtedly the double s, which is fairly unusual in Spain. "Picasso" is of Italian origin, as you know. And the name a person bears or adopts has its importance. Can you imagine me calling myself "Ruiz"? "Pablo Ruiz"? "Diego José Ruiz"? Or "Juan Nepomucene Ruiz"? I was given I don't know how many names. Have you noticed, by the way, the double s in the names of Matisse, Poussin, and Le Douanier Rousseau?'

He surely did not choose these three artists' names at random.

Matisse ... Since they had been introduced by the Steins in 1906, since he had first seen *Woman with a Hat* hanging on a wall in the Steins' apartment on the Rue de Fleurus before they came to Bateau-Lavoir, Picasso had been convinced that Matisse was his greatest artistic rival. An enduring rivalry that was to prove vital to his work. 'When one of us dies, there will be things that the other will never be able to tell another soul', he confided to Françoise Gilot.

Poussin ... Picasso's engagement with his work began in 1901 and lasted many years. In 1962, he projected slides of Poussin's work onto a wall to compose his own variations on *The Rape of the Sabine Women* and *The Massacre of the Innocents*.

Le Douanier Rousseau ... In his review of the Salon des Indépendants published in *La Revue des lettres et des arts* on 1 May 1908, Apollinaire wrote, 'Mr Rousseau's exhibition is at once moving and amusing. This self-taught artist undeniably possesses natural talent, and it seems to me that Gauguin would admire Rousseau's blacks. However, le Douanier is sadly lacking in broader cultural knowledge. We must not indulge his naivety. It lends his work a touch too much randomness, even absurdity.'

This criticism did not put Picasso off buying a *Portrait of a woman* by Rousseau from the antique dealer Père Soulié's shop on the Rue des Martyrs. Perhaps he was thinking of Degas, who, on seeing a painting by le Douanier at one of the Salons, asked if this work, more than any other, might represent the birth of modern painting? A few months later, a dinner was given at Bateau-Lavoir in his honour. Among those who attended the event at Picasso's studio were Fernande Olivier, Max Jacob, Apollinaire and Marie Laurencin, Georges Braque, Gertrude and Leo Stein.... Maurice Cremnitz sang: 'This Rousseau's paintings / tame nature itself / with his magic paintbrush.' André Salmon wrote in the journal *Bravo* (no. 32) in 1931: 'We wanted very sincerely to bring great joy to an old man whom we believed to be a genius and to whom life had been cruel. It was a great success.' The 'old man' was only sixty-four years old.

Matisse, Poussin, Rousseau ... They all have a double 's'. Like Picasso. Like *Yo Picasso*. I, Picasso. But if he is undeniably Picasso, which Picasso is he? In 1901, he painted his own portrait four times. And these four images of himself, all painted in the same year, have nothing in common. Some time in the spring of that year, he painted the first, *Yo Picasso* (47), for the exhibition that opened on 25 May at Ambroise Vollard's gallery on the Rue Laffitte. The exhibition featured more than sixty paintings and numerous drawings. Did Picasso perhaps paint this work at the last minute? It is true that, as Gustave Coquiot wrote in *Le Journal* one week before the private view, Pablo Ruiz Picasso was 'an artist who paints twenty-four hours a day'. This *Portrait of the Artist* was the first entry in the list of works exhibited. Such confidence, perhaps even arrogance, from a painter who was not yet twenty. Confident in his capabilities, in his talent, he meets the viewer's gaze and sets about dismantling tradition. A preparatory sketch shows him, as this revered tradition dictates, sitting in front of an easel (46). In the final painting, however, the easel has been replaced by a jumble of colours, which could perhaps represent paint on a palette, although this interpretation is far from certain. And, as no one had dared to do before, Picasso painted a slash of green running from his temple to his chin. It serves as a counterpoint to the broad red ascot tie that covers his chest. Does this self-portrait show his desire to be worthy of the gallery that, in 1895, put on the first exhibition of Cézanne's work?

A painting completed that summer shows him sporting a moustache as in *Yo Picasso*, as well as a beard – indicated by small dabs of dark paint around his chin. This time he is standing, wearing a black coat and a top hat. An elegant gentleman with a white scarf and a flower in his buttonhole, he is surrounded by prostitutes in a brothel (50). Two of the women have bare breasts, but, to indicate that this house of ill repute still has a touch of class, he takes care to show that all three women are wearing hats, so that the viewer does not take them for the kind of women who go out 'bare-headed'. It is for the same reason that the woman by his side in the portrait of himself in a top hat is wearing an admiral's hat decorated with a flower (49).

Towards the end of that summer, he painted himself again. Just his face this time. Front on. His head perched atop a stiff white collar (51). A few brushstrokes suffice to indicate a dark jacket and a black tie. This figure has nothing in common with the man whom the sculptor Maillol met: 'He was thin, he was skinny, he looked very much like a young woman.'

Finally, towards the end of the year, Picasso painted a man with a beard, moustache, and dark hair. His coat, secured with a single button, is a solid block of dark paint, made up of variations on the same blue that forms the shadows around his eyes and beneath his cheekbones. The same blue that covers the background, giving no indication of the room in which he stands (53).

In the *Revue blanche*, the critic Georges Faillet – who wrote under the pseudonym Félicien Fagus – closed his article about the Picasso exhibition at Vollard's gallery with these words: 'As well as the greats of the past, we can easily identify many likely influences: Delacroix, Manet (appropriately, given that he was influenced by Spanish artists), Monet, Van Gogh, Pissarro, Toulouse-Lautrec, Degas, Forain, perhaps Rops.... Each influence is fleeting, slipping away as soon as it is captured: we can see that his energy and impulsiveness have not allowed him time to develop his own personal style; his character is in this energy, this youthful, impulsive spontaneity (we must remember that he is not yet twenty and that he paints up to three canvases a day). The danger, for him, lies in this impulsiveness, which may well lead him to a simplistic kind of virtuosity. Prolific and productive go hand in hand, as do fierce and energetic. And it would be most regrettable, given he shows signs of such brilliant potency.'

Could this blue self-portrait be a response to Fagus's criticism? Perhaps, with his characteristic impulsiveness, he was seeking to shrug off the influences of the 'greats from the past' and 'develop his own personal style'.

The National Exhibition of Fine Arts that opened in Madrid on 29 April featured one painting by Picasso: *Woman in Blue*. This painting, number 963 in the catalogue, was given an honourable mention. However, it was not returned to Picasso when the exhibition closed. More than half a century later, it was discovered tucked away in a forgotten corner of a storage space. The woman, who is wearing a large hat and an enormous crinoline embellished with a double band of ribbons, is a courtesan, an extravagantly adorned prostitute. Does she set the tone for Picasso's Blue Period, in which he focuses on this seedy world of poverty, destitution, and despair, where absinthe is the only escape? Blue is the only colour for painting gaunt, emaciated, wan faces and figures clothed in rags. (For a cash-strapped artist such as Picasso, the fact that Prussian blue was the cheapest pigment would not have been a minor consideration, although we should not make too much of this.)

Picasso never sold this blue self-portrait. Never. Is that because it was the first painting that truly showed Picasso by Picasso? The Blue Period, which began in 1901, is the first period of Picasso's that can be said to owe nothing to anyone but him. In 1971, Aragon published a 'Discourse for the grand days of a young man named Pablo Picasso' in *Les Lettres françaises*. In it, he paid tribute to 'a young man forever called Pablo Picasso, who began to be himself long ago with his blue song of poverty and love.'

By its very nature, an artistic period does not last for ever. Picasso could not shake off his characteristic 'impulsiveness'. It drove him to adopt a new style, to begin a new period.

Monkey and Pharaoh

In 1903, with a few strokes of ink on a torn-off scrap of paper, Picasso drew himself as a monkey (71), with a paintbrush tucked behind one ear and a mechanical pencil behind the other. This is the only one of his self-portraits that is accompanied by the simplest of captions: 'Picasso par lui-même' (Picasso by himself).

There seems no doubt that he had seen Chardin's *The Monkey Painter*, which was exhibited at the Salon in 1740. In it, the monkey sits in front of a painting on an easel, wearing a tricorn hat. But Picasso does not follow this composition. He could not care less about the eighteenth-century painters' reworkings of, for example, Abraham Teniers's monkey scenes. Just as he did not care that the phrase 'monkey painter' came from the words *ars simia naturæ*, written by a certain Filippo Villani in Florence at the end of the fourteenth or start of the fifteenth century. But perhaps he was aware that Chardin may have painted a monkey because he was one of those at the Royal Academy of Painting who were not afraid to denounce a system that trained mere copyists and plagiarists. Artists who were not capable of individuality. This caricature is a warning. A clear statement that Picasso would not stoop to imitation. As for the grand masters, they were there to be plundered and defied. While he may have seen Chardin's *The Monkey Painter* at the Louvre, he was clear in his approach to museums: 'In museums ... there are only unsuccessful paintings.... You laugh, but pay attention, see if I'm right; what we now call "master works" are those that broke the rules handed down by the masters of that time.'

Was it because he was recognized as a 'master' in his own time that he never ceased to break the same 'rules' he had established? Perhaps the answer can be found in the words said to Claude Roy by a 'seller of fishing equipment, nets, sou'westers, boots and cork': 'Picasso? Well, Picasso (he said this in a southern French accent, with great conviction), he does Picasso things!'

That same year – or perhaps the following year, 1904 – in the corner of a sheet of paper on which he had drawn many female nudes and written the word *caridad* ('charity') above a figure of a portly, well-off man in a top hat giving money to a skinny, bearded man with dishevelled hair, Picasso drew himself as a Pharaoh (74). The Egyptian royal headdress (*khepresh*) that he wears is somewhat reminiscent of a sugarloaf hat or a papal tiara. Picasso the Pharaoh ... is this depiction meant to show that he exercises absolute power over the art of painting? Or that his work will always be indecipherable, impossible to understand, as Egyptian hieroglyphs were for centuries?

Au Lapin Agile

This work was painted in 1905 (97). In the background is a moustachioed figure, with a vertical line of beard down the middle of his chin. This is Frédé. In 1903, Frédéric Gérard – known as Père Frédé, or simply Frédé – took Lolo, his faithful donkey, along with his mice, his crow, and his monkey and moved into Au Lapin Agile with his mistress Berthe Sébource, who had bought the place from the former cancan dancer Adèle Decerf. The establishment was originally called 'Le Rendez-vous des voleurs' (Where the thieves meet), then became known as 'Le Cabaret des Assassins' (The murderers' cabaret) towards the end of the Second Empire. Its infamy was not due simply to the names it had been given since 1860; it was thanks to Mother Adèle. But the name under which it became famous was 'Au Lapin Agile'. The origin of the name lies in a cartoon by André Gill, of a rabbit in a green frock coat and red scarf leaping out of the saucepan where it was about to be turned into a stew. Over time, 'Au Lapin à Gill' (Gill's rabbit) became 'Au Lapin Agile' (The nimble rabbit). Later, Berthe went to great lengths to drive out the pimps and madams – the mother superiors who were considered even worse than their male counterparts – and other robbers, and as a result the clientele changed. From then on, it was artists who frequented the establishment, which had become a cabaret. Poets, painters, writers. Charles Cros, Aristide Bruant, Toulouse-Lautrec, Alphonse Allais were all spotted there. Jehan Rictus was one of the first to sing there.

Frédé sits in the background of the painting with his guitar – he played both guitar and cello, although judging by some reports, it seems he was not blessed with great talent. He is wearing clogs and – if his woolly hat with ear flaps is anything to go by – perhaps he is playing one of Rictus's songs: 'Shit! Winter is here, with all its hardships / The time when you can't go around naked / Those who hold the handle of the frying pan / Are going to leg it to the south!'

Picasso himself soon became a regular visitor to Au Lapin Agile. The cabaret at 22 Rue des Saules was only ten minutes' walk from Bateau-Lavoir, at 13 Place Ravignan, where he moved in May 1904. Fernande Olivier, who was gradually growing closer to him, remembered: 'The Lapin Agile was the place where all the artists went. On summer evenings they sat on the terrace. In winter they sat in the dark, smoke-filled room.'

Germaine also appears in the painting, a glass set in front of her, leaning one elbow on the bar and resting her chin on her hand. She was twenty-five and had met Picasso when he first arrived in Paris, at the studio belonging to Isidre Nonell, for whom she modelled. Casagemas soon fell hopelessly in love with Germaine. She was already married to a man named Florentin and turned him down. Was her rejection the reason why, when they were dining at the Hippodrome on 17 February 1901, an inebriated Casagemas shot at her? The bullet grazed her temple. Convinced that he had killed her, Casagemas turned the gun on himself and shot himself in the head. It is safe to say that this young woman played a significant role in the life of the Harlequin sitting next to her, a Harlequin who is none other than Picasso. The lock of hair that escapes from his admiral's hat and hangs down over his forehead is the giveaway.

This is a remarkable self-portrait by Picasso. (There is no need to go into the rumours that after Casagemas's death, Germaine became his mistress. Perhaps there is some truth to them. But what do we gain by repeating such gossip?) Germaine had already modelled for him in 1901, sitting at a table with her chin resting on her hands, beside another Harlequin, this time wearing a tight black hat and an outfit with blue squares. In 1904, in an etching composed with Max Jacob, Picasso had drawn himself as a Harlequin (91), with an admiral's hat on his head, his eyes fixed on the skull in his hand, the other hand on his hip. Why not depict a subject that had fascinated both Degas and Toulouse-Lautrec?

Those who knew him at the time spoke of his fervour and his great energy. How, then, could he admit that he identified with this servant or clown from the commedia dell'arte, who is characterized as clumsy and lazy? The figure's only good quality was said to be his great skill in the art of scheming. As for his Columbines, or lovers, they were only passing through....

Picasso had clawed his way out of desperate poverty thanks to Pere Mañach, Berthe Weill, and Ambroise Vollard, who had sold four of his paintings in 1901 for 225 francs, as well as *Le Moulin de la Galette* for 250 francs. The art dealer Clovis Sagot bought numerous paintings when he visited Bateau-Lavoir in February 1905, and many were also sold at the exhibition at the Galerie Serrurier that same month. However, Picasso's life at Bateau-Lavoir was still one marked by hardship.

Perhaps the blue squares – some dark, some light – that the Harlequin wears in the 1901 painting may constitute a last trace of this 'watery painting, blue as the depths of an abyss, and piteous', as Apollinaire described it in the newspaper *La Plume* on 15 May 1905. Or perhaps we should see in the coloured diamonds of this self-portrait what Jean Cocteau wrote in his poem 'Rue Schœlcher': 'Don't worry, my old Pablo / Your Harlequin was already wearing / Cubism in his diamonds.'

Hand

The muses welcomed this painter into their circle,
And directed his hand,
So that he could impose human order
On the sweet disorder of the world.
Jean Cocteau

We must not, of course, disregard Picasso's hand, his incomparable hand, which Jacques Prévert described in one of his poems as 'the hand that turns a face into unfamiliar territory and stares closely at the features of a landscape'. Picasso's hands, both his right and his left, were an endless source of fascination for those who saw them with their own eyes.

Sabartés wrote: 'He was constantly cutting out paper figures. He has become so skilful at it that he no longer even needs scissors. Plenty of people have seen him tearing out shapes from those paper tablecloths that are used in certain restaurants, using nothing more than his fingertips. Everyone who eats with him has seen this.'

Robert Desnos: 'Picasso's hands! You must see them obeying the orders of his eyes, which have such an intense gaze that they seem to animate motionless shapes. His hands never stop creating; creativity streams from them like everyday speech streams from the mouths of ordinary mortals. For his hands, the act of creation is as simple, as natural as that.'

Paul Éluard told Claude Roy 'that he had seen Picasso training himself to draw a face with his eyes closed, then in complete darkness and holding his piece of paper the wrong way round. It wasn't simply because he enjoyed setting himself a physical challenge, a game to test his virtuosity. He was determined to achieve a state of free automatism in his hands, to reach the moment where it could not be said that his mind guided his hand, or even that his hand guided his mind, because they were one: a hand-mind, a mind-hand.'

This led Claude Roy to conclude that: 'His hand, which executes everything he wants it to without fail, sometimes draws symbols that he did not intend, that he was not aware of intending. He is the first to express surprise.... That is Picasso. And it's true that he achieves everything he wants to with his hands, with his hand. You might say that nature doesn't resist him. When he is drawing and painting, it is as if he is playing, imitating if he so desires, rivalling the masters, finding himself, leaving himself behind and finding himself again.'

Picasso drew his own hand in 1902 (56), in 1907 (114, 115) and again in 1919 (138–40). In 1942, he made a plaster cast of his hand (153), which was later used to make a bronze sculpture; he also made a sculpture of his forearm and closed fist, in iron, wood, and plaster (154). We must surely conclude that he had never forgotten the words of his father, which he repeated to Sabartés: 'It is with the hands that we see the hand.' 'That is Picasso', as Claude Roy said. A drawing of his hand, a cast of it ... both are self-portraits.

Brassaï wrote, 'Curiously, I find this eliminated, prohibited hand as subject and as object in many casts and impressions, as if Picasso had shifted to his hands the attention he once granted to his face. With his left hand, he had made a whole series of charcoal sketches, gouaches, and pastel drawings "from nature" about twenty years earlier. Here, he pressed them into fresh plaster and made casts, a closed fist at the end of a strong wrist, as if he wanted to seize all its concentrated power. I also see a cast of his right hand, executed, I think, by someone else. It stands alone and autonomous, a monument of supreme potency, equilibrium: fleshy palm, Mount Venus sensually jutting out, wilful thumb, fingers pressed tight against one another, preventing any light from passing between them. And what clarity, what cleanness, in the deeply etched lines that furrow that large palm of a craftsman, dominated by the line of fate that rises straight as a rocket to the base of the middle finger.'

Forelock

Picasso painted the lock of hair that fell over his forehead for the first time in 1896. A messy, dishevelled fringe (8). In a sketchbook from 1899, he drew it as a series of dark diagonal charcoal lines across his forehead (16). While he was staying in Barcelona, he drew himself in the middle of a page of sketches and studies, wearing a hat and sitting with his legs crossed in front of him (21). His hair falls over his temple. As it does in a pencil drawing of 1901, which shows him standing with his hands in his coat pockets, a hat on his head (36). That same year, in the drawing of himself with Francisco de Asis Soler that he did for the periodical *Madrid, Notas de arte*, it once again falls across his forehead (40). As it does in the pen-and-ink drawing that shows him in profile with Àngel Fernández de Soto and Sebastià Junyer-Vidal. It appears again and again until 1906, when he suddenly had his hair cut short. After that, it does not reappear until 1907, in the drawing on which he wrote '*Bonjour Mlle Cone*'. In the self-portrait from that same year that Vollard bought (116), it is painted with precise, distinct brushstrokes. Aside from a few exceptions, it appears in all his self-portraits. Until ...

Brassaï writes: 'It has become a habit of his to sign rare books, as a way of making them unique.... Almost all the noteworthy books in his treasure chest have been written on or decorated.... However, he had another reason for showing me this book.... Underneath the portrait, he had written three words in his jerky, exuberant handwriting ... and these three words represented a historic event in his life.... I read on the flyleaf: 'NO MORE FORELOCK! Paris, 12 May 1945'. His famous black forelock, which escaped from his hat and frightened his family, the black crow's wing that he had drawn a hundred times, caricatured, even sculpted, which fell sharply from right to left across his forehead and almost swept into his left eye before reaching his temple, this forelock has been gone for some time. All that was left were a few sparse hairs, more symbolic than anything, hairs that couldn't hide his baldness but that he carefully preserved as the last remnants of his youth.... It was not until this morning that he worked up the courage to break with the past by giving his dead forelock a solemn burial in this book by Mallarmé.'

This forelock, which had become a kind of symbol, allows us to recognize Picasso, to identify him beyond all doubt. If he had not been denied French citizenship in 1940, the year in which a law introduced on 25 November by the Vichy government made it obligatory, perhaps the police authorities would have considered it necessary to include the word 'Forelock' on one of the identity cards that listed 'Identifying features'.

But this forelock is not enough to identify Picasso. Although ... In 1917 or 1918, he draw a cartoon of himself (130). Just a few lines. A figure in profile. A trapezium indicating a large coat, a sleeve with no hand emerging from it, a hat that is as tall as a top hat but has a peak like a cap. A pipe in his mouth, indicated by a simple line that ends in a circle. One dark eye. And, between his ear and the peak of his hat, a few parallel lines representing ... his forelock.

From 1897 to 1903, he often parted his hair in the middle. In 1906, he had it cut short. It looks like a black helmet in his 1943 self-portrait *The Sailor*. And in his last self-portraits, he is bald.

I do not think Brassaï was making too bold a claim when he described the three words he found on the flyleaf of the book by Mallarmé – 'NO MORE FORELOCK! Paris, 12 May 1945' – as 'a historic event in his life'. If Picasso's work is autobiographical – as many of those who knew him over the years claimed without the slightest hesitation – is it truly conceivable that he would not have marked this 'historic event' with a self-portrait? Perhaps the words of Jean Cassou might offer an answer: 'Picasso is a foreigner, a stranger in this country, but what is most foreign about him is his strangeness.'

Autobiography

'His work has always been profoundly autobiographical.' A very confident claim about Picasso from Daniel-Henry Kahnweiler. It is supported by the following sentence from 'Picasso and the Human

Comedy, or the Avatars of Big Foot', an article by Michel Leiris published in 1954 in *Verve*, no. 29–30. This double edition printed a suite of 180 drawings by Picasso. 'Whatever themes Picasso has handled in the course of his various periods, they have almost always been closely associated with his life.'

On reading Leiris's words, I cannot help but be reminded of a comment by Aragon about that same 'admirable suite of drawings completed between 28 November 1953 and 3 February 1954' and printed in *Verve*. In the edition of *Les Lettres françaises* dated 18 November–17 December 1954, he wrote about them: 'We have this rather simple idea that only young men truly appreciate female beauty. Or that, for a man who is past thirty, the act of depicting female beauty must always be tinged with regret. We forget that when Ingres painted *The Turkish Bath* in 1859, he was six years older than Picasso is now. Given that *The Turkish Bath* is the work of a man in his eighties, we must stop looking to an artist's private life for a means of explaining their paintings.'

I am inclined towards Aragon's view that we should not rely on autobiographical readings, if only because of Vermeer. Does it matter in the slightest that we know nothing – or almost nothing – about his life in Delft between 1632 and 1675?

But could two self-portraits, both dated 11 August 1940, offer an insight into what we might call 'the artist's private life'? They are both pencil drawings on paper (150, 151), each measuring sixteen centimetres by eleven. A few months earlier, on 3 April, Picasso had sent a typewritten letter that read, 'To the Keeper of the Seals, I humbly petition you for citizenship and commit to paying the necessary fees. Yours sincerely', followed by his signature, Picasso, and handwritten address: Paris, 23 Rue La Boétie, 8th arrondissement.

On 25 May 1940, the French authorities sent a note to the relevant department about this 'individual RUIZ Y PICASSO, called 'Picasso', born 25 October 1881 in Malaga (Spain), of Spanish nationality'. They had no shortage of reservations about his application. Their first reason for scepticism was: 'Since 1918, he has lived at 23 Rue La Boétie, where he occupies two floors and pays an annual rent of 28,000 francs, including taxes. An artist, he paid 700,000 francs in tax on his income for the year of 1939, but that did not prevent him from asking his landlord for a reduction in the rent, claiming that his earnings had been affected by the hostilities.'

How could they trust an individual who was capable of such an act? But this shameless request was by no means the authorities' most serious objection.

Picasso was 'reported to be an anarchist in 1905' and in 1914, although he was then thirty years old, 'he did not serve our country during the war'. However, 'during the civil war in Spain, he sent considerable sums of money to government forces every month'. All the signs indicated that he had settled in France because he was 'able to earn millions (which it seems he has invested abroad) from his work as a "self-proclaimed modern painter"' – the quotation marks are the writer's own. The note also claimed that he was 'a Soviet sympathizer' and that he had 'told certain people that when he dies, his collection will be left to the Soviet government and not the French government, which shows that this foreigner has a strange way of expressing his gratitude to the country that has allowed him to create for himself such an extraordinary situation, which would certainly never have been attainable for him in Spain.' There was only one possible conclusion: 'In summary, taking into account all the information at our disposal, this foreigner has no claim to citizenship: what is more, according to our findings, he should be regarded as suspicious from a national perspective.' It goes without saying that this 'national perspective' was that of the Vichy government, which had chosen to collaborate with the Nazis.

At what point did the 'suspicious' Picasso learn of this decision? Is it possible that he was notified of it on 11 August 1940? Was that what drove him to urgently draw his face, the face of a man whom the French state had refused citizenship? A refusal that would inevitably make him vulnerable to a range of nebulous, worrying threats. As Pierre Daix wrote, 'As in 1918, when he heard the news of Apollinaire's death, and in 1938 after the Anschluss, Picasso drew himself facing tragedy and danger. He imbued these drawings with all the seriousness of the fate that awaited him: Spain living under the heel of Franco, France under Hitler.'

Daix wrote these words for his *Dictionnaire Picasso*. The brief comment appears on pages 69 and 70. The warning that opens his book is dated 'Paris, Autumn 1995'. And the imprint page has the date November 1995. The note written by the French authorities on 25 May 1940 was seized by the Germans in 1944, taken to the USSR in 1945 and returned to France, along with other archive documents, only in 2001. It was not discovered until 2004, almost ten years after Daix's *Dictionnaire Picasso* was published. A dictionary that does not include an entry for 'Citizenship'. In the passage (on pages 426–8) that describes Picasso's life during the 'World Wars', Pierre Daix does not mention the application for citizenship submitted in 1940. When he met Picasso in November 1945, did the artist never speak of it? What exactly led Picasso to draw himself 'facing tragedy and danger'? It is impossible to say for sure.

Another question to ponder: could two paintings, both dated to the same day, 29 December 1953, be seen to illustrate the relationship between life and art? One is called *The Shadow* (157), the other *The Shadow on the Woman* (158). A few years after he painted them, Picasso showed *The Shadow* to one of his friends and said: 'It was our bedroom. Do you see my shadow? I had just moved away from the window. Now do you see my shadow and the sunlight falling on the bed and the floor? Do you see the toy carriage on the chest of drawers and the little vase on the mantelpiece? They are from Sicily and they are still in the house.' In this painting, the shadow of Picasso's head falls just behind the small of the reclining female nude's back, while in *The Shadow on the Woman*, it covers her body. And the toy is nowhere to be seen.... Who played with it? Claude, who was born in 1947? Paloma, born in 1949? Who is the woman lying nude in this bedroom at the time the picture was painted? Françoise Gilot? She had left Picasso three months earlier.... She took the children to Cannes for Christmas and did not come back to their villa La Galloise in Vallauris for New Year's Eve. Why would he paint her nude after she had left him, when he had never done so during the years when they were together? Could this woman be Geneviève Laporte, who had come back into his life two years earlier and whom he saw regularly in Paris and Saint-Tropez? In a drawing that is dated 29 July 1951, he drew himself in profile, holding up a mirror to her (156).

The identity of the reclining nude – whether it is Françoise Gilot or Geneviève Laporte – changes the meaning of these paintings entirely. The only thing of which we can be certain, because Picasso himself confirmed it, is that the shadow is his own. But because it does not show his face in profile, it does not evoke Gyges the Lydian tracing his shadow in the firelight, the event that Pliny claims – according to Vasari – to be the invention of painting. Does the 'presence' of this shadow make the work a self-portrait?

Absence

When asked what evidence he had for his claim that Picasso's work was profoundly autobiographical, Kahnweiler did not hesitate: 'I cannot think of any artist whose work is as autobiographical as Picasso's. There is not a single face that is not a portrait of his beloved at that time. He never invents a face: it is always the woman he loves. I often said there was a time in his life, from 1912 to 1914, when it was impossible for him to paint a portrait because of what he wanted to do.'

Not even, over the course of those years, a portrait of himself.

The only model who is always available to a painter, the only model who they can be sure will never recoil, offended or disappointed, on seeing the finished portrait, is themselves. Their own image is what artists have always measured themselves against, time and time again, to establish their visual identity.

Over the course of many years, it was with the aid of a photograph or a mirror, rather than painting the recurring settings of the Jas de Bouffan or the Mont Sainte-Victoire, that Cézanne became Cézanne. It was through the portraits that Vincent van Gogh painted of himself after he moved to Paris in 1886 – while it is possible that he painted himself before then, there remains no trace of any such self-portrait, aside from a few pencil sketches that date to his stay in Anvers – that van Gogh became van Gogh.

Picasso said, 'As if I don't know Cézanne! He was my one and only master! Don't you think I've looked at his paintings? I spent years studying them. He was like the father of us all. He was the one who protected us.'

And he said, 'Since van Gogh, we have all been self-taught – one could almost say we are primitive painters. Tradition has become bogged down by convention, so we have to recreate an entire language. And every painter of our time is entitled to recreate this language from A to Z. We cannot impose any fixed criteria on them, because strict rules no longer apply. From a certain perspective, it is liberating, but at the same time it is terribly limiting: when an artist starts to express his personality, what he gains in freedom, he loses in order, and it's very difficult no longer being able to rely on a rule.'

Was Picasso thinking of the 'master' Cézanne when he drew or painted a portrait of himself? Or was he embodying the self-taught artist who invented his own rules for what painting should be, what he wanted it to be? Whatever the answer, his self-portraits form a vital part of his tireless quest to recreate the language of painting.

Work

> *This one was one who was working and he was one needing this thing needing to be working so as to be one having some way of being one having some way of working.*
> Gertrude Stein

On 23 April 1936, Sabartés received the following letter: 'I am writing to you straightaway to let you know that from this evening onwards, I am giving up painting, sculpture, etching, and poetry and dedicating myself entirely to singing. A handshake from your devoted friend and admirer – Picasso.'

It seems he did not stick to this resolution.... Over the course of more than eighty years, Picasso worked constantly. Michel Leiris wrote, 'In the entire history of art, there has never been anyone who produced such a great quantity of works of such great quality.'

But it seems surprising that – aside from the first self-portrait he drew in 1894 and the last, dated 3 July 1972 – there are only two in which he depicts himself at work, with the paintbrushes and palette that have been artists' tools of the trade for centuries. The first example dates to 1901, a study for what would become *Yo Picasso*, in which he reaches towards the canvas set on the easel in front of him, with a brush in his hand (46). The second was painted when he was in Gósol in 1906. In it, he wears a white shirt and holds a palette in one hand, but there is no paintbrush to be seen in his other hand (109). If we accept that *The Young Painter* of 14 April 1972 (165) – in which he wears a wide straw hat reminiscent of the one van Gogh wore to paint outdoors – is Picasso, then this self-portrait is the only one that shows him holding both palette and paintbrush. In 1915 and 1916, he took many photographs of himself in the studio on the Rue Schœlcher, but only one shows him holding a brush (122). There are more brushes on the floor, diagonal lines poking out from tins of paint, standing in for a palette.

As for his drawings ... A few self-portraits appear here and there among the studies he drew in 1896 (4) and 1897 (or 1899?). In 1906, he sketched himself again and again, seeking to pin down his features on the page (100–5). It seems that he saw two of the drawings from 1917 – one showing him sitting in a wooden armchair (132), the other in a straight-backed chair (1) – as full works in their own right. If not, why would he have dedicated one to Jacqueline? Perhaps we should view these self-portraits, which are few and far between, as anomalies, rare exceptions that – as he knows better than anyone – do not reveal anything about the reality of his practice.

'You have to pile up work after work, to work like a machine and not deviate from the straight line. Everything must yield to stubbornness.' Picasso did not need to read these words by Gustave Flaubert in order to make painting yield to him.

Unless it was the other way round. In his *Diary*, Leiris noted that on 27 March 1963, Picasso wrote in a sketchbook: 'Painting is stronger than I am, it forces me to do what it wants.' Leiris is far from convinced: 'It is impossible to say whether he is the one who lives for and through painting, or whether it is painting that lives in him and is naturally embodied in everything around him.' He only agrees with Picasso's claim if it is seen as a kind of 'artistic alienation, in which the artist is forced outside of himself by art, which becomes his master at the same time as he masters it.' Leiris concludes, 'We might compare him to Rimbaud and his "*I* is an other."' A comparison that Picasso himself made. In 1955, on the Rue des Grands-Augustins, he told Kahnweiler, 'I never know what I am going to do. I begin a painting and it becomes something entirely different. It's strange how little the artist's will counts for.... He was certainly right when he said, "I is an other."'

However, Picasso – whether he is the 'I' or the Other – certainly piled up work after work: 'It's when I rest that I feel tired. Some people drink Pernod all day long. For me, my Pernod is my work.'

He knew that in his adopted city of Paris – where a quarter of a century earlier the Impressionists had destroyed and overthrown all the deeply rooted, fossilized certainties of art – the artist's craft no longer had anything in common with what it had been for centuries before: 'In the past, paintings progressed in a linear manner towards their finished state. Every day the artist added something new. A painting was made up of a series of additions. For me, a painting is a series of destructions. I create a painting, then I destroy it. But in the end, nothing is lost; I may have scraped off the red in one place, but I added it back in elsewhere.'

It would be a strange kind of magic trick that consists of nothing more than scraping off red in one place and adding it back in elsewhere. What kind of destruction does he mean?

In 1918, Picasso told Apollinaire, 'Art can be achieved only through a great amount of work, physical and material work as well as mental work.' But he also admits, 'Despite myself, what I want to grasp interests me more than my ideas.' So he wanted to acknowledge intellectual work but was not interested in his ideas.... Does this contradiction simply mean he was using everything at his disposal? Or does it constitute the thesis and antithesis of a dialectical exercise that led him to this conclusion, which Leiris records in his *Diary* of 15 March 1962: 'I scorn all my knowledge and only rely on what comes to me from unknown sources within my being.'

'Unknown': the choice of adjective is both deliberate and crucial. Because it is this unknown with which Picasso is constantly grappling, from one work to the next. Sometimes with a great sense of urgency: 'The freedom of painting is the freedom of liberating something within myself. I have to be quick, it doesn't last.'

Time and again, he is surprised by moments of clarity: 'Every evening, I was impatient to get back to work, *I wanted to know what was going to happen*.' Claude Roy chose to put those last words in italics to reflect Picasso's tone of voice when he said them. He added: 'When I was working on this series of drawings, every day as I picked up my sketchbooks, I said to myself, 'What else am I going to teach myself that I didn't know before?' And when it is no longer I who is speaking, but the drawings I have created, when they slip from my grasp and taunt me, that is when I know I have achieved my goal.'

Picasso put a hand to his forehead: 'Everything that happens is there. Before it reaches the nib of the pen or the hairs of the paintbrush, the most important thing is to have it in your finger-tips, with nothing lost, in its entirety.' As he said to Zervos, 'When I'm working, I don't know what I'm going to do. It's not a case of indecision, it's the fact that the work is constantly changing as it comes together. At the start of every work, there is someone who works alongside me. Then, towards the end I feel like I have worked without a collaborator.'

Who is this 'someone who works' alongside him? Who is this 'collaborator'? Is it 'I', the Other? Or is this Other the connoisseur he referred to, saying, 'You work, and there is a connoisseur standing behind you who decides: that's good, that's bad, that's finished now. A kind of guardian angel who stops you from going on ... You are just working, and you never know if it's good or bad.'

Whether it is 'good' or 'bad' is not important in the least. Picasso's work is about being surprised, the chance occurrence, the unexpected. Perhaps because what he discovers in his work is often the opposite of what he intended. Because the work that suddenly appears in front of him is not the one he set out to create. It reminds me of these words from Fernando Pessoa: 'The only man who is happy is the one who does not search; because only the man who does not search may find.' Picasso must therefore have been happy.

Again and again, he said the same thing: 'For me, searching has no place in painting. The important thing is to find.' 'People tend to take me for a seeker. I do not seek, I find.' Although that may not be entirely true, judging by this admission: 'It's like doing a chemistry experiment. I work on certain subjects as people do in a laboratory. Sometimes the experiment is successful: then I move on to a different one so as not to repeat myself. I am always trying to discover new things.'

Although some of these discoveries eluded him: 'Success is the result of all the things you don't manage to find.... Otherwise you become your own connoisseur.' Picasso was undoubtedly a connoisseur of his own work, a collector of it. Shortly after the war, Jean Cassou went to his studio on the Boulevard des Grands-Augustins and saw the paintings that Picasso was giving to the Museum of Modern Art: 'They were paintings from all his periods.... Paintings that were important to him, that he had kept for himself and refused to sell.' Similarly, when André Malraux visited the villa Notre-Dame-de-Vie, 'in the dining room there was a self-portrait from his Rose Period' (106).

In 1923, Picasso told an American journalist: 'The different styles I have used in my art should not be seen as an evolution or as steps towards some unknown ideal. Everything I have ever made was for the present and with the hope that it would always remain in the present. When I have found something to express, I have done it without thinking of the past or the future. I have never made use of tests or experiments. Every time that I have had something to say, I have said it in the way I felt it should be said.

Different subjects naturally require different means of expression. That does not imply either evolution or progress; it simply means aligning the idea you want to express and the means of expression.'

Picasso did follow one rule: 'In painting, you can try anything. You have the right, even. But only if you don't start over again.' Picasso never started over again.

And he was always Picasso: 'My inner self must be in my painting because I am the one who created it. I don't need to torture myself to achieve that. Whatever I do, it will be present in it. Perhaps even too much ... It's the rest that's the problem.' What is this 'rest', if not what happens while he is working? 'If a machine recorded everything I think while I am painting!' If such a machine had existed, perhaps it would have recorded the sense of inevitability he felt as he worked. And perhaps it would have recognized a kind of predestination, or even tragedy. 'I am unable to do anything other than what I do.'

Picasso asked Sabartés, 'Have you ever seen a finished painting? It is no longer a painting, but something else. It is a sad moment when you say that you have finished.... Finishing a work? Completing a painting? What a stupid idea! Finishing something means being done with it, killing it, tearing out its soul, stabbing the *puntilla* into the bull at the end of the fight. Finishing it, or finishing it off, as we say here, means administering the thing that is most vexing for both the painter and the painting: the coup de grâce.'

Later, he explained to Brassaï, 'Finishing something off, executing it – don't those phrases have a double meaning? They mean completing something, of course, but don't they also mean killing it, administering the coup de grâce? I produce a lot of paintings because I am looking for spontaneity, and once I have expressed something to my satisfaction, I no longer have the courage to add anything to it.'

But it was not just about courage. 'Paintings are never finished, in the sense of suddenly being ready to be signed and framed. They tend to stop at a certain moment, because something has happened to interrupt the continuity of their development.'

It is these works that were interrupted in the middle of their development by 'something' – something that only Picasso could recognize – that I am interested in. This 'something' that made him decide now was the moment to put down his pencil, his paintbrush, because he knew that his self-portrait was what it was supposed to be. But was this 'something' always the same thing? Picasso said, 'I have succeeded when what I create starts to speak without me.' What does it say then?

There is no use waiting for Picasso to provide the answer ...

He said, 'I don't plan a painting in advance. While I am painting, it changes depending on what I am thinking. Once it is finished, it changes again, depending on who is looking at it and how they feel at the time. A painting lives its life, like a living being, undergoing changes just as daily life changes us. This is natural because a painting only lives through the person looking at it.'

Alone. I am alone before Picasso's self-portraits. You are alone before these same self-portraits.

And perhaps that is the purpose of a self-portrait, to make us examine our own solitude.

Solitude

> *Every man is a crowd, but in a crowd every man is alone.*
> Jacques Prévert

'You cannot achieve anything without solitude. I have carved out a solitude for myself that no one suspects. It is very difficult, now, to be alone because we have watches. Have you ever seen a saint wearing a watch? I have searched everywhere but have not found one, even among the patron saints of watchmakers.' These words from Picasso are quoted again and again, because they express something vital.

I cannot help but wonder if, more than any of his other works, his self-portraits are the expressions of this solitude.

Perhaps the only accurate description of these self-portraits is the following lines, which appear in Gertrude Stein's 1924 poem 'If I Told Him, A Completed Portrait of Picasso': 'He he he he and he and he and and he and he and he and and as and as he and as he and he. He is and as he is, and as he is and he is, he is and as he and he and as he is and he and he and and he and he.'

But who is *he*? Could Picasso's carefully guarded solitude be seen as a deliberate technique? Let me explain. Fernando Pessoa offered the following vital insight: 'Art is isolation. Every artist must seek to isolate others, to make them want to be alone.'

Likeness

The page had been turned. Picasso said to Brassaï, 'Objective reality must be carefully folded, the way one folds a sheet and locks it away in a closet for once and for all'. A clear break with the past ... There was a very simple, very important reason to consign this ancient tradition of *mimesis*, or imitation, which had been around since 400 BC, to the history books: 'We have to wake people up. To disrupt their way of recognizing things. We have to create unacceptable images. Images that make people angry. We have to make them understand that they live in a crazy world. A world that is not reassuring. A world that is not what they believe it to be.'

So the purpose of painting is to conjure, to divert, to plant decoys, to play tricks, and to create illusions.

Picasso was thinking of how images could benefit the public. And these 'unacceptable images' were intended to awaken their consciousness.

Speaking of the importance of looking closely at his subjects, Picasso told Sabartés, 'We don't pay enough attention.... If Cézanne is Cézanne, it's because when he stands in front of a tree, he looks closely at what is before his eyes; he stares at it, like a hunter who has an animal in his crosshairs. If he captures a leaf, he doesn't let it go. Then once he has the leaf, he moves on to the branch. And the tree will not evade him. Even if he only captured the leaf, that's still something. Often, a painting is nothing more than that.... You have to give it your full attention.... Ah! If only everyone was capable of that!'

In 1895, Ambroise Vollard went to Cézanne's apartment on the Rue Hégésippe-Moreau to have his portrait painted. He recalled: 'In the centre of the studio, there was a stool placed on a small platform supported by four posts. Cézanne invited me to sit on it.' Vollard had his doubts about the stability of the set-up. Cézanne reassured him, 'I put the chair there myself for you to sit on. Just be careful to keep your balance. Anyway, when you're posing, you shouldn't be moving.' But Vollard fell asleep and soon tipped over backwards. Cézanne reacted angrily: 'You idiot! You disturbed the pose! You have to pose like an apple. Does an apple move?'

We may well imagine that Vollard told this anecdote while posing for Picasso, who painted his portrait in 1910. But by then Picasso had known for some time that the model he was painting was and could only be an apple. And that this apple had to submit to the art of painting. Just like any other object.

'Of course, when I paint a cup, I will show you that it is circular, but it may be that the painting's overall rhythm and construction force me to depict this circle as a square,' he told Kahnweiler.

He adopted the same approach for faces:

'What is a face, when it comes down to it? A photograph of a face? Its make-up? Or the face as represented by some painter? What is in front? Inside? Behind? And the rest? Doesn't everyone see in their own way? I have only ever painted what I saw and felt.... Physical objects? I don't know what you mean. In painting, everything is a symbol. So it is the meaning that counts and not the process. However, there is a big difference between the symbol and the word. The word 'chair' doesn't mean anything. But if you paint a chair, it is already a symbol. It could have infinite meanings.... Look at these drawings: they didn't become what they are because I wanted to depict the superficial appearance of objects in a stylized way. It's simply because the superficial appearance did away with itself. Nothing I did was deliberate. Of course, for that, there is no key other than that of poetry.... If the lines and shapes rhyme and move, they do so in the same way as a poem.' It was no accident that Picasso wrote in chalk on the door of his studio at Bateau-Lavoir: 'The Poets' meeting place'.

He told Brassaï, 'I always focus on likeness. A painter must observe nature, but should never confuse that with painting. Nature can only be translated into painting through symbols. You must always aim for a close likeness in order to create a symbol in the end. For me, surreality is not, has never been anything other than the deep resemblance that goes beyond the shapes and colours through which things present themselves.'

What *symbols* might Picasso's self-portraits be? And what *surreality* do they reveal in him? One of the few answers that might satisfy comes from Prévert: 'Sometimes he enjoys playing tricks. He disguises himself and becomes someone else, without saying anything, someone that everyone recognizes. But he never takes a bow once the performance is over.... Picasso likes reproductions but he does not like the kind of painting that is only reproduced in captivity. He knows that professional art critics cannot see the art of painting in a painting, especially when it is free and beautiful and laughs in their faces.' We have been warned!

Style

In 1948, over dinner in the restaurant at the Colombe d'Or hotel in Saint-Paul-de-Vence, Prévert introduced Picasso to André Verdet. Picasso leaned forward to kiss the identification number that had been tattooed on Verdet's forearm when he arrived at Auschwitz. A gesture that cemented the close friendship between the poet and the painter. During one of their conversations, Picasso told Verdet, 'Perhaps I am fundamentally a painter without a style.... Style is often something that traps the painter within the same vision, the same technique, the same formula for years and years, sometimes their whole life. We recognize their work without hesitation but it's as if they are always dressed in the same clothes, or the same cut. However, there are great painters who have a distinctive style. As for me, I move too much, I shift too much. You see me here but then I have already changed, I am already somewhere else. I never stay in the same place and that's why I don't have a style.'

He had probably already told Françoise Gilot, 'God is simply an artist like all the others.... He doesn't really have a style.' The example of God was one he returned to again, proclaiming in front of Malraux:

> 'Down with style! Does God have a style? He created the guitar, the harlequin, the basset hound, the cat, the owl and the dove. Like me. The elephant and the whale, sure, but the elephant and the squirrel? It's chaos! He created things that did not exist. So do I! He even created painting. So do I.'

Picasso, this artist who 'moves too much', who 'shifts too much', is an anomaly in the history of painting, which, over the centuries, has only ever known 'great painters with a distinctive style'. His painted self-portraits – from *Yo Picasso* in 1901 (4) until his last in 1972 – are all different. Might they be the most irrefutable proof of his desire to constantly reinvent painting, proof that the only way to do so was to be unfaithful to every style? Including those that he created himself. An unprecedented approach in the history of painting. A deliberate choice that he explained to Malraux: 'After all, you can simply work against something. Even against yourself. It's very important. Most artists make themselves a little cake mould and then they bake cakes. Always the same cakes. They are very happy. A painter should never do what people expect of him. A painter's worst enemy is style.'

Picasso's self-portraits are the result of his battle with this enemy. During his Blue Period, his Rose Period, his cubist period, when some classed him as a 'primitivist', then suddenly 'Ingres-like', 'neoclassical', when some thought he was 'surrealist', and so on … when Picasso imitated the masters, from Delacroix to Grünewald, from El Greco to Manet, from Velázquez to Poussin, and so on … like no other artist before him, Picasso *finds* something and immediately turns away from what he has found: 'My old paintings don't interest me any more…. I am much more interested in those I haven't created yet.'

In 1954, Aragon wrote a preface, entitled 'Oedipus Rex', for the exhibition *Picasso – two periods: 1900–1914 and 1950–1954*, which featured at the Maison de la Pensée Française from 9 June to 28 September. He opened with these words: 'It is more difficult to speak about Picasso than about anyone else. As soon as you make a claim, he has immediately contradicted it. And yet he is more himself than ever, defying commentary as ever, with his enormous heap of works behind him, which here we view through the lens of their beginning and their end.' He went on: 'To be honest, given the diversity of his output, what strikes me is not so much the way Picasso's work changes, but his consistency.'

Which leads to this paradoxical conclusion: it is the very changeability of Picasso's work that makes it endure. Perhaps we should therefore view Picasso's self-portraits as symbols of these changes that look like him. That is, until he does away with the idea of likeness. When he paints himself, he is not so much seeking to *represent* Picasso as he is seeking to be *a* Picasso. In 1906, when he showed his recently completed portrait of Gertrude Stein to his friends, they cried out in protest. Unperturbed, Picasso replied: 'Everyone thinks she doesn't look like her portrait, but don't worry, she'll work out how to make herself look like it.' Because she knew she had to become *a* Picasso.

Overpainting

'After the 1930s, Picasso's work shows hardly any signs of overpainting or retouching. Drawings follow one after another, innovative, immediate, frenetic, decisive. They seek no destination other than what will come after them.' Jean Clair seems very confident in interpreting the lack of overpainting in this way. But what if the portraits that Picasso was constantly creating of himself – the sketches, drawings, etchings, and paintings – were a kind of overpainting? I cannot help but think of what Picasso said to Brassaï: 'I always have to seek perfection.... Of course, this word, for us, no longer means the same thing.... For me, it means going from one painting to another, always going further, further.'

Could Picasso's self-portraits be evidence of this quest?

Studios

Judging by what many people said about him, there is one thing that never changed throughout Picasso's entire life. Only one. His studio was always an absolute mess, always in utter disarray, always full of clutter.

Turning off the Boulevard de Clichy, you climb the hill to Montmartre. You take the Rue Germain-Pilon, turn right onto the Rue des Abbesses, then left onto the Rue Ravignan. You finally arrive at the Place Ravignan, now called Place Émile-Goudeau. It probably does not mean much to you that it has been renamed after the author of *Ironic Poems*, published in 1884 by Paul Ollendorff. However, if you think about this collection, about the year 1884, that is because it is the same year that Kahnweiler was born. In 1907, Kahnweiler followed this same route to arrive at no. 13 Place Ravignan: Bateau-Lavoir. It seems unlikely that anyone quoted Goudeau's poetry to Picasso, because his lines may have been taken as a commentary on the paintings he was working on at that time: 'We ascended into the strange blue / Of a summer's night widowed of sleep'.

One story as to how the Bateau-Lavoir got its name claims it came from a narrow corridor that was like the gangway of a ship Bateau – and the wood used in the building, which had been salvaged from a demolished washhouse – Lavoir – on the banks of the Seine. Others say that it was Max Jacob who came up with 'Bateau' because he thought the corridor looked like a gangway, then he added 'Lavoir' as a joke because the brick-and-wood building, which had been rather haphazardly turned into studios for impoverished artists in 1889, had only one tap. But the origin of the name does not change anything.

On one of the doors, written in blue chalk were the words: 'The Poets' meeting place'. This was Picasso's studio. On pushing the door open, you would have been met with the same scene that Kahnweiler described: 'I went into this room, which served as Picasso's studio. No one will ever be able to imagine the poverty, the lamentable state of these studios on the Rue Ravignan.... The wallpaper hung off the wooden walls in strips. There was dust on the drawings, the canvases were rolled up on a sagging sofa. Next to the stove, there was what looked like a mountain of built-up lava; that was ash. It was dreadful.'

Shaken by the terrible storm that struck Paris on 4 August 1904, Fernande – the partner of the sculptor Laurent Debienne, who rented another studio in the Bateau-Lavoir – pushed open Picasso's door and was confronted by the same mess:

> 'It was the end of his Blue Period. There were large unfinished paintings all over the studio and a sense of work being done everywhere, but my God, the mess! There was a bed base on four legs in one corner. A little cast-iron stove covered in rust with a yellow earthenware basin on top for washing ... In another corner, a poor little trunk that had been painted black served as a rather uncomfortable seat. A straw chair, some easels, canvases of all sizes, tubes of paint scattered across the floor, paintbrushes, gasoline containers, a bowl of aqua fortis, no curtains.'

A little over a year later, in early September 1905, Fernande separated from Debienne and moved in with Picasso. Her first priority was to get the place cleaned up: 'To make the studio habitable for me, Picasso and Apollinaire spent the whole day cleaning, sweeping it with a broom doused in oil, then bleach, then cologne!'

At Bateau-Lavoir, Fernande was known as Fernande de la Baume. She was born Amélie Lang and was the widow of a man named Paul-Émile Percheron, but some people called her Fernande Bellevallée. Although she may have changed names as often as she changed lovers, now she is remembered as Picasso's lover and model, Fernande Olivier, the woman who appears both nude and clothed in *La Toilette*. Simply Fernande. That is, until she left Picasso for the futurist Umberto Oppi. But then Picasso moved on to Éva, who went by the name Marcelle Humbert.

The poet Jacques Baron described 23 Rue La Boétie, where Picasso lived with Olga, as follows: 'It was neither messy nor magnificent, it was chaos: paintings of all sizes, finished and unfinished, many turned to face the wall, scruffy chairs of all kinds, paintbrushes, tubes of paint, pots of paint of course, that goes without saying, but in all sorts of strange places, discarded magazines and journals, wire and all kinds of scrap metal, empty dented tin cans.'

Brassaï's surprise on meeting Picasso in the studio that he had set up in an apartment above the one where he lived with Olga – she could not tolerate mess – was similar to Baron's: 'Before me was a simple man, without the slightest affectation, arrogance, or posturing. His naturalness and kindness immediately put me at ease. I also looked around the strange place: I had expected an artist's studio and instead found an apartment that had been transformed into a pigsty.'

Kahnweiler was confronted by the same jumble, the same incongruous assortment of dusty objects, wherever Picasso worked: 'I remember going to the Rue des Grands-Augustins, looking at the dilapidated ceiling and thinking: "Oh, it's just like the Rue Ravignan." He essentially recreated the Rue Ravignan everywhere, its mess and everything that came with it.'

The cleaning spree of September 1905, when Picasso and Apollinaire swept the floor with oil, bleach, and cologne, seems to have been the first and last of its kind. Picasso told Brassaï: 'I always forbade everyone to clean my studios, dust them, not only for fear they would disturb my things, but especially because I always counted on the protection of dust. It's my ally. I always let it settle where it likes. It's like a layer of protection. When there's dust missing here or there, it's because someone has touched my things. I see immediately someone has been there. And it's because I live constantly with dust, in dust, that I prefer to wear gray suits, the only color on which it leaves no trace.'

Georges Limbour visited Picasso shortly after he moved to a villa in the Californie neighbourhood of Cannes, on a hill overlooking the city and the bay. He wondered: 'Is Picasso still moving in? Has he left? The room that I can see through the windows (and those I can glimpse through the open doors inside) is jammed full of boxes, old newspapers and wrapped-up pieces of pottery that you can just make out through their torn packaging, terracotta vases and cups that haven't been painted yet; there are baskets, stepladders, pieces of wood, sculptures, all covered in dust. And from what I can see of the other rooms, it seems they are just as messy, a jumble of incongruous objects, dominated by a few paintings resting on a piece of furniture or hanging on a wall.... More boxes, furniture facing every which way, an old rocking chair, it looks like the kind of bric-a-brac you find at a flea market. Sculptures of heads set on the floor, with that pensive look that sculptures take on in attics, their eyes veiled by accumulated dust.'

Claude Roy wrote: 'You should not go looking for an artist's face in his daily life, but in his work. It is only possible to take a photograph of Picasso's soul in his studio.'

It was this confident claim that led me to quote these descriptions of Picasso's studio, which do not change whether it is the one set up in Bateau-Lavoir or on the Place Ravignan.

Picasso's studio ... Always the same. The same jumble of junk and masterpieces. According to Sabartés: 'Picasso keeps everything. It's not inconceivable that you might find the outfit he wore for his first communion in one of his studios!' But keeping everything of his own did not stop him from also collecting other people's things, as he told Brassaï: 'I pick up everything, especially what other people throw out. Do you know what nickname Cocteau gave me one day? "The King of Ragpickers"!' Could Picasso's studio be seen as a metaphor for his self-portraits?

Success

There is one rule that Picasso always refused to break. He told Brassaï: 'One must have the courage of one's vocation and the courage to make a living from one's vocation. The "second career" is an illusion! I was often broke too, and I always resisted any temptation to live any other way than from my painting. I too might have done drawings for satirical magazines like Juan Gris, Van Dongen, or Villon. *L'Assiette au Beurre* offered me eight hundred francs per drawing, but I was intent on earning my living from my painting. In the beginning, I did not sell at a high price, but I sold. My drawings, my canvases went. That's what counts.' While this self-imposed discipline may have meant that he went without for many years, in the end it turned out to be profitable.

Years after she had lived a life of poverty, hardship, and deprivation alongside Picasso at Bateau-Lavoir, Fernande Olivier allowed herself a moment of nostalgia: 'Where has that time gone, the time when Picasso and his friends lived off hope and illusions? What has happened to the prices from that time, which allowed us to survive for a month on fifty francs, and sometimes even find enough money for paint?'

Those hard times were in the past, replaced by fame and success. Should we criticize Picasso for having achieved that?

'But success is an important thing! People often say that an artist should work for himself, for "the love of art", and scorn success. That's not true! An artist needs success. Not only so that he can survive, but so that he can produce work. Even a rich painter must have some success.'

And Picasso soon became rich, very rich. On hearing that his 1901 self-portrait had been auctioned for $500,000, he asked, 'What does a Rolls cost?... Can you see Van Gogh in a Rolls? They're crazy! I did that when I was nineteen years old! $500,000! $500,000! Can you explain that?'

What kind of bizarre, masterful act of metamorphosis could transform a self-portrait into a Rolls-Royce? It would not have been impossible for Picasso. For proof of this, we need look no further than the old, dismantled bicycle from 1942, which had no idea that its saddle and handlebars had been transformed into a bull's head.

Sailor's shirt

In its 2 May 2018 edition (no. 1469), the *Quotidien de l'art* announced an upcoming auction due to take place at Christie's in New York on 15 May. The works to be auctioned included a painting by Picasso, dated 28 October 1943. Its title: *The Sailor* (155). The painting's write-up said that it had belonged to the Galerie Louise Leiris, then the Kootz Gallery, then been part of the editor Henry Abrams' collection until it was bought by Victor and Sally Ganz in 1952 for $11,000. Almost half a century later, in 1997, it was auctioned – also by Christie's – for $8.8 million. Twenty-one years later, it was valued without the slightest hesitation at $70 million.

The painting is oil on canvas, measuring 129.3 centimetres by 80.7 centimetres, and it was painted in Picasso's studio on the

Boulevard des Grands-Augustins. It has no subtitle. None at all. However, the sailor's outfit has been widely interpreted as one of Picasso's games of dress-up, meaning the sailor is Picasso himself and this painting is therefore one of his few self-portraits.

Picasso did say, 'Yes, it's me' about another portrait of a sailor, the one called – despite his admission – *Maya in a Sailor Suit* (148). When he confirmed it was him, he even unbuttoned his shirt to reveal a blue-and-white-striped jumper, saying he wore it all the time. Can the blue-and-white-striped jumper in this painting therefore be anything other than irrefutable proof that this portrait of a sailor by Picasso is – in fact, must be – a self-portrait? What about the *Seated Man*, dated 3 April 1966, this bald, bearded man, who is also wearing a striped sailor's shirt (162)?

Picasso posed in a similar sailor's shirt for Robert Doisneau, standing behind a window with his palms flat against the glass. And he is wearing the same sailor's shirt in another Doisneau photograph, which shows him sitting at a table, with bread rolls on either side of a plate standing in for his hands. However ... However, he wore a mackintosh to be photographed by Man Ray. And when he posed for Lucien Clergue, he was wearing a checked shirt. He posed shirtless for André Villiers. And wearing a double-breasted suit with a pocket square for Cecil Beaton.

Surely we cannot help but wonder whether his claim 'Because I always wear a sailor's jumper' is enough for us to be certain that a portrait of a sailor is a self-portrait by Pablo Picasso.

The painting's eventual buyers knew that self-portraits by Picasso were few and far between. And they knew better than anyone that anything rare is expensive. We must be careful when we use the term 'self-portrait' in an art world that is so given to speculation.

The Young Painter

Picasso died on 8 April 1973. A few months earlier, he and Jacqueline had asked René Char to write a foreword for the catalogue of the exhibition that was due to open at the Palace of the Popes in Avignon in May. The painter and the poet had known each other for almost forty years. In 1936, Char's *Dépendance de l'Adieu* was published by Éditions G.L.M., accompanied by a Picasso drawing. In issue I/IV of *Cahiers d'art*, his poem 'Enfants qui cribliez d'olives' was also printed alongside a drawing. The edition of *Transparents* published by P.A.B. in 1967 also featured four etchings. A lasting, faithful friendship.

Char's foreword, 'Picasso in the Summer Winds', closes with these words: 'On 8 April, a stupid little bird tapped its beak on the windowpane seven times, making me turn from the morning's work to the midday alarm. Was it bringing the news? At 4 o'clock, I heard. The terrible eye had ceased being solar to draw even closer to us. Life paints us and death draws us in 201 paintings.'

One of these paintings is *The Young Painter* (165). Char wrote: 'Today we may allow ourselves to dream that this childlike painter without a wrinkle, wearing a hat that is dear to him, holding a palette and paintbrush in his hands, is him, Pablo Picasso: a prescient father has just anointed him king. And the night of poverty that is beginning is a night full of stars.'

When Char discovered this painting at Notre-Dame-de-Vie, did Picasso tell him that at the age of nineteen, before he first went to Paris, he had painted a (lost) self-portrait that he had named *Yo el Rey* (I, the king)? And so as to leave no doubt, he had signed it three times: 'I, the king; I, the king; I, the king'. This young painter – left-handed because he was painting his reflection – this young painter holding a palette, this *Young Painter* painted on 14 April 1972, this painting that Char recognized as a self-portrait ... could it be seen as invoking the portrait painted seventy years earlier? 'We may allow ourselves to dream.'

After all, throughout the twentieth century, there was a fashion for artists depicting themselves as children. In 1927, one of many examples, Alberto Savinio chose to do so when he painted his portrait based on a photograph of himself taken in 1897. Similarly, in 1948–9, Diego Rivera painted himself wearing short trousers in the middle of *Dream of a Sunday Afternoon in Alameda Park*, a fresco painted on the walls of the Pardo Hotel in Mexico City. In 1950, Salvador Dalí painted *Myself at the Age of Six When I Thought I was a Girl Lifting with Extreme Precaution the Skin of the Sea to Observe the Dog Sleeping in the Shade of the Water*. In 1970, Fernando Botero painted his *Self-Portrait on the Day of my First Communion*. As for Arshile Gorky, in 1936 he painted himself with his mother, depicting himself as a young boy of around ten when in reality he was already thirty-one or perhaps thirty-two years old.

Perhaps, for a painter, time holds no sway over his image.

Subject

While passing through Rome, I met Jean Leymarie at the Villa Medici, where I had had the privilege of working with him when he was the invaluable, generous director of the French Academy in Rome. At some point during our conversation, I told him about the promise I had made to Jacqueline Picasso a few weeks earlier, when I had said I would write a book about Picasso's self-portraits. He put a hand on my shoulder and smiled. Then he told me how in his book *Picasso: Métamorphoses et unité*, which was due to be published by Skira the following year (1985), he had written that Picasso had warned him never to write a book about him because 'you would have to write one every day'.

As I was about to leave, standing on the doorstep of the loggia, he caught hold of my arm and reminded me of the warning that I had pinned up on my office wall when I was a fellow at the Academy. It was a postcard with a reproduction of the self-portrait that Salvator Rosa painted when he was around thirty years old, in about 1645. (This painting is in the collection of the National Gallery in London.) The artist had painted himself holding a tablet with the following inscription:

> *AUT TACE*
> *AUT LOQUERE MELIORA*
> *SILENTIO.*
> (Keep silent, unless your speech is better than silence.)

I come back to Picasso's self-portraits again and again. It is impossible to tell what his life was like from them alone. Could this series of paintings be seen as an autobiography? That question has been discussed to death.... The answer is no. Perhaps, sometimes, they are anecdotes. Nothing more. They are not even an 'illustration' of his various periods. There is no self-portrait from his Rose Period, or from his cubist period. His 1907 self-portrait is in no way comparable to the *Portrait of Vollard* he painted in 1910. And there is no self-portrait that hints at his political leanings. Picasso the communist? What to make of the red butterfly in the *Sailor* painted in 1938 (148)? When asked, 'Didn't you deliberately paint it red because of the colour's political symbolism?', he responded with a sigh: 'Not especially. If there is a political meaning, it comes from my subconscious.' He knew what was important: 'Every poet, every artist is an individual. Only the Russians are naïve enough to believe that a painter or a writer could serve society or the state. That is why Mayakovsky committed suicide. Rimbaud and Apollinaire could not exist in Russia, and neither could I.'

Picasso, 'who is a sworn enemy of anything that might resemble a system', according to Sabartés, was 'this man who so troubled the world of appearances', according to Aragon.

Aragon never renounced his communist sympathies, despite the gulags, despite the brutal repression of the uprisings in Budapest in 1956 and of the Prague spring in 1968, probably because he viewed these events in the same way as Khrushchev described Stalin's cult of personality, as 'superficial abscesses on the perfectly healthy organ of the Party'. He sparked criticism from the French Communist Party when he published Picasso's portrait of Stalin shortly after his death, as it was not considered a sufficiently heroic depiction, and he had to apologize. He was not wrong when he claimed that Picasso 'never ceased to create modern unease'.

'Create', not depict. It is the unease of a world that had seen all its certainties destroyed by the twentieth century. The new century had promised a brave new world that failed to appear. The promise of better days to come, of unassailable empires, instead gave birth to censorship, torture, terror, war, massacres, deportations, and extermination camps.

'People say: a painting, it's about colour. Yes, but that's not true. A painting is a subject. No one dares say it any more.' The subject that Picasso painted, drew, etched, sculpted, and moulded more than any other was tragedy. Sabartés wrote: 'He believes Art to be the child of Sadness and Pain.'

Over the years when I was trying to track down each one of Picasso's self-portraits, from sketches to paintings, again and again I was surprised to find that a page torn out of a sketchbook or a ripped-up scrap of paper had not been lost but had been preserved in a museum or a private collection. As I examined them, interrogated them (without eliciting a response), I could not stop thinking about these words from Albert Camus: 'The artist constantly lives in such a state of ambiguity, incapable of negating the real and yet eternally bound to question it in its eternally unfinished aspects.'

In late 1968, the Galerie Louise Leiris exhibited a series of 347 etchings that Picasso had completed over the course of a few weeks, from 16 March to 5 October of that same year. Seven months of hard work during which he used a variety of techniques, from aqua fortis to aquatint. He worked tirelessly, drawing, scraping, erasing, varnishing, retouching.... At the age of eighty-seven. A series of 347 plates that represent this real that he was eternally bound to question in its unfinished aspects, and that he finally perfected.

In the first plate of the *Suite 347*, (seventh edition of an aqua fortis etching, measuring 39.5 centimetres by 56.7 centimetres, dated 22 March 1968), Picasso appears on the left (164). As he does again on the eighth plate, with a walking stick in his hand. This one is an aqua fortis etching measuring 42.3 centimetres by 34.2 centimetres, dated three days later, 25 March (163). In both of these etchings, he is a spectator. In the first, a man with long hair stands behind him and he is looking at a kind of Hercules figure. Between them lies a nude woman, her back turned to the viewer, while in the background is a woman riding a horse, surrounded by onlookers in the tiered seats of a circus. In the second, Picasso appears as a dwarf, standing behind a bearded man who is wearing what seems to be a stage costume. On the right is a group of four nude women, one of whom is voluptuous and out of scale, as is the nude young child who sits in the centre. He is smiling, as is the other bearded man whose face appears just above him, next to one of the women's breasts. In both etchings, Picasso seems to look beyond the other people who appear with him. He is looking instead at the procession of all the figures he has gathered together in this series of etchings.

Those figures – what they were, what he wanted them to be and what they could be – appeared again and again. La Celestina, the madam accompanied by a nude young woman, the sailor in the brothel, the Harlequin, the musketeer with a deeply lined face, Don Quixote with Dulcinea standing in a cart, Raphael making love to La Fornarina, a pharoah bent over a woman's genitalia, King David (probably) confronted the Bathsheba's beauty, a nude acrobat standing on a ball, a painter and his model ... Always sensuality, the intensity and brutality of desire. The origin of the world is the only subject that matters. As Prévert said, 'Fixing your gaze on life means contemplating death. Picasso is a force of nature who has a weakness for life.'

The two self-portraits from 1968 are the last ones Picasso produced until the four that he drew in June and July 1972 (166–9), less than a year before his death on 8 April 1973. And these two self-portraits, of an artist whose gaze roams over his work, seem to offer a conclusion: 'Finally, I have imitated the whole world, except for myself.'

1895

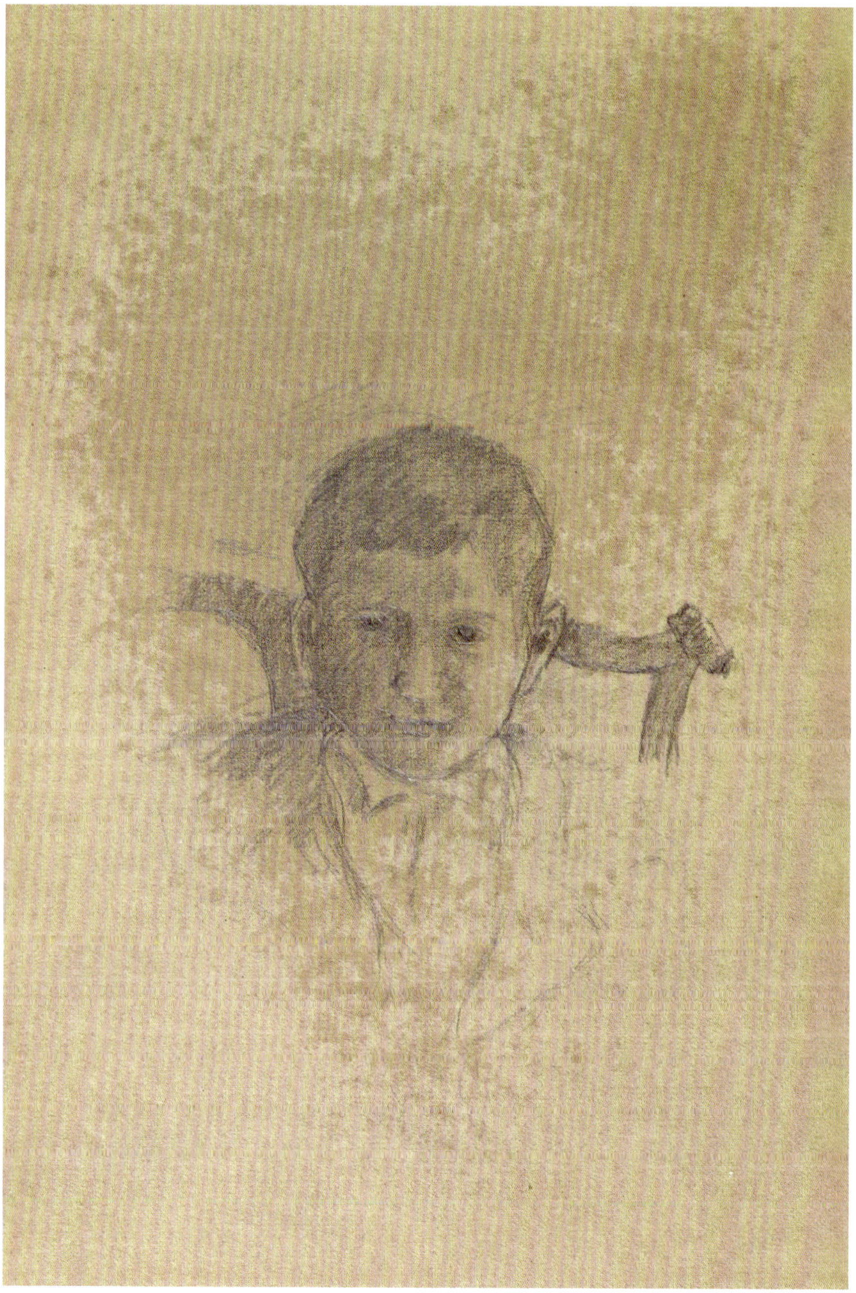

1896

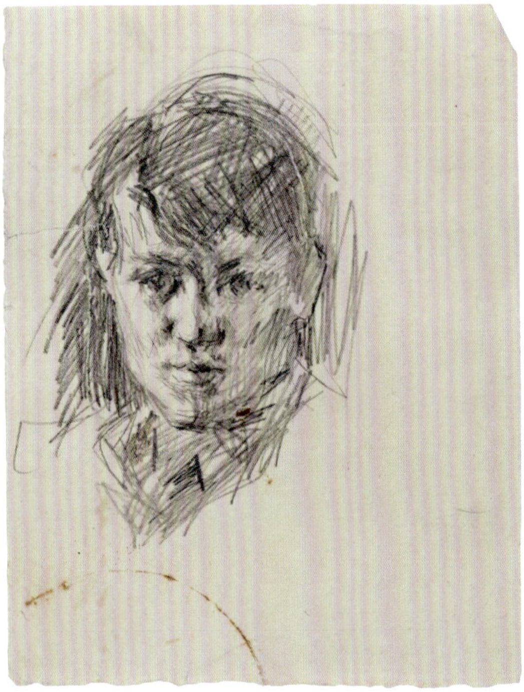

3

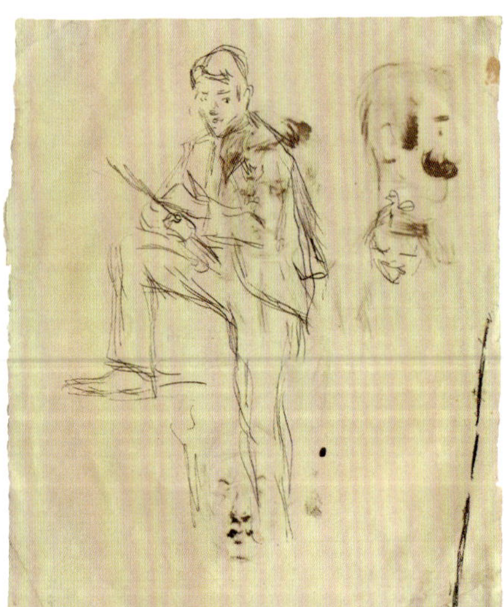

4

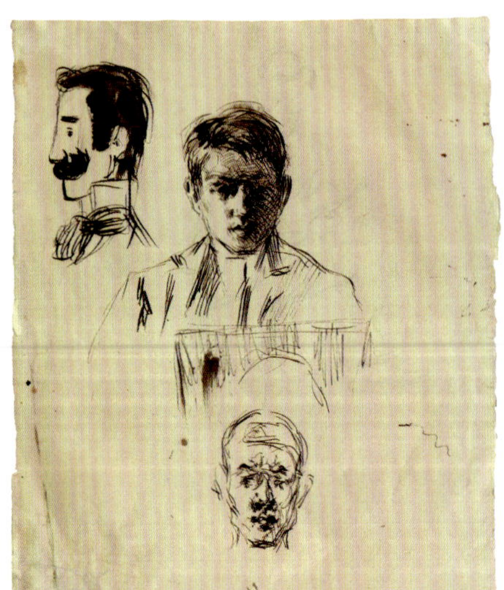

5

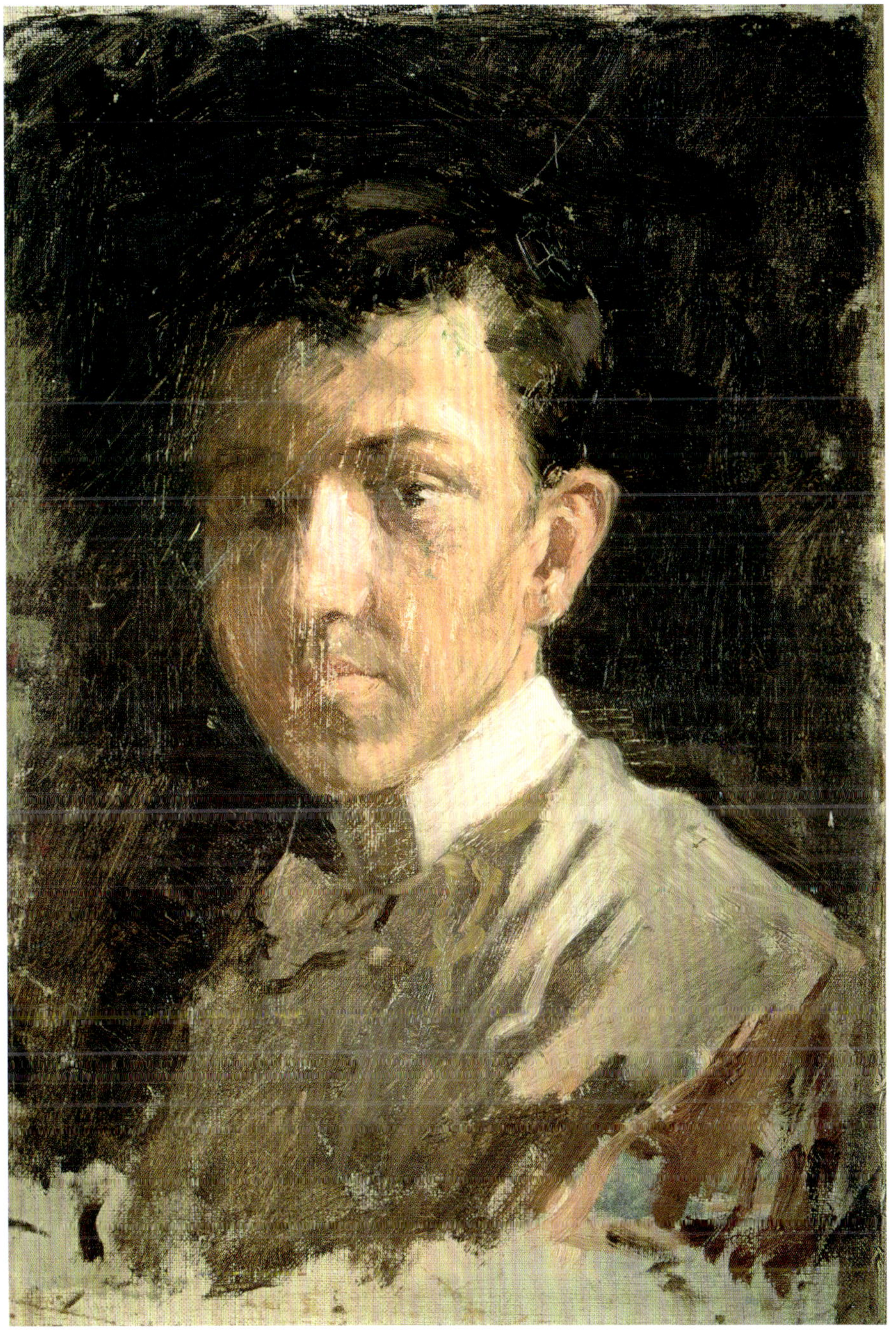

6

1896

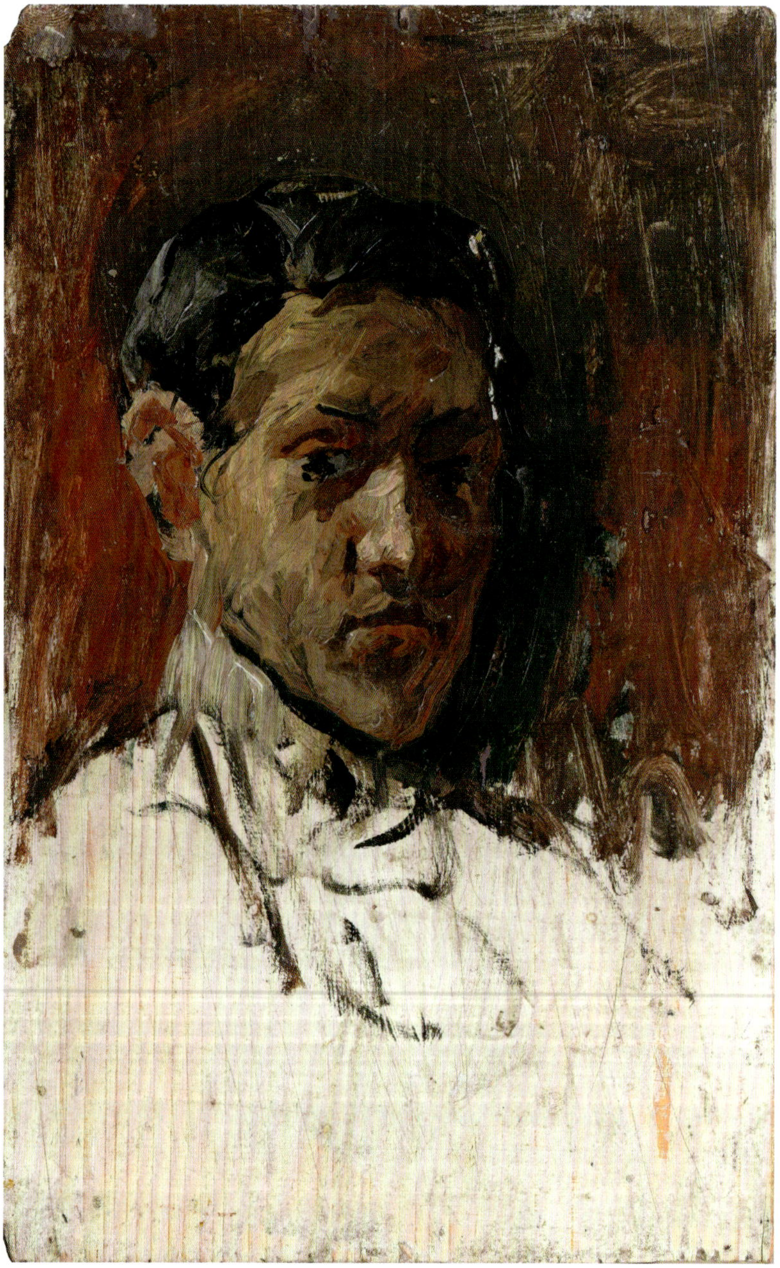

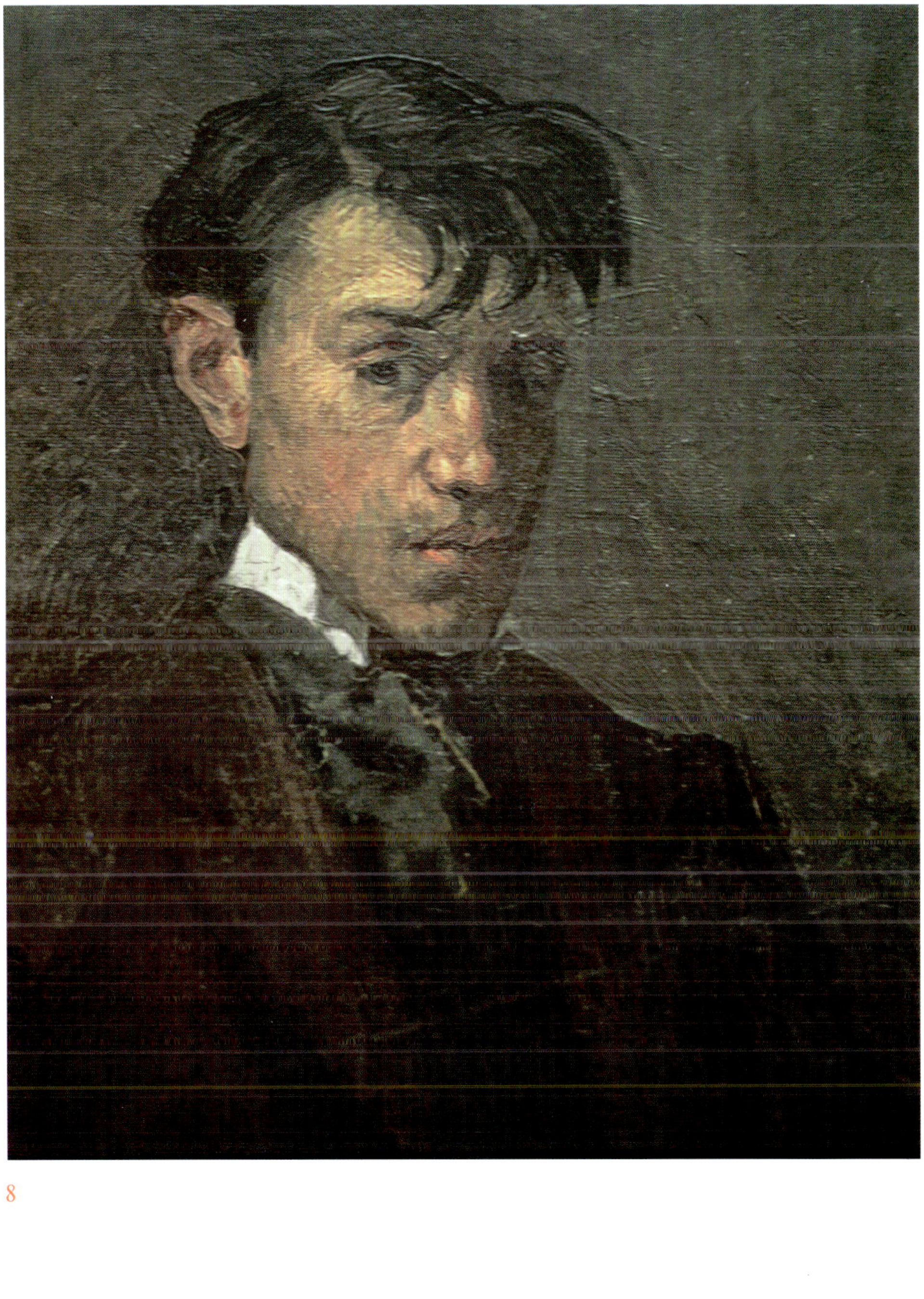

1897

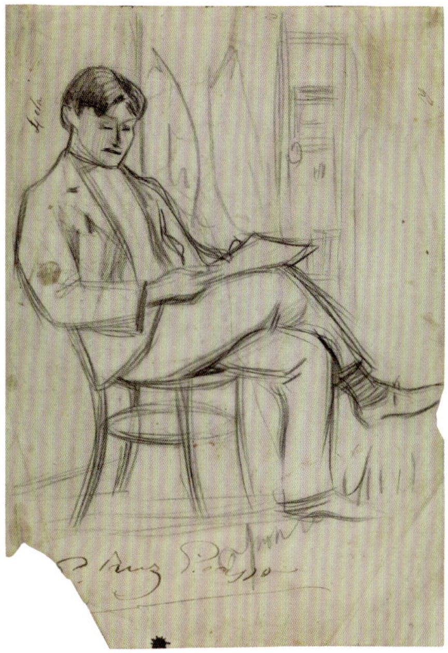

10

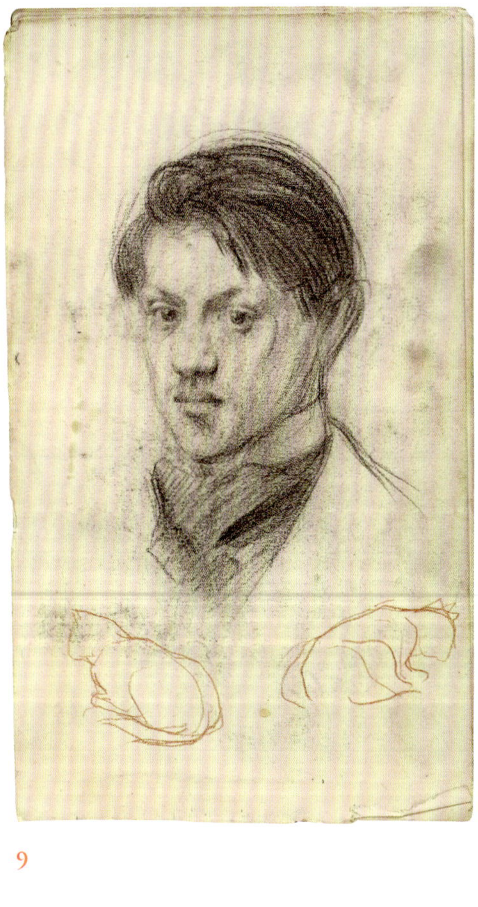

9

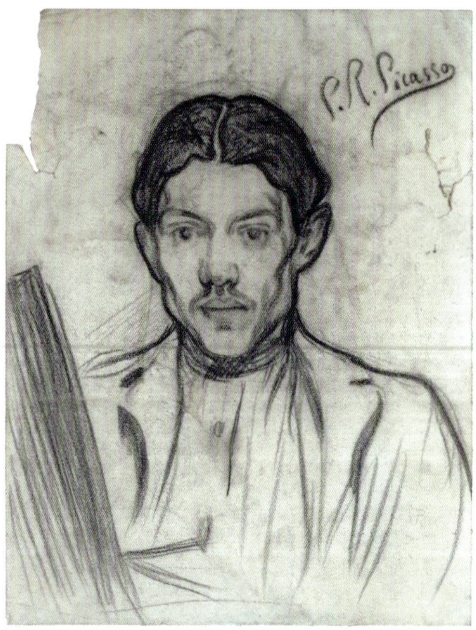

11

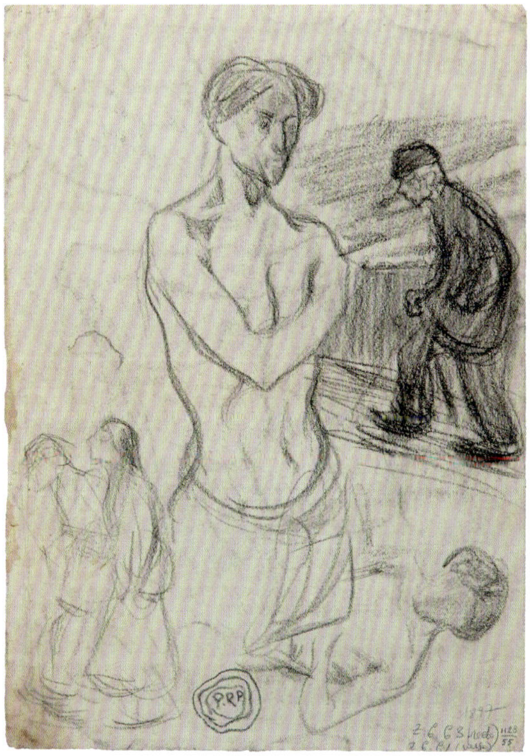

12

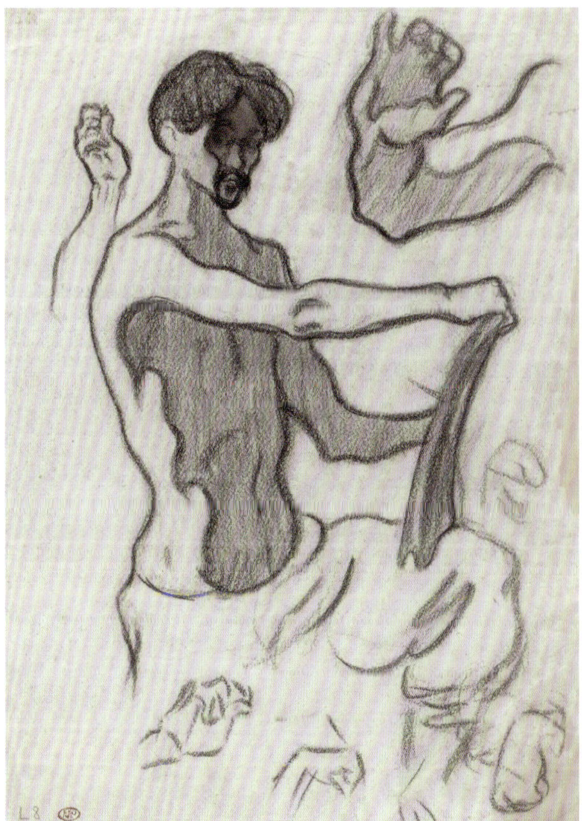

13

1898

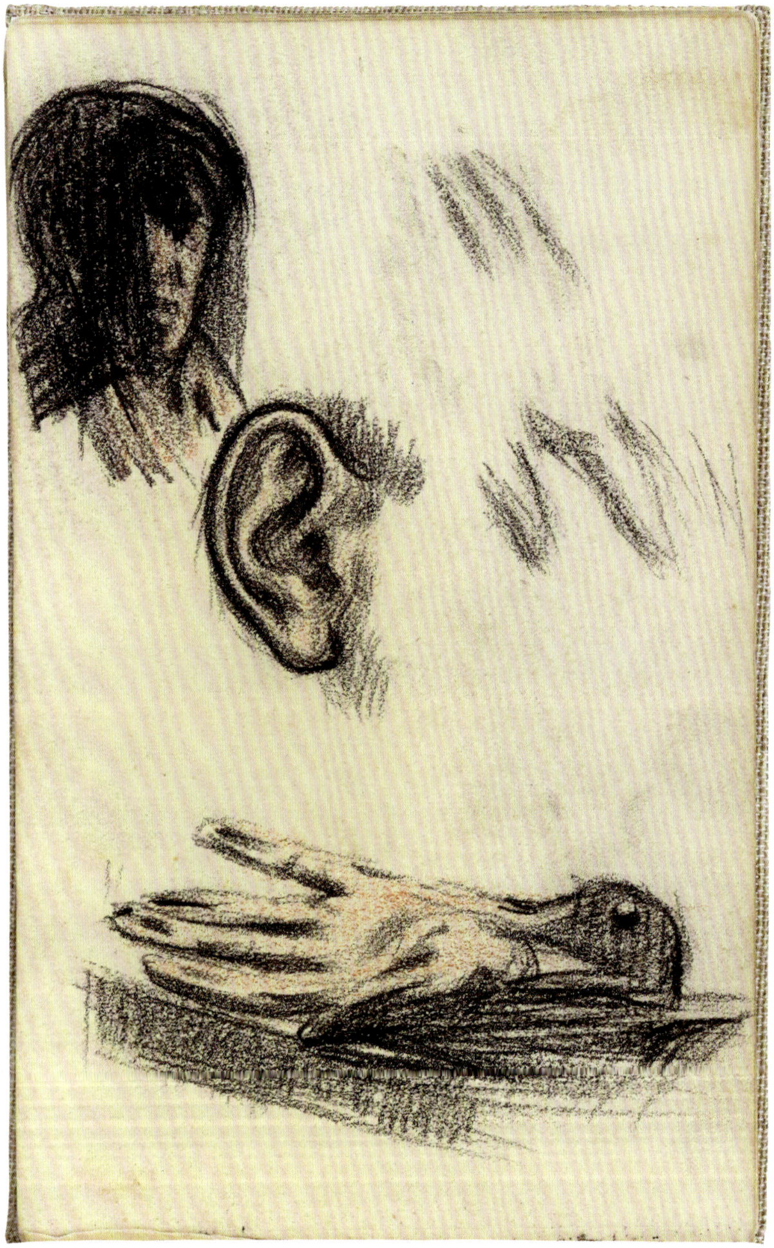

1899

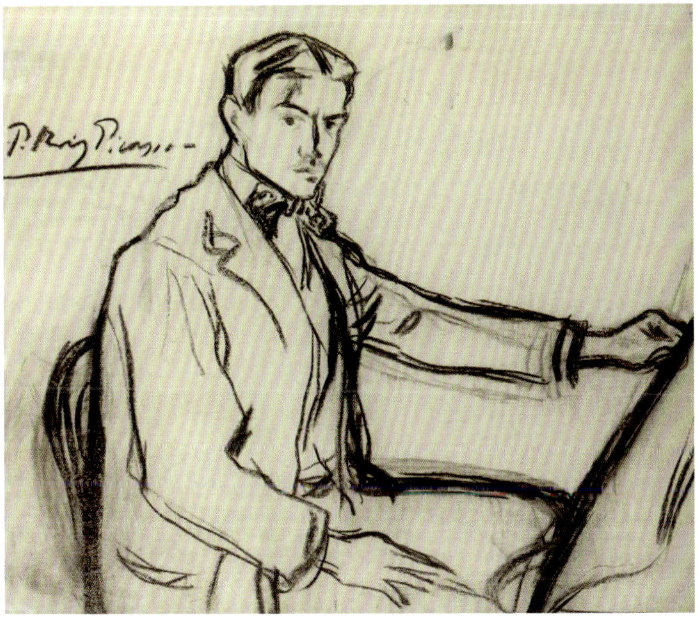

15

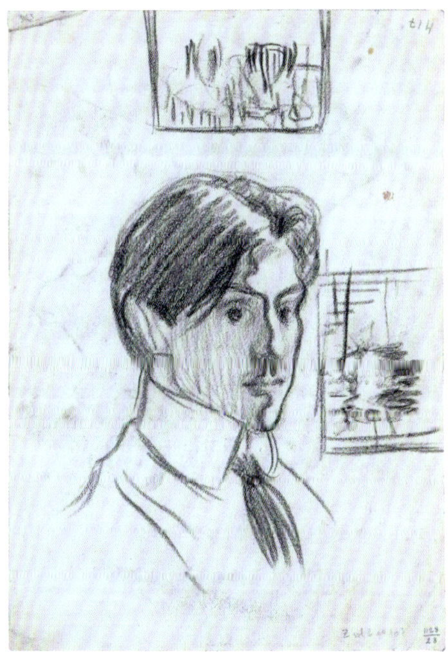

16

1899–1900

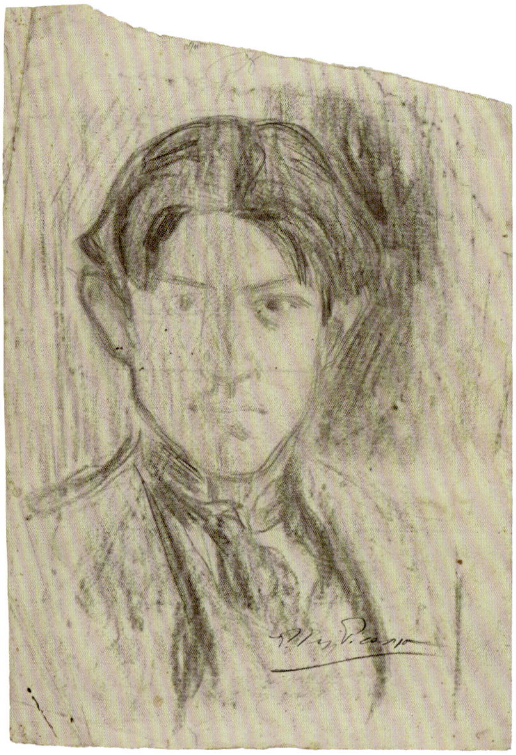

17

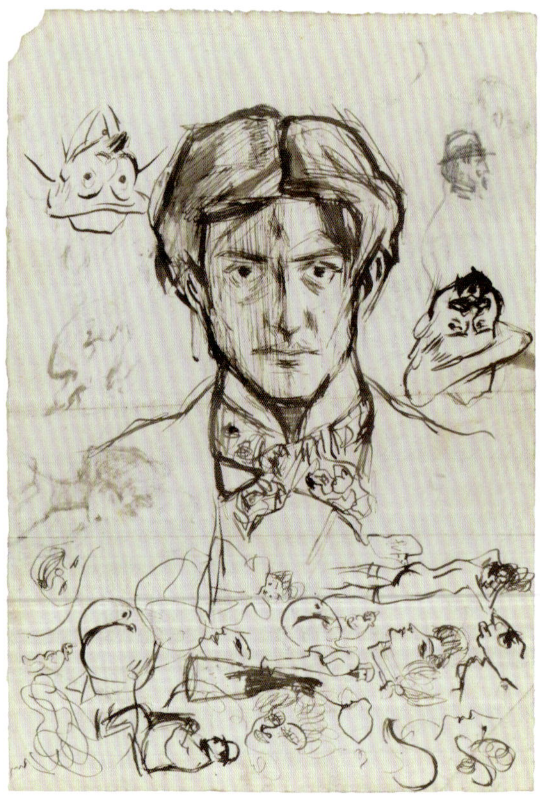

18

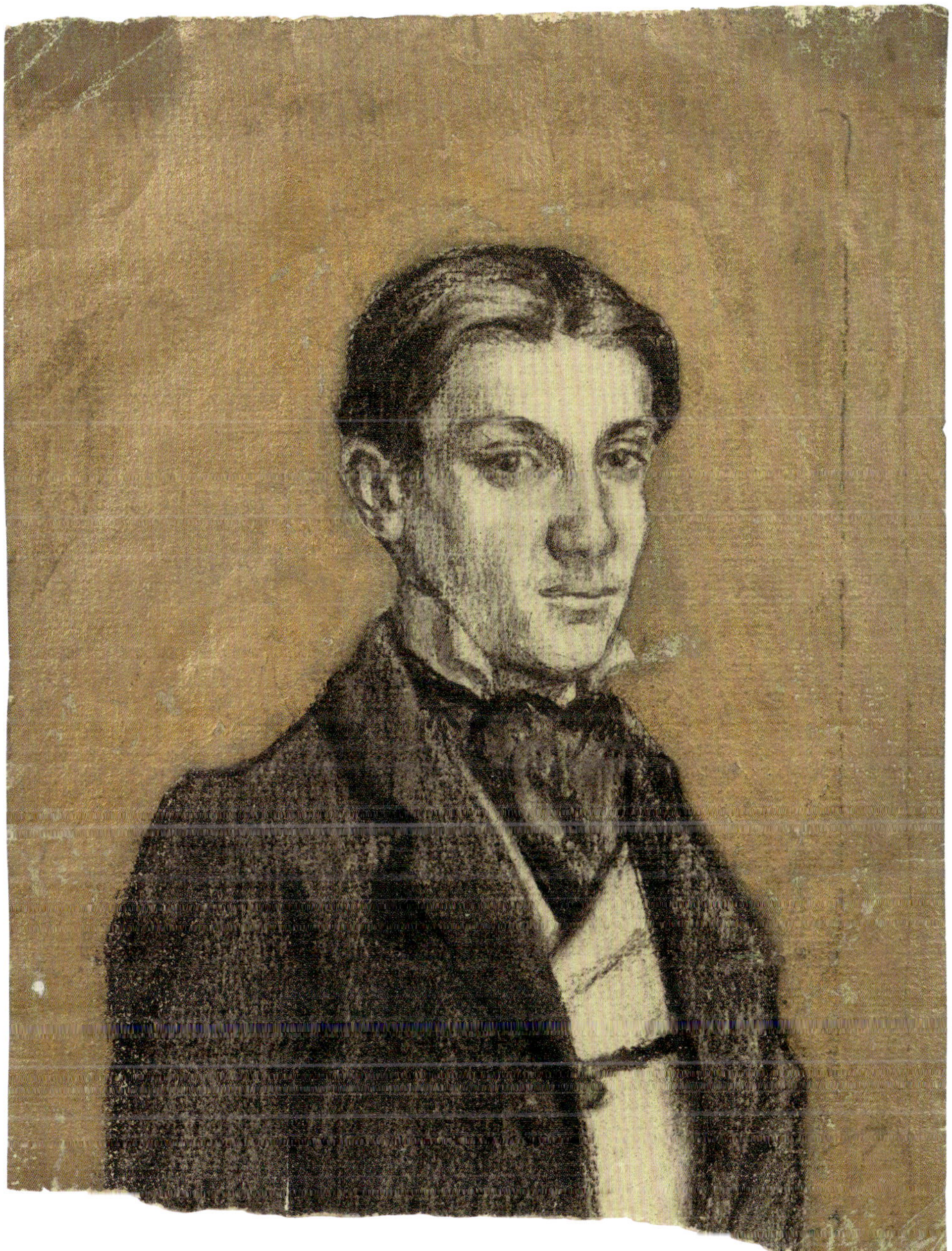

19

1899–1900

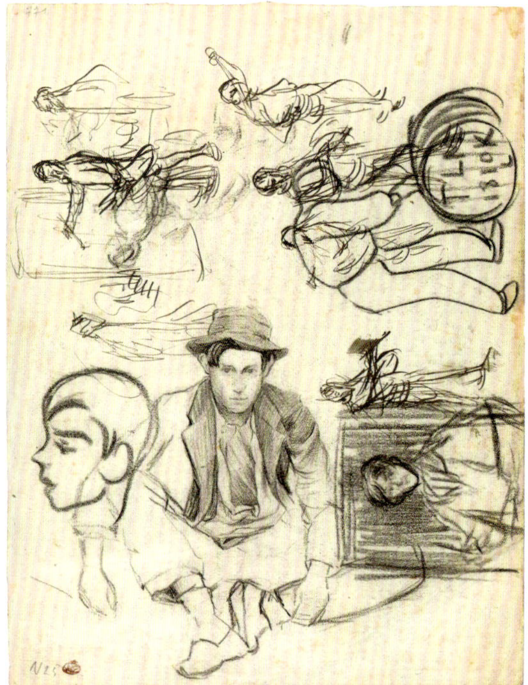

21

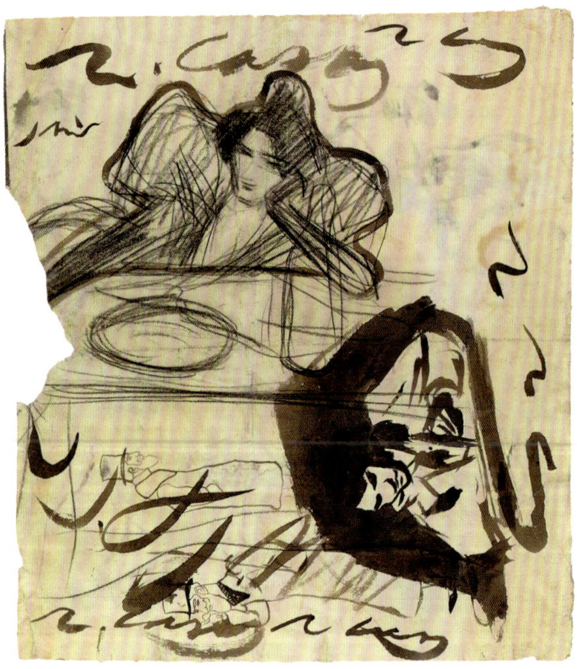

20

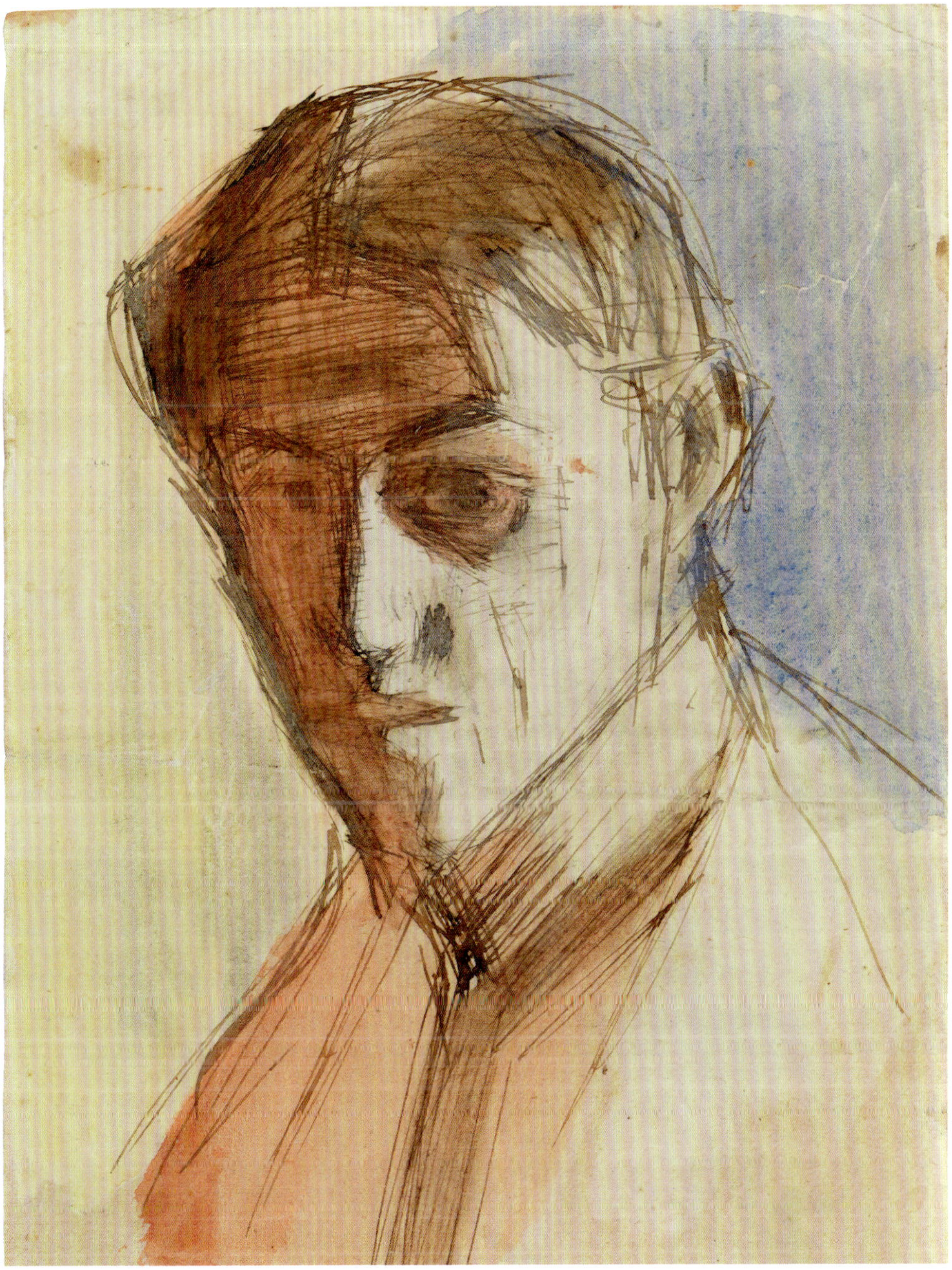

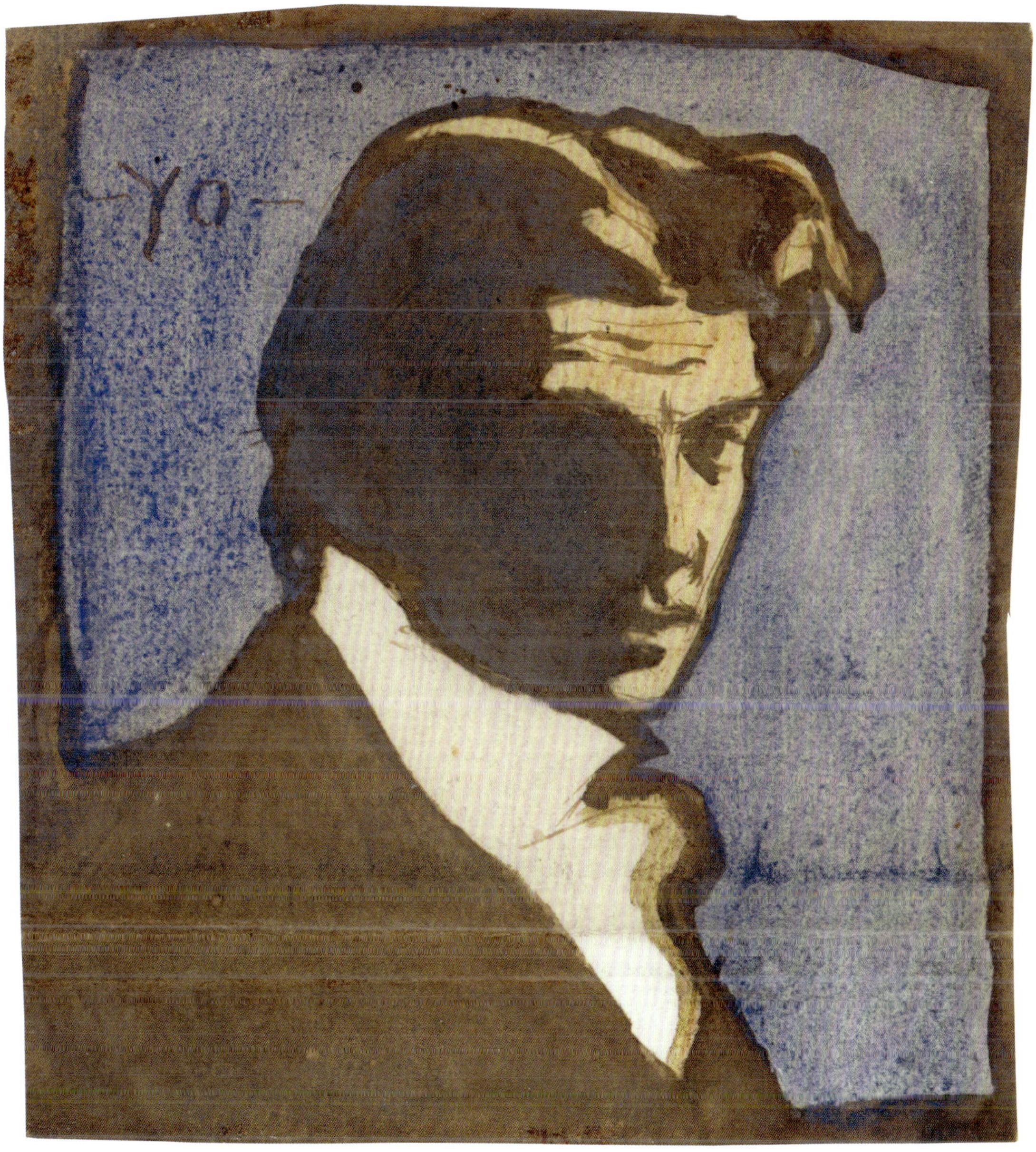
YO

1900

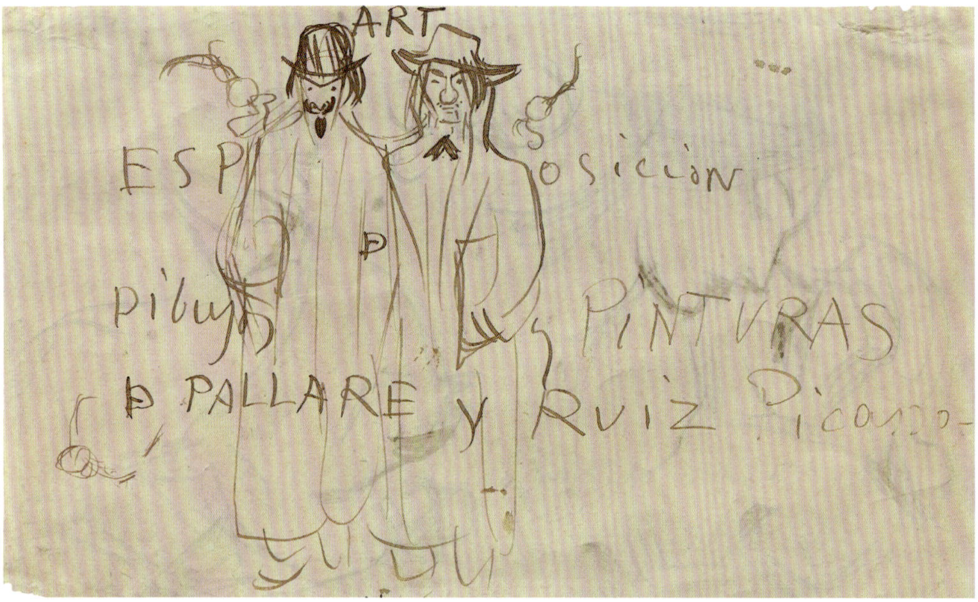

24

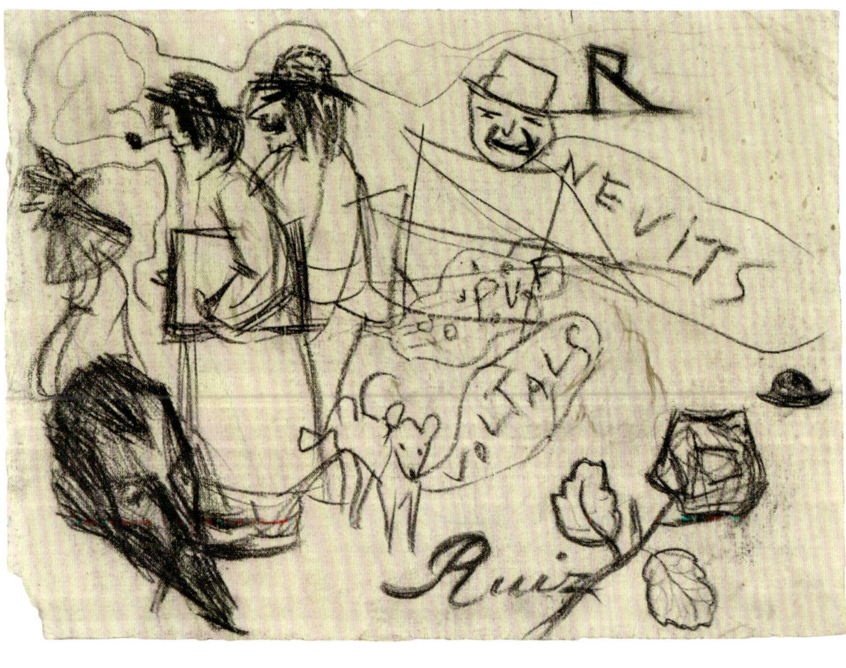

25

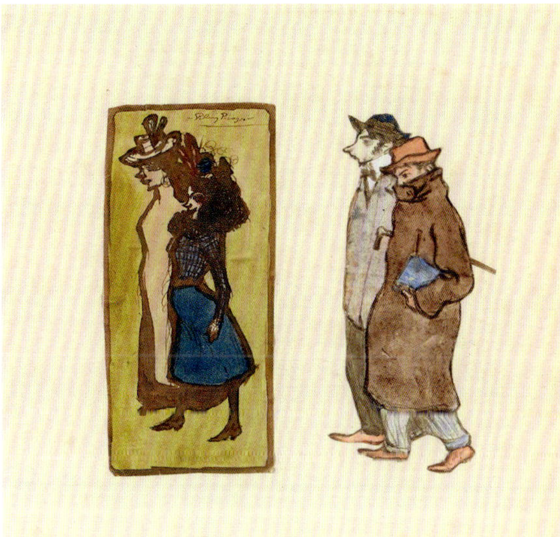

26

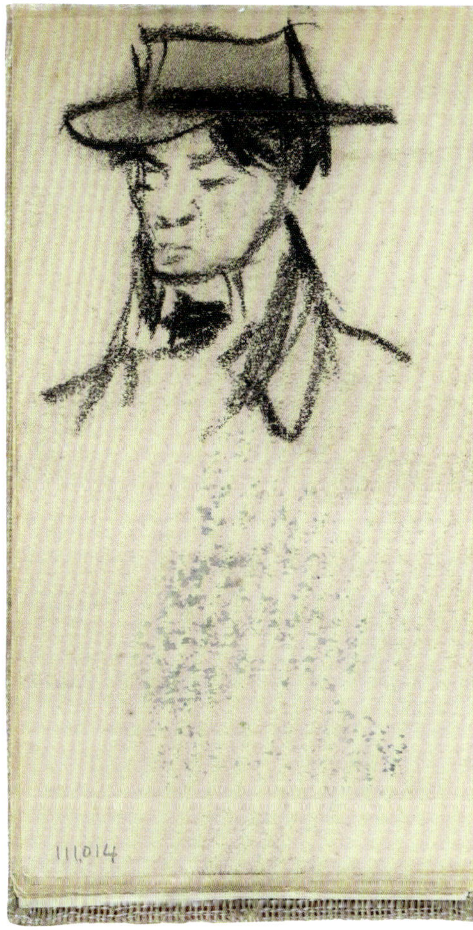

28

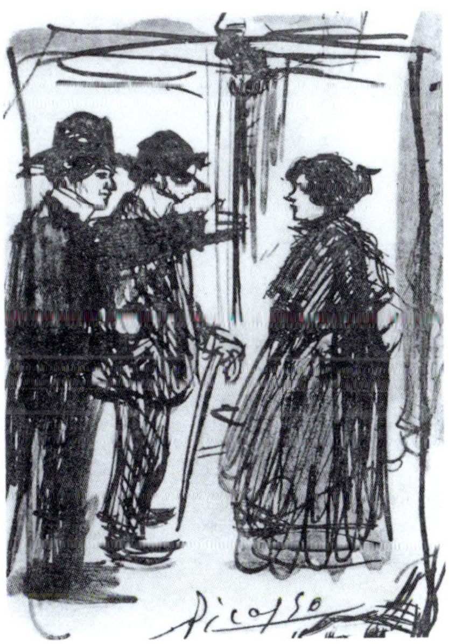

27

1900

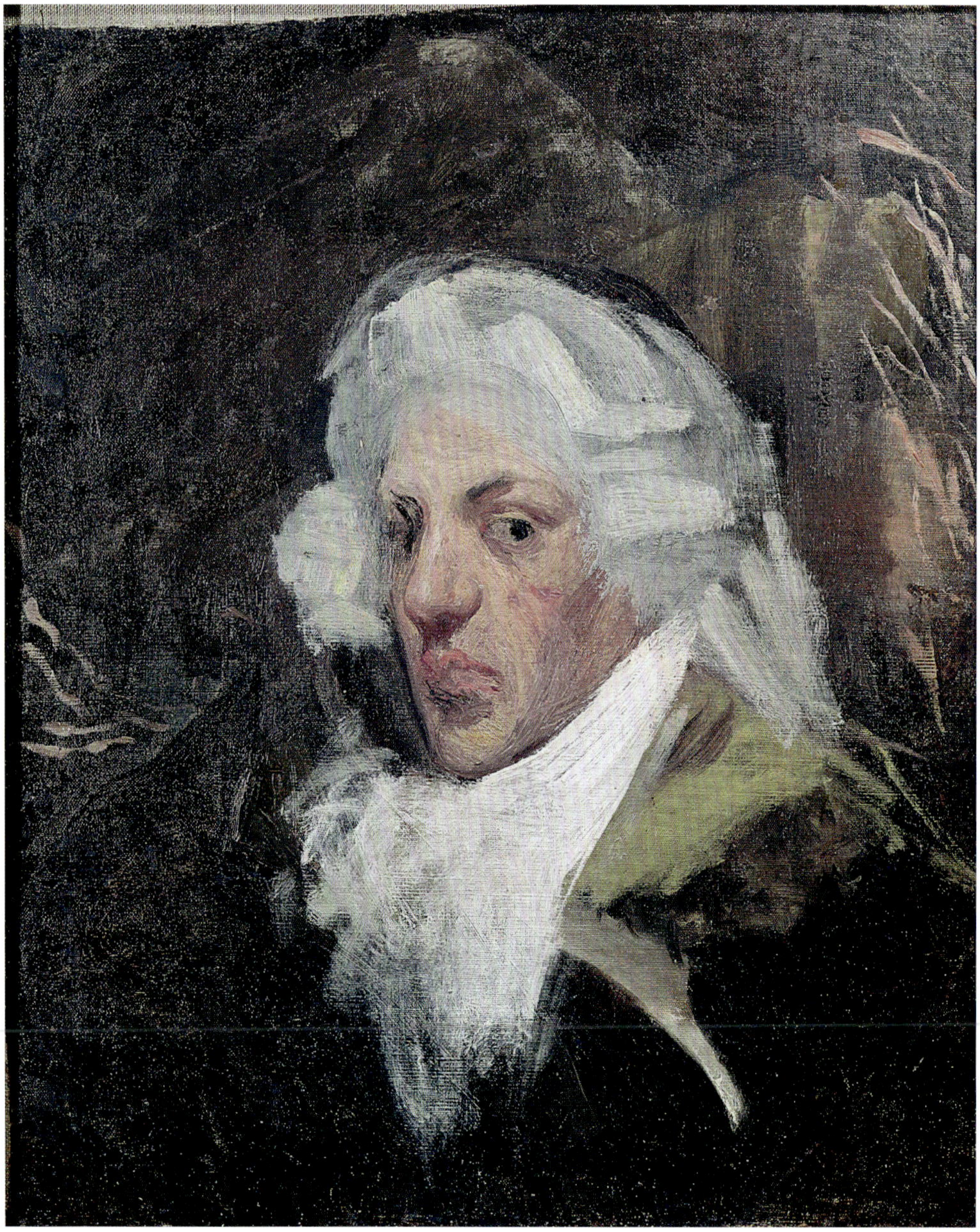

29

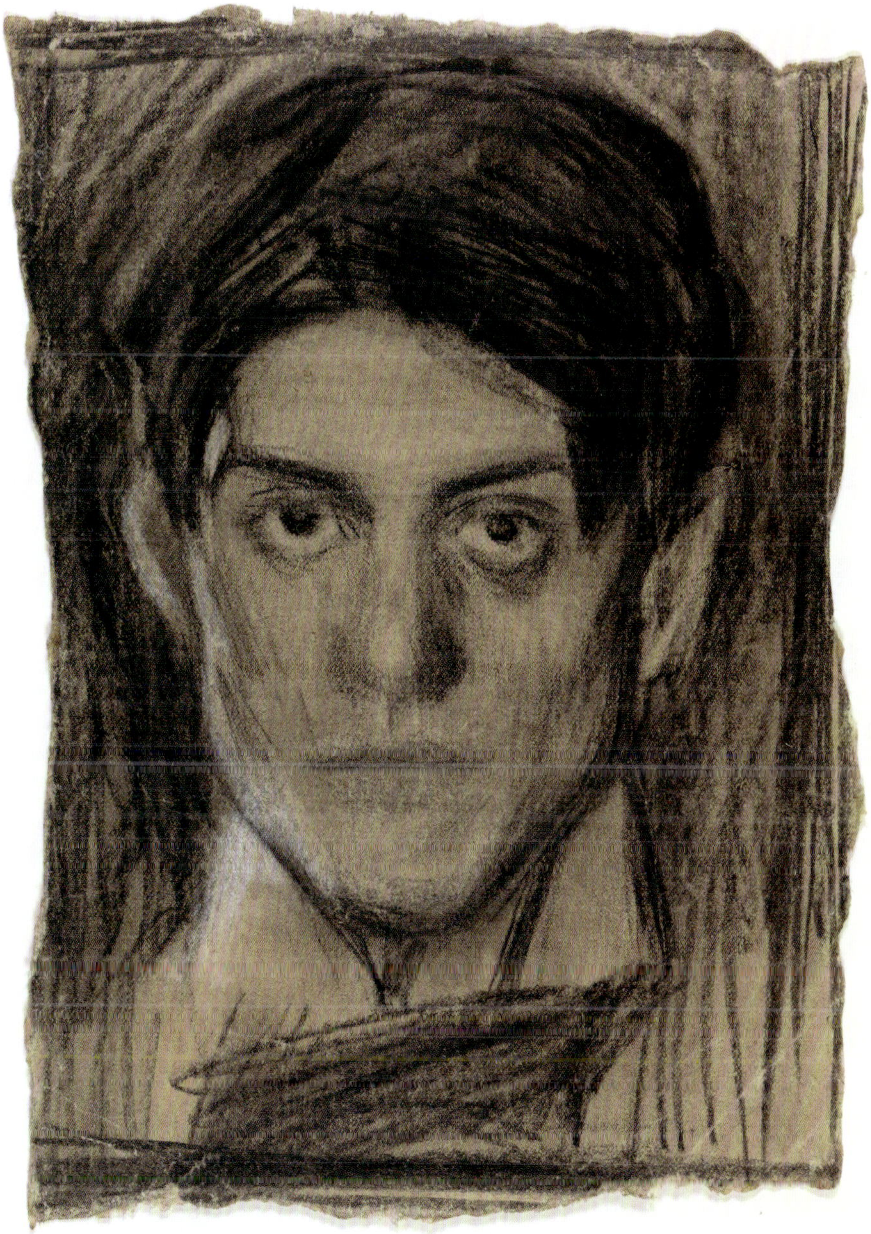

1900

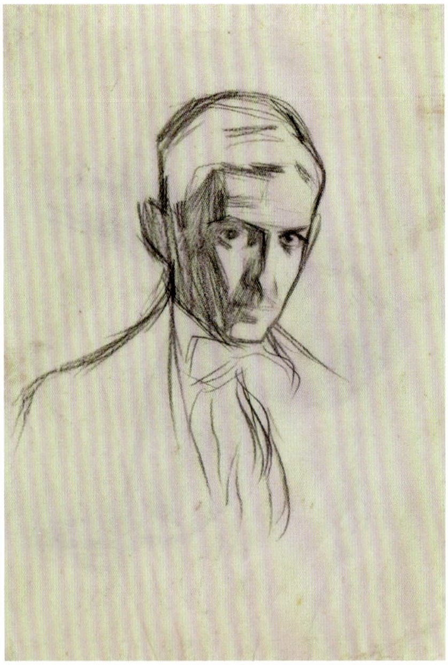

31

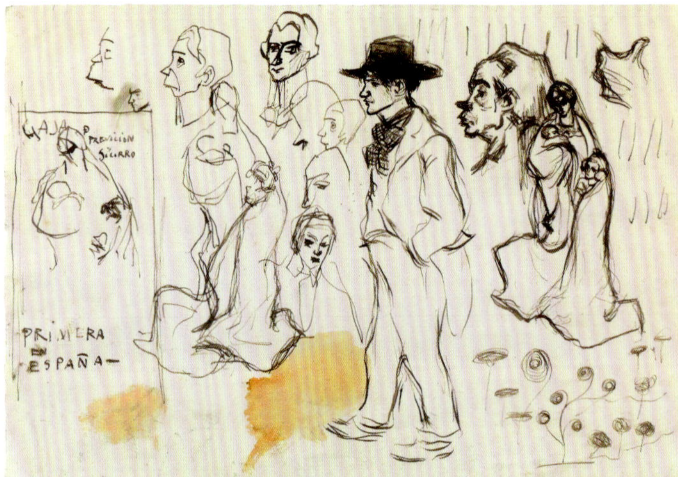

32

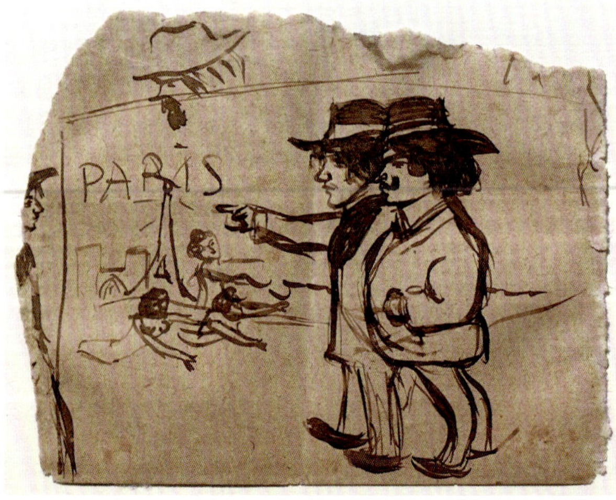

33

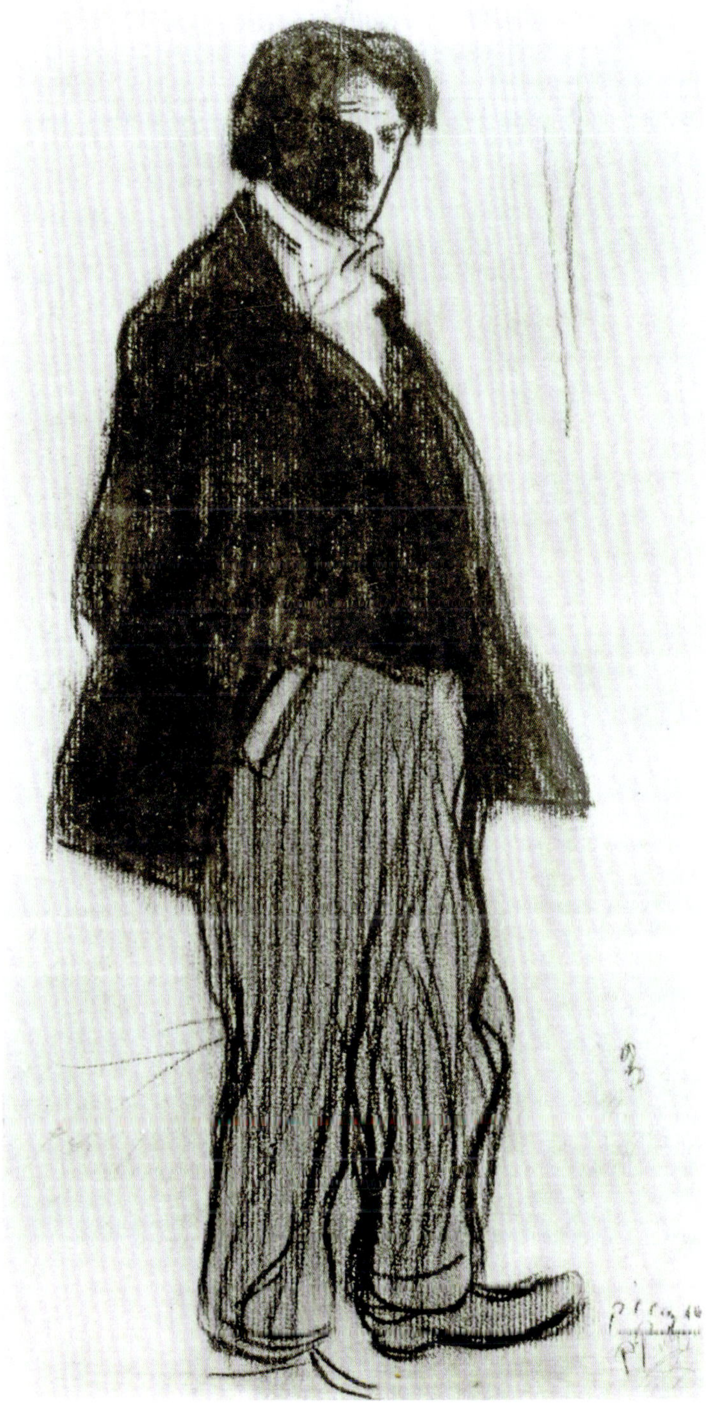

1901

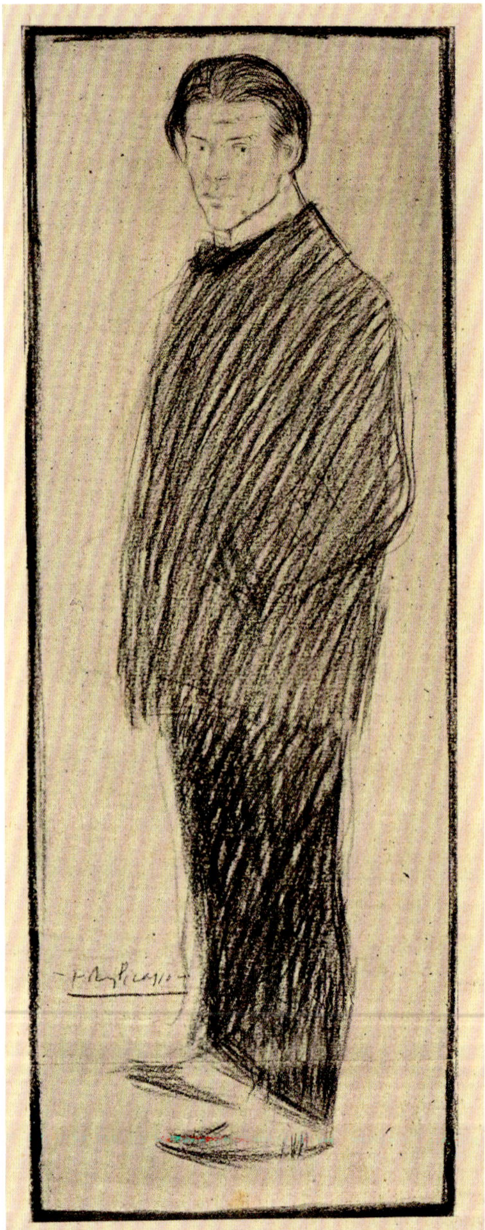

35

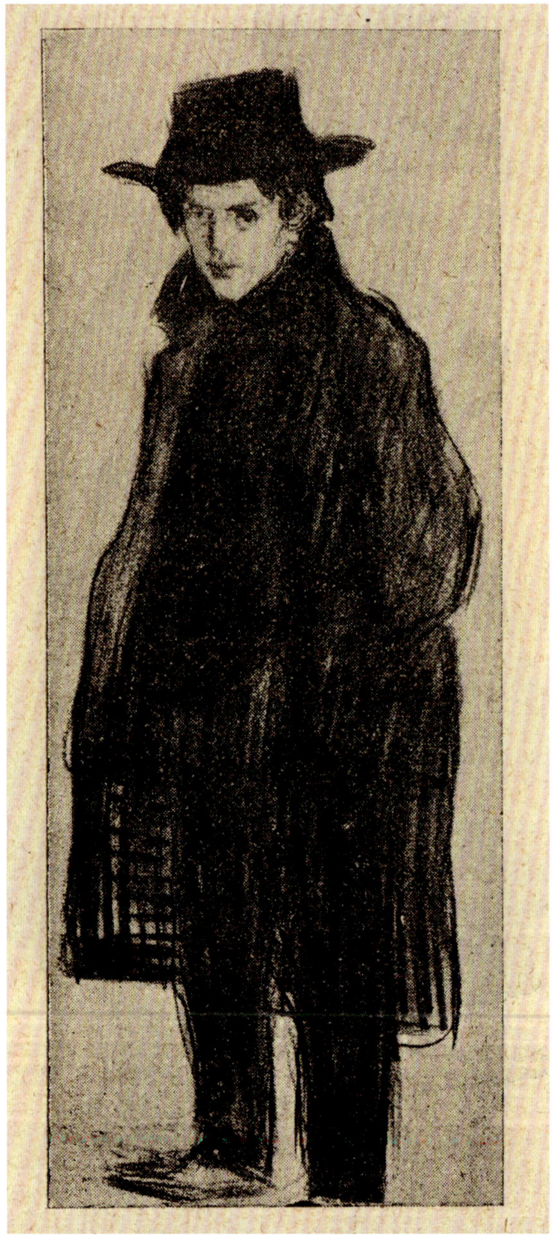

36

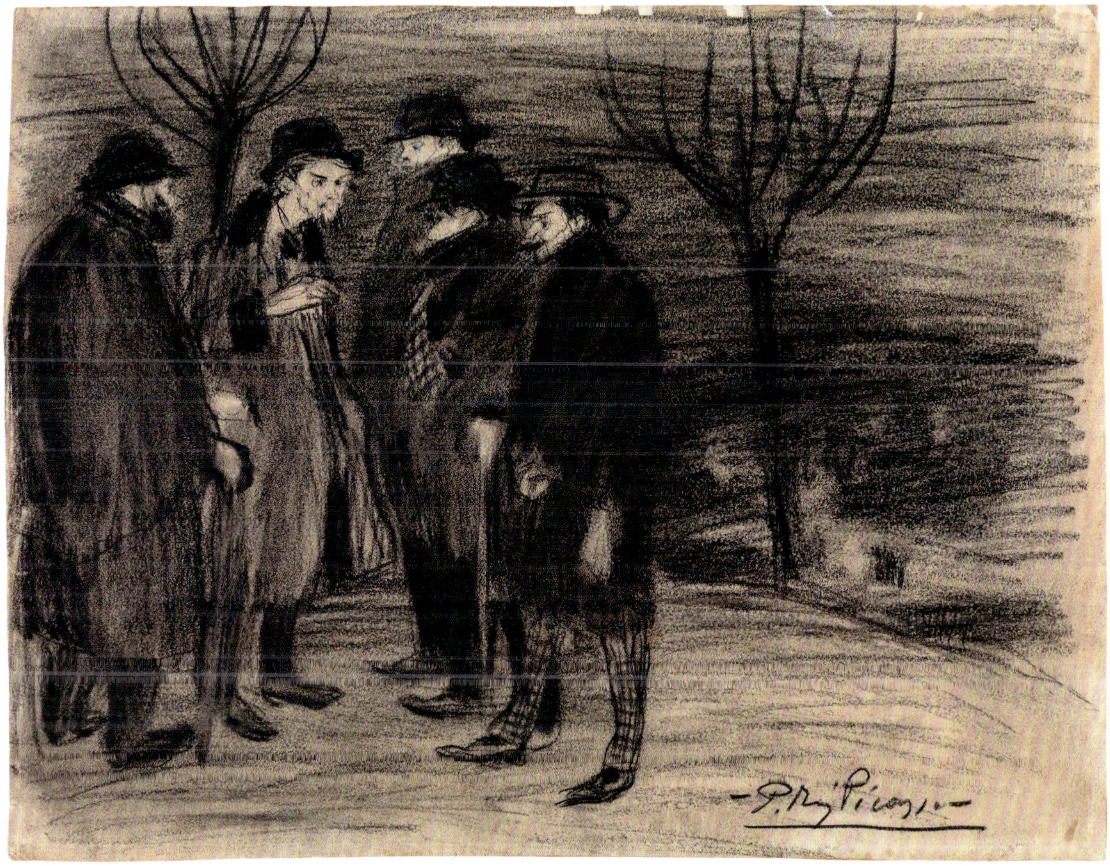

37

1901

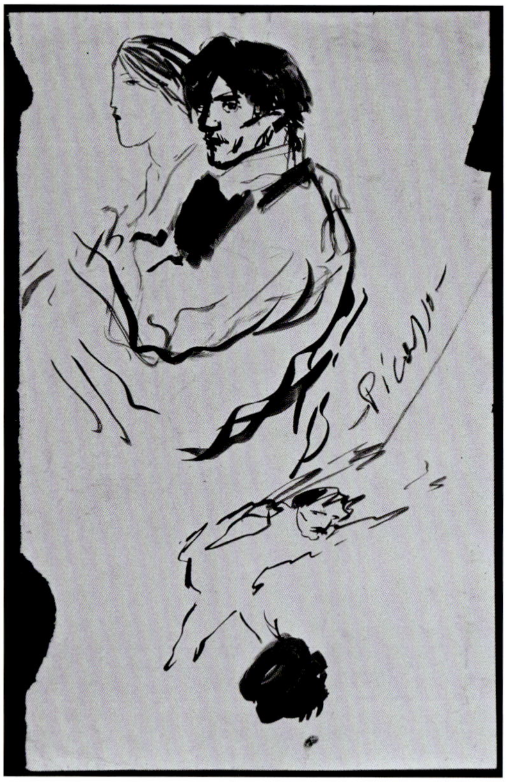

38

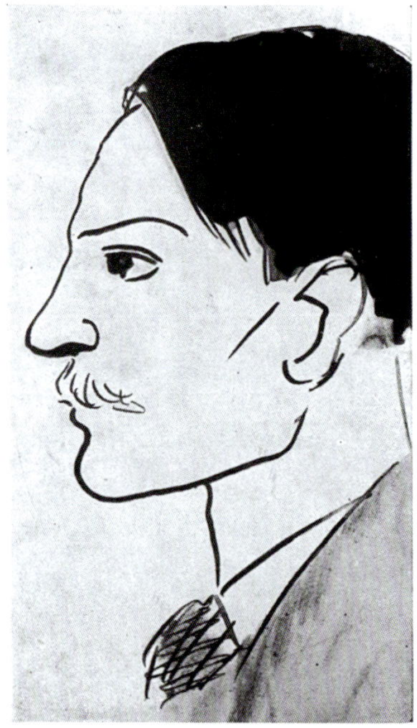

39

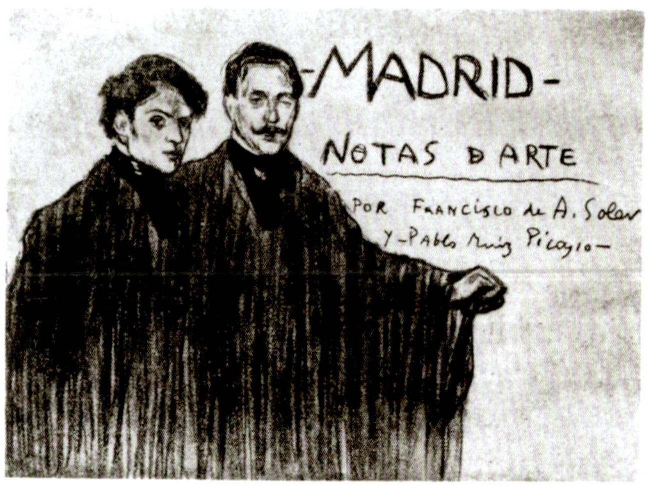
-MADRID-
NOTAS D ARTE
POR FRANCISCO de A. Soler
Y-Pablo Ruiz Picasso-

40

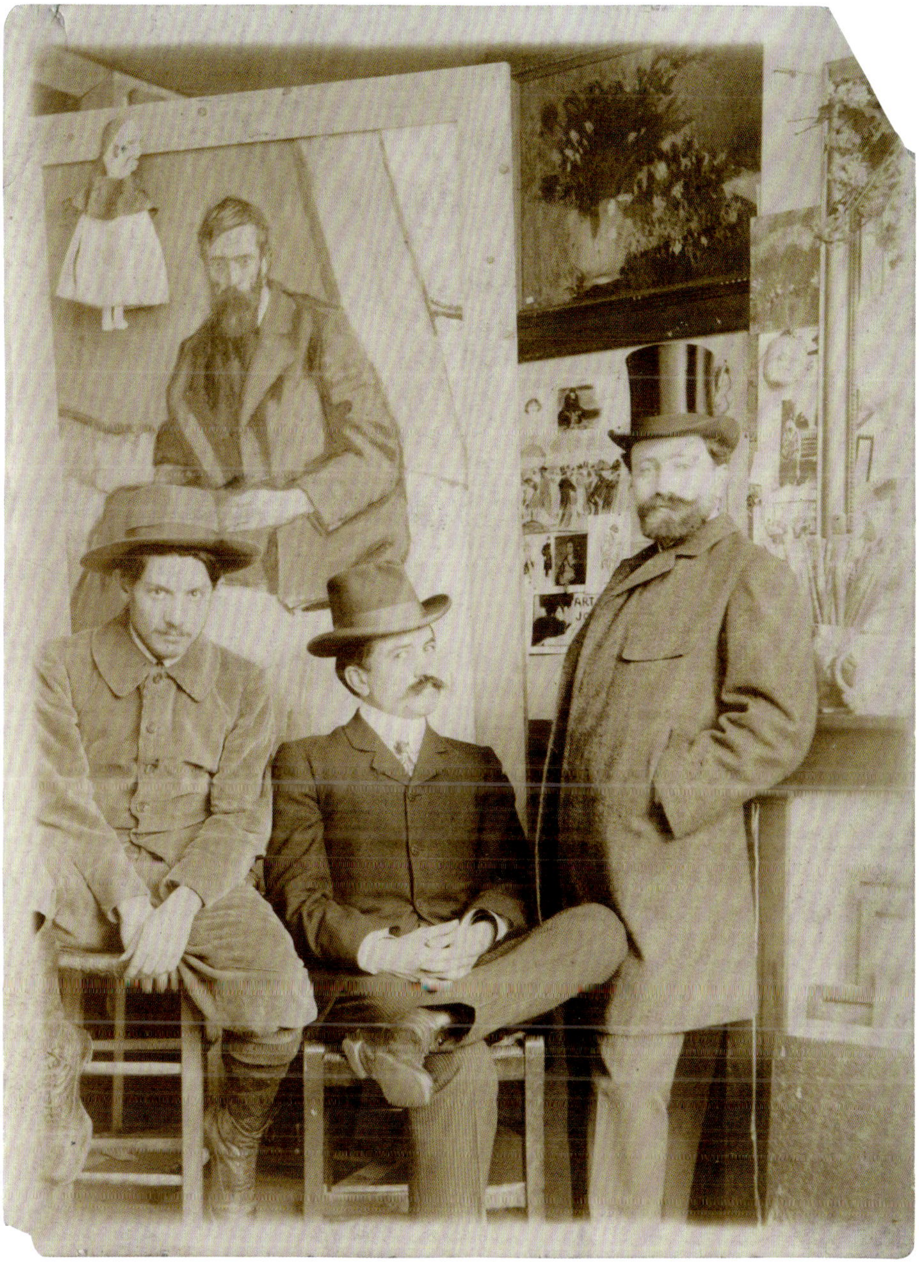

1901

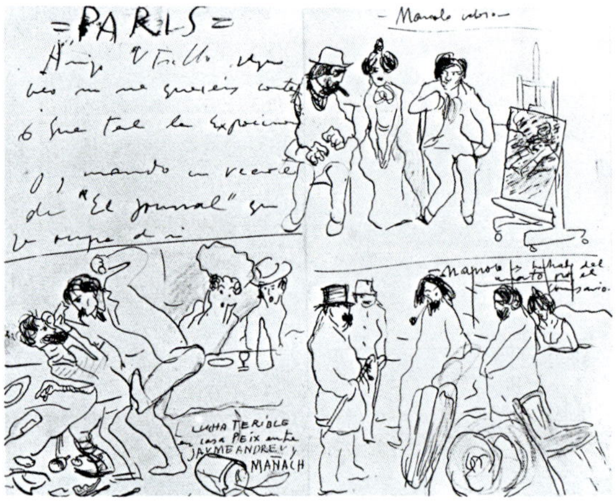

42

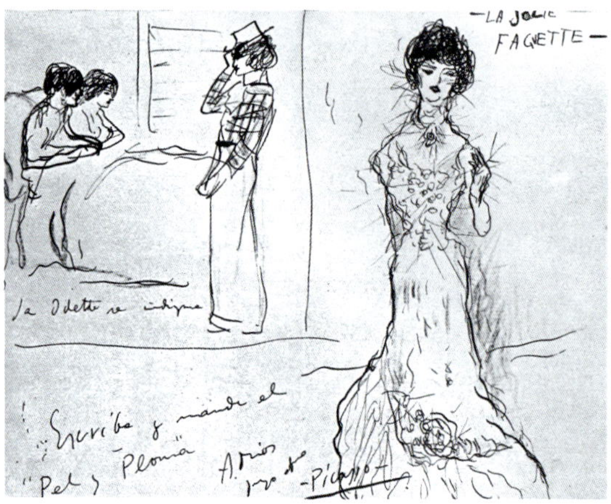

43

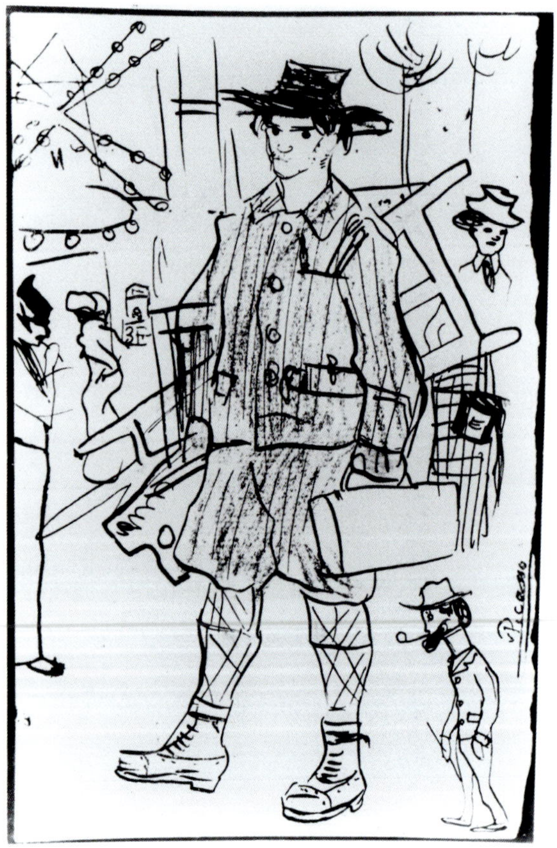

44

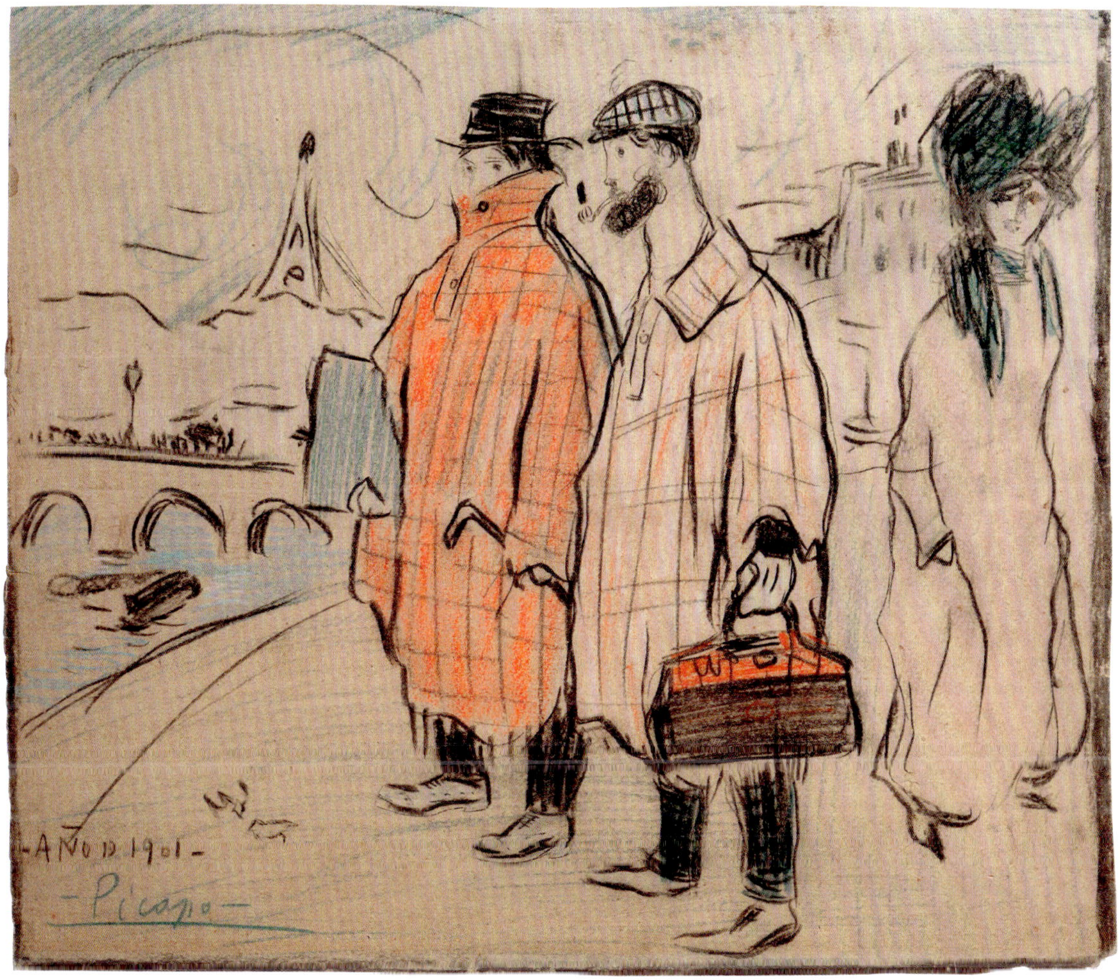

45

1901

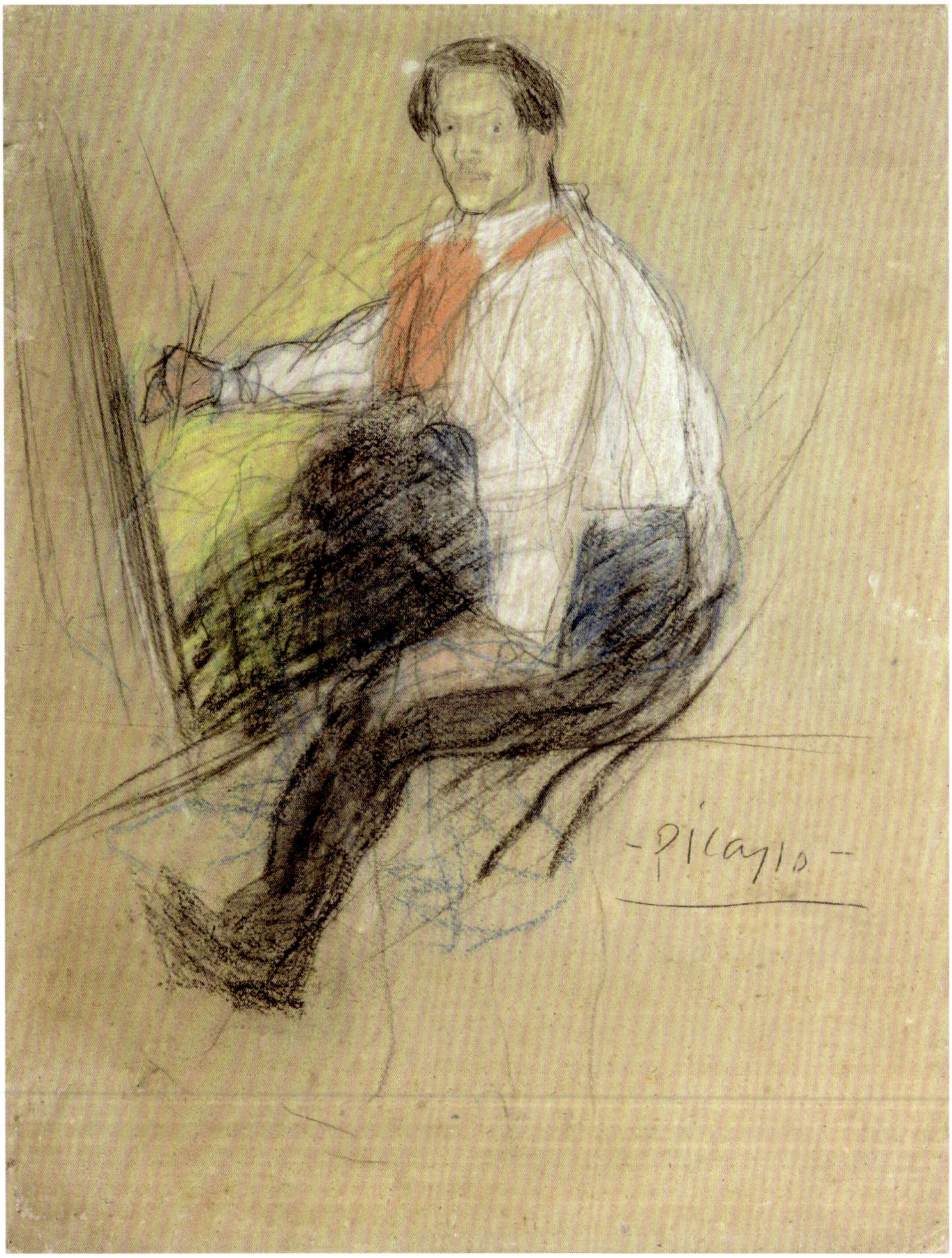

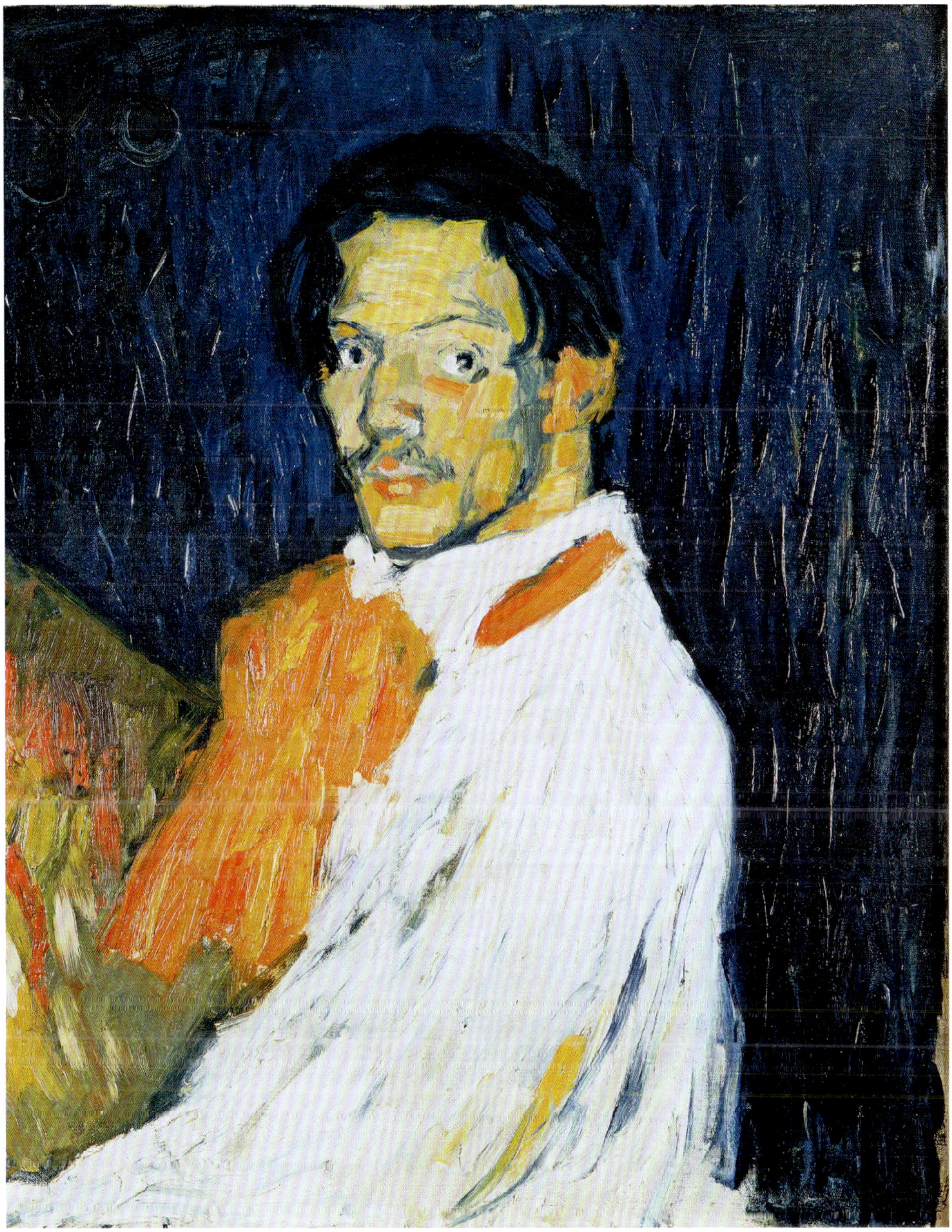

47

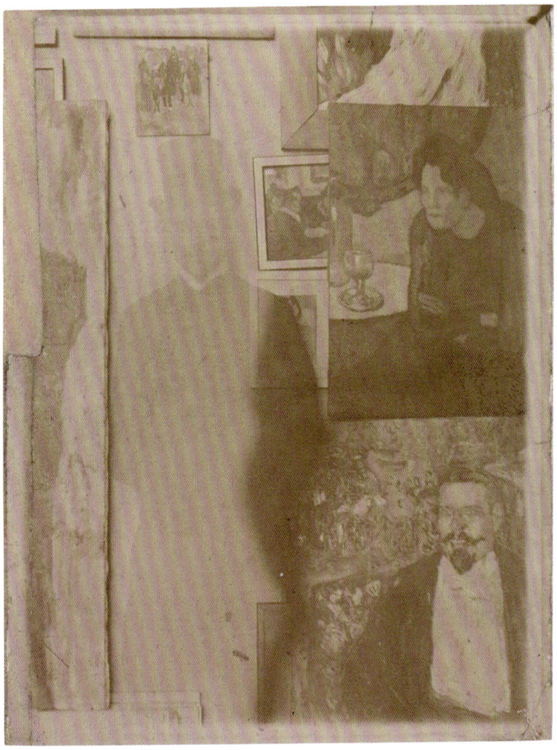

48

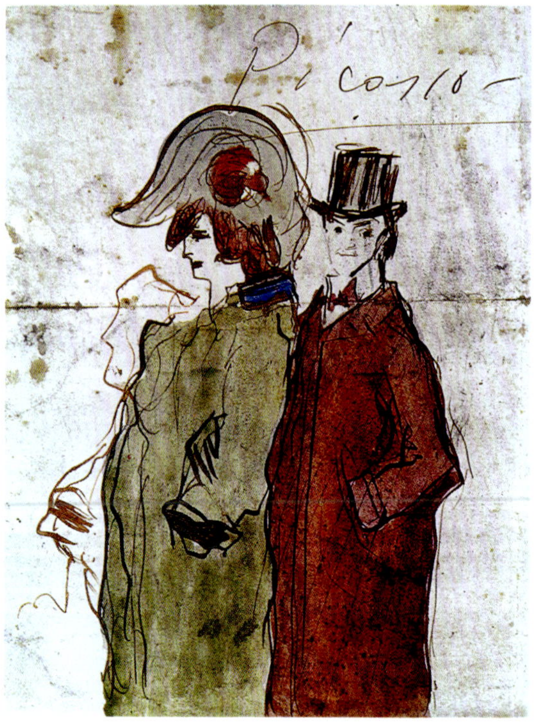

49

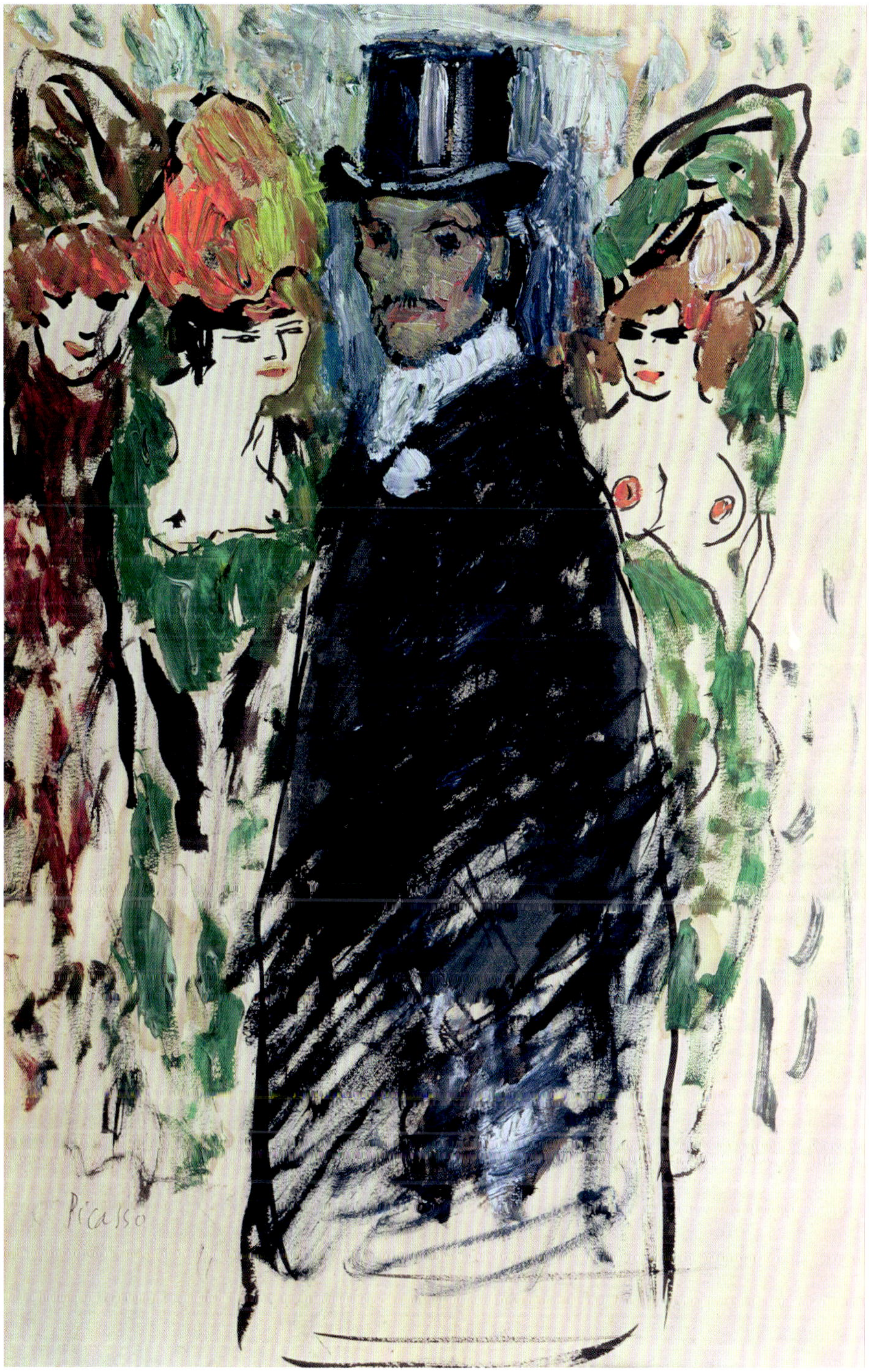
Picasso

1901

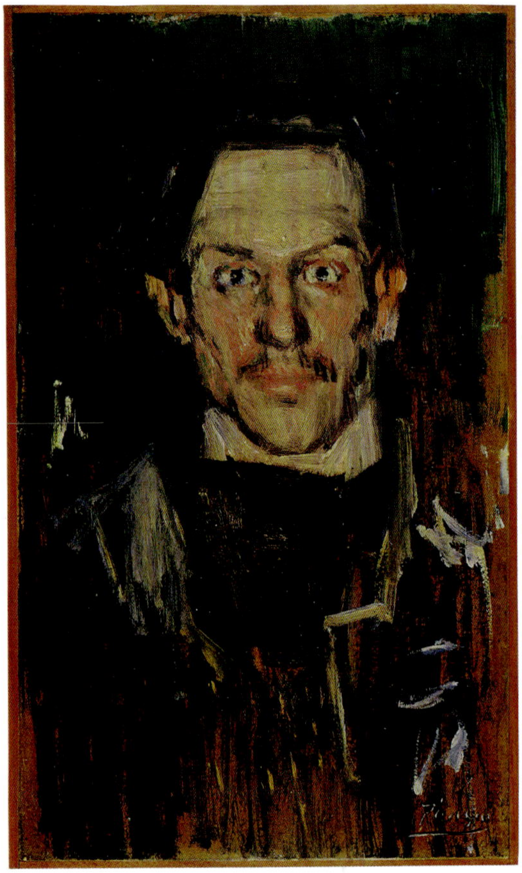

51

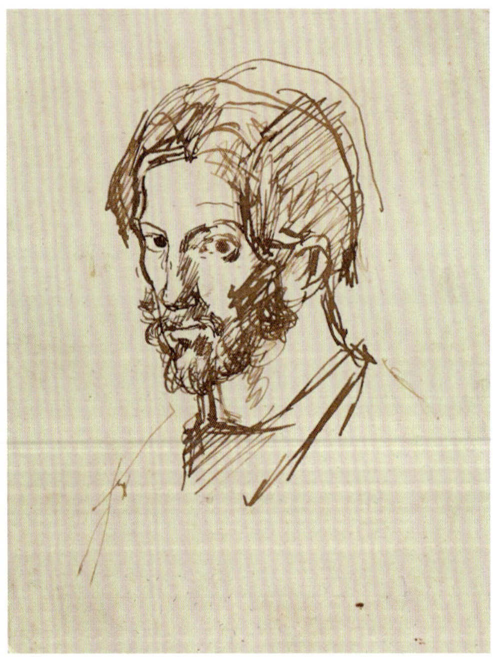

52

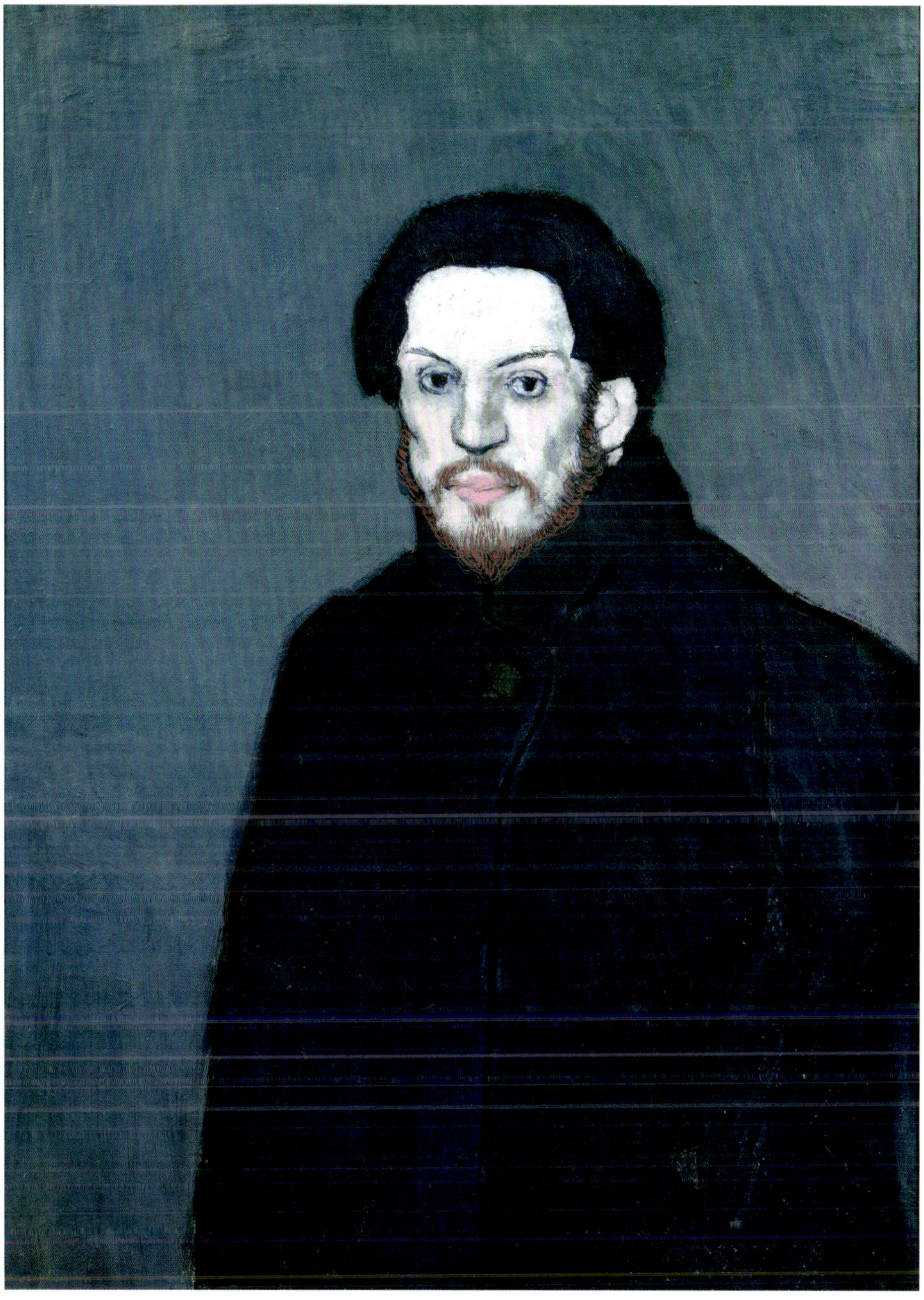

1901–1902

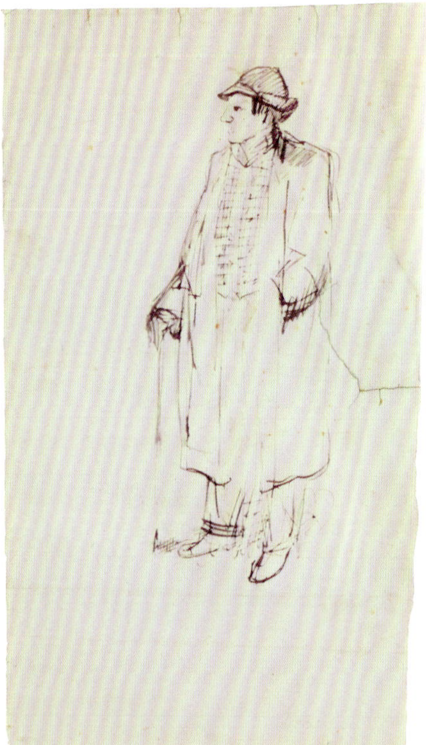

54

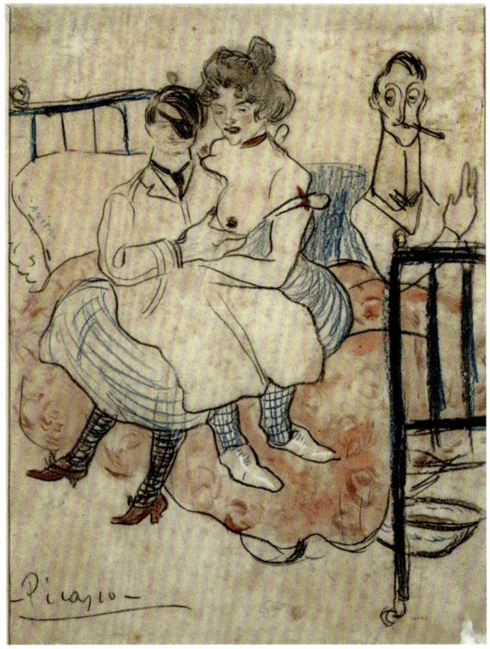

55

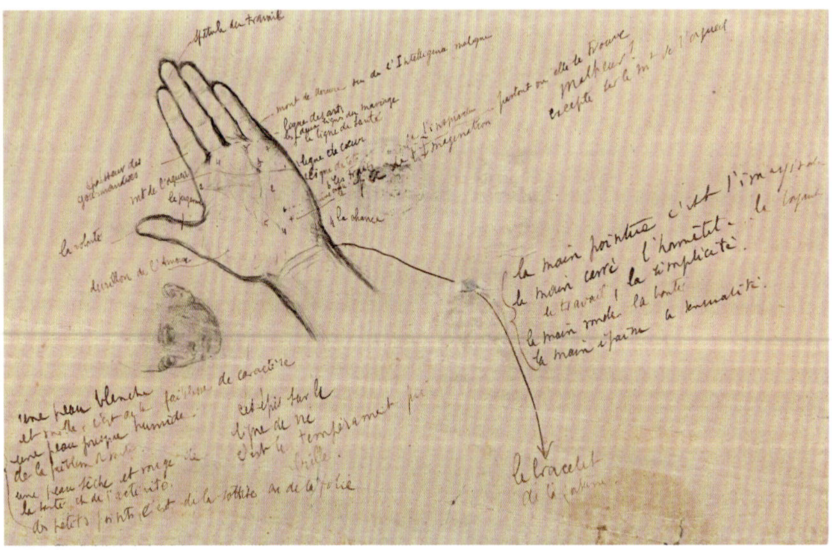

56

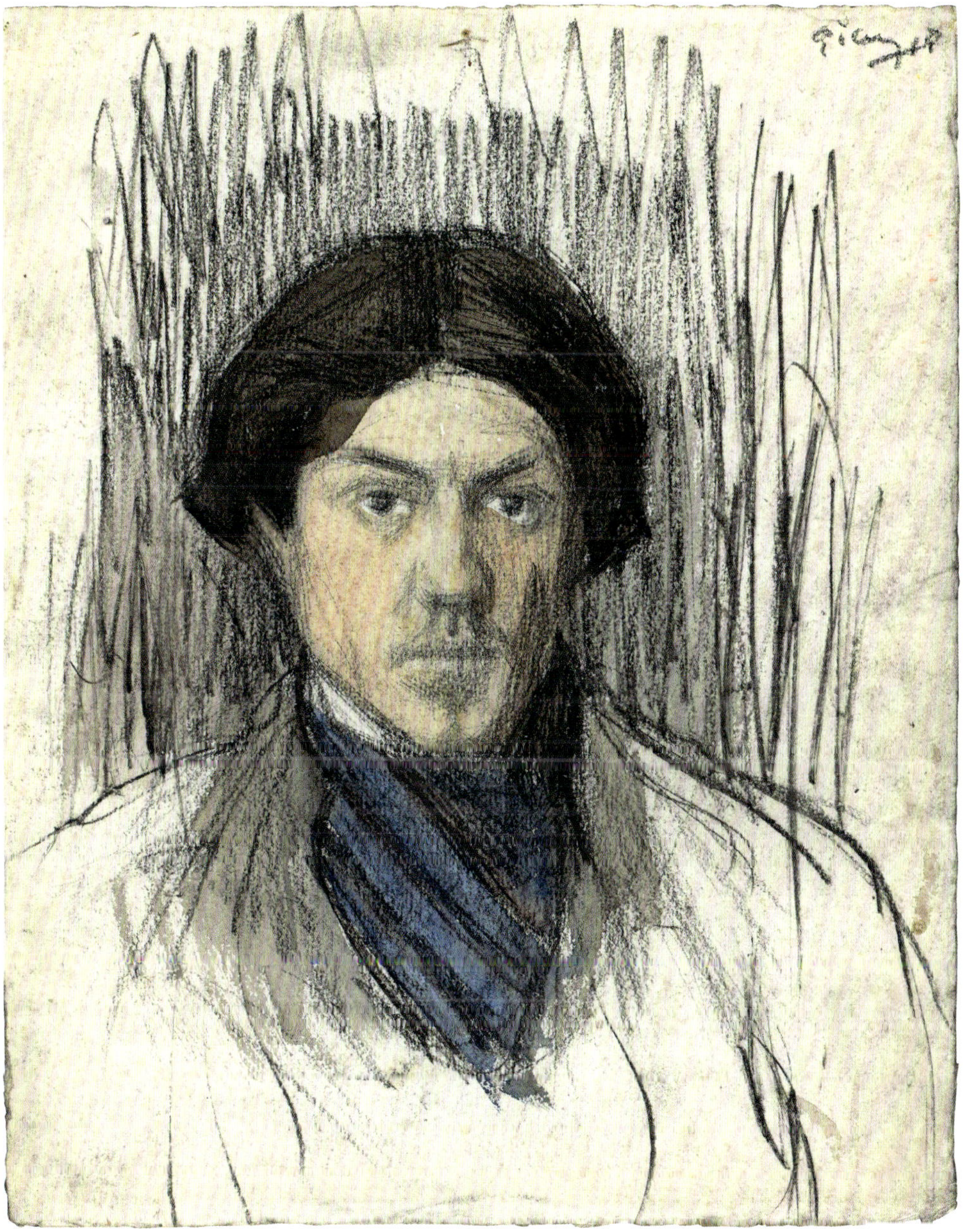

57

1902–1903

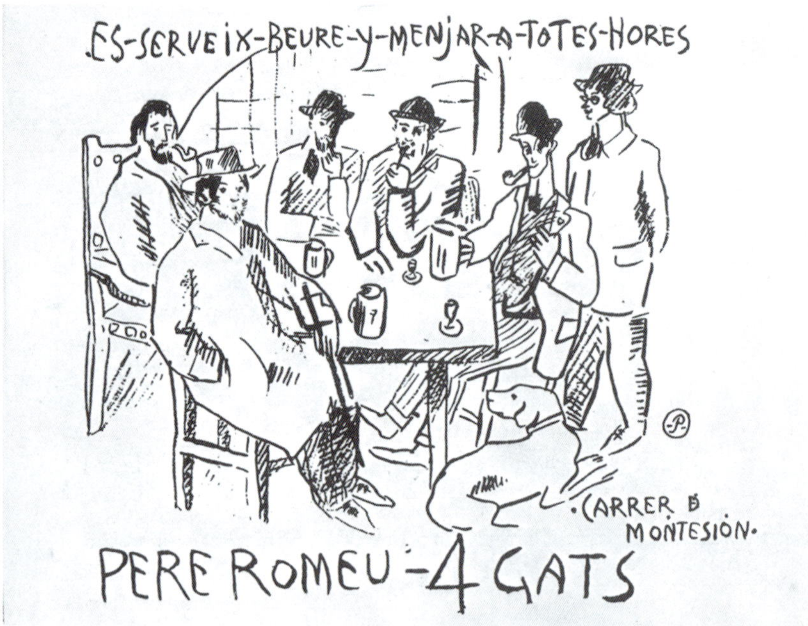

58

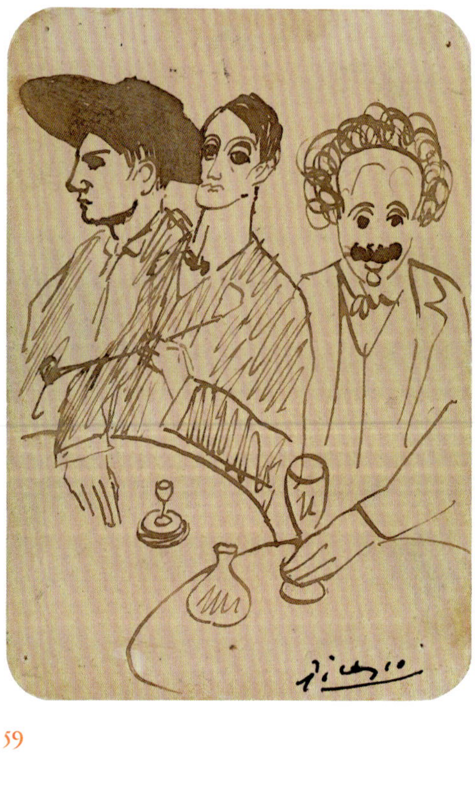

59

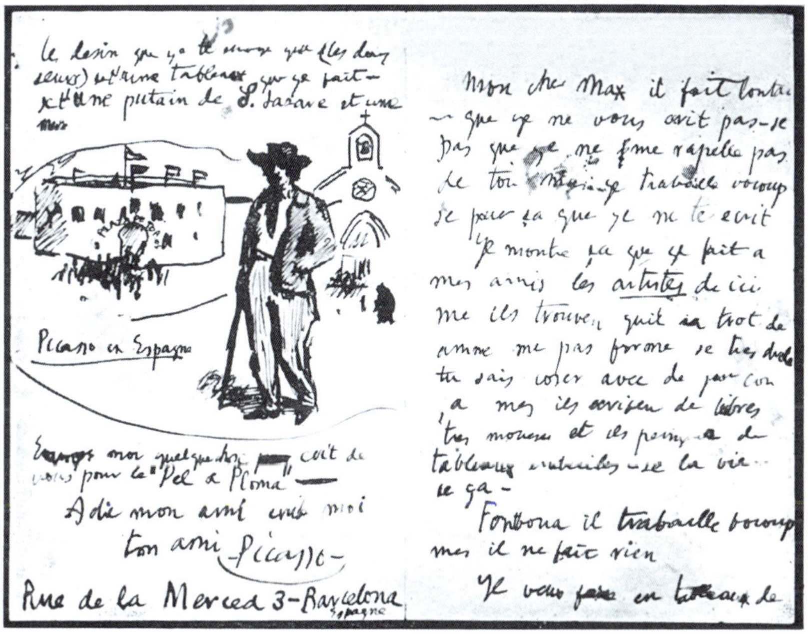
le desin que ye te envoye (les deux seues) est une tableaux que ye fait — est une putain de S. Lazare et une mere

Picasso en Espagne

Envoye moi quelquechose ecrit de vous pour le "Pel & Ploma" —

Adie mon ami ecris moi

ton ami Picasso —

Rue de la Merced 3 – Barcelona
Espagne

Mon cher Max il fait lontemps — que ye ne vous ecrit pas — se pas que ye ne me rapelle pas de toi mais ye traballe vocoup se pour ça que ye ne te ecrit

Ye montre ça que ye fait a mes amis les artistes de ici me ils trouven quil ia trot de ame me pas forme se tres drole tu sais coser avec de pour con a mes ils ecrisen de libres tres mouves et ils peinten de tableaux imbeciles use la vie se ga —

Fontbona il traballe vocoup mes il ne fait rien

Ye vous fais un tableaux de

60

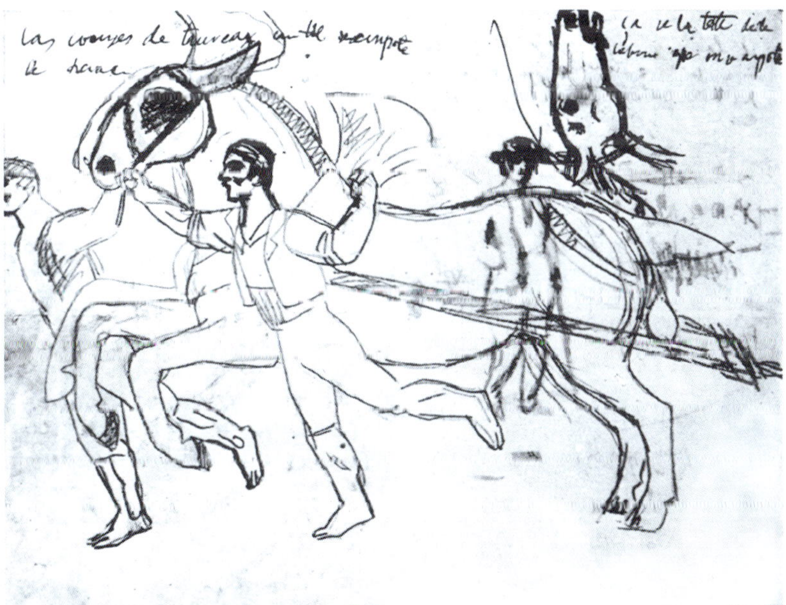

61

1902–1903

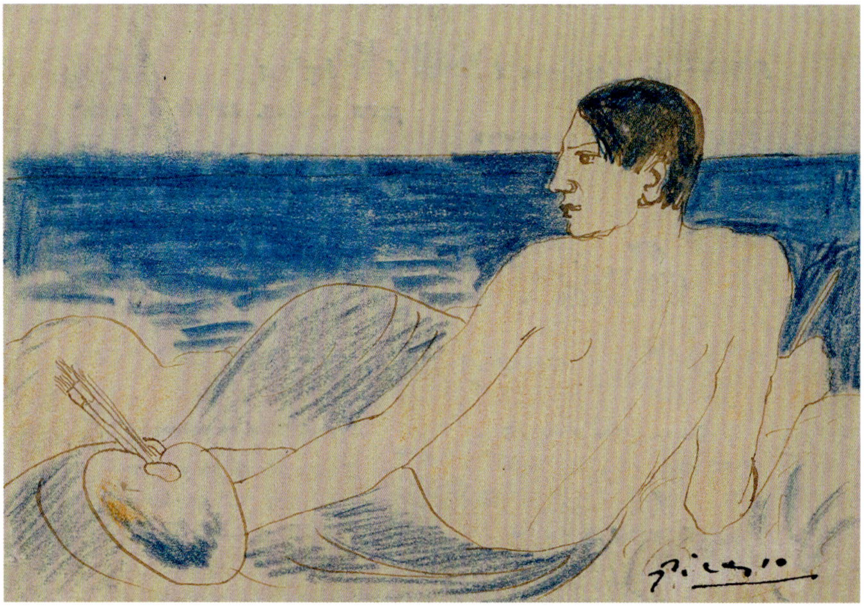

62

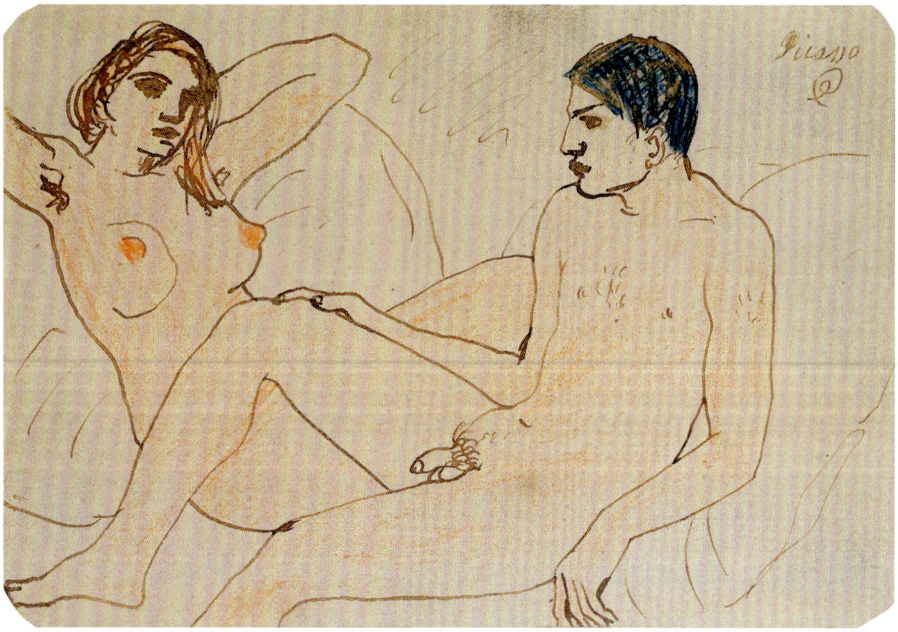

63

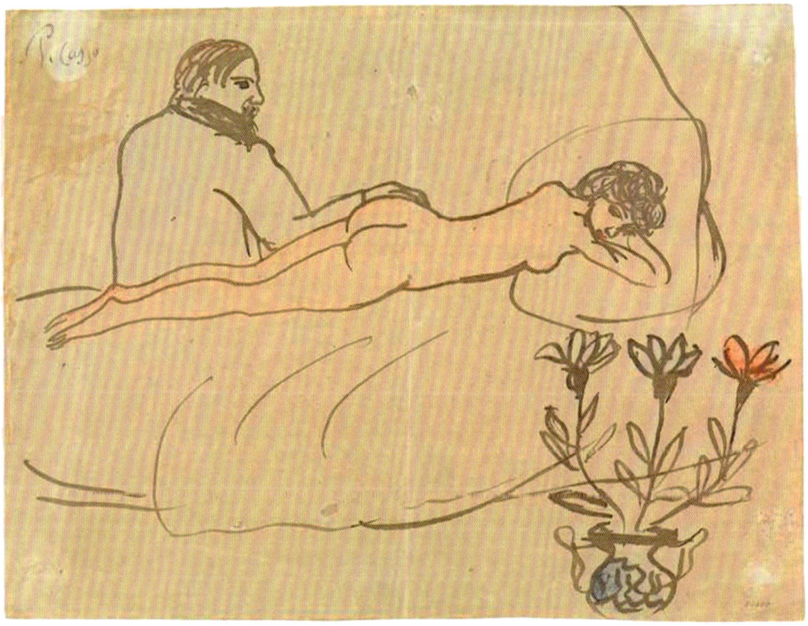

64

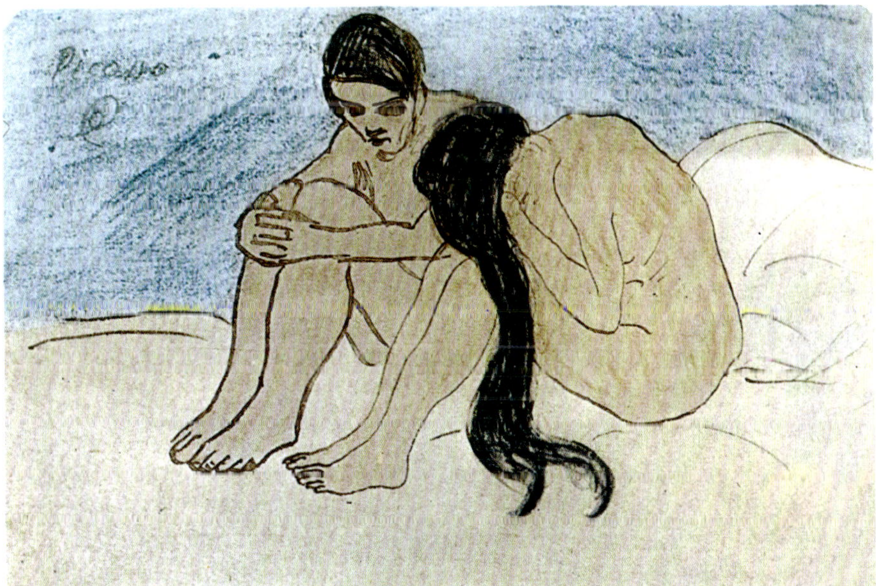

65

1902–1903

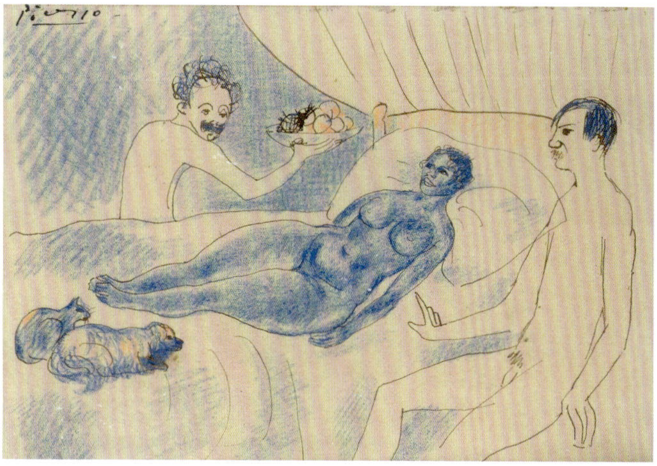

66

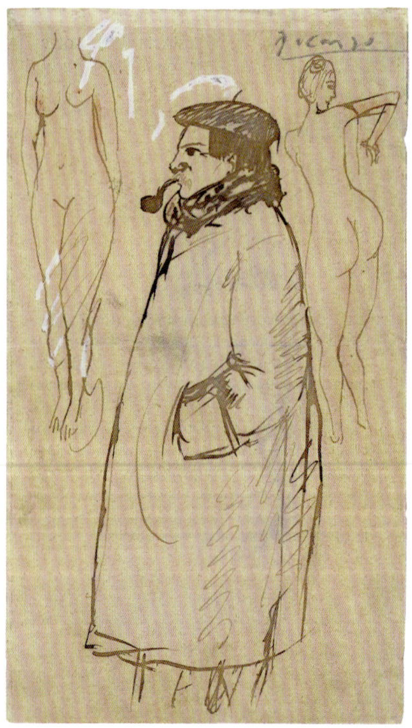

67

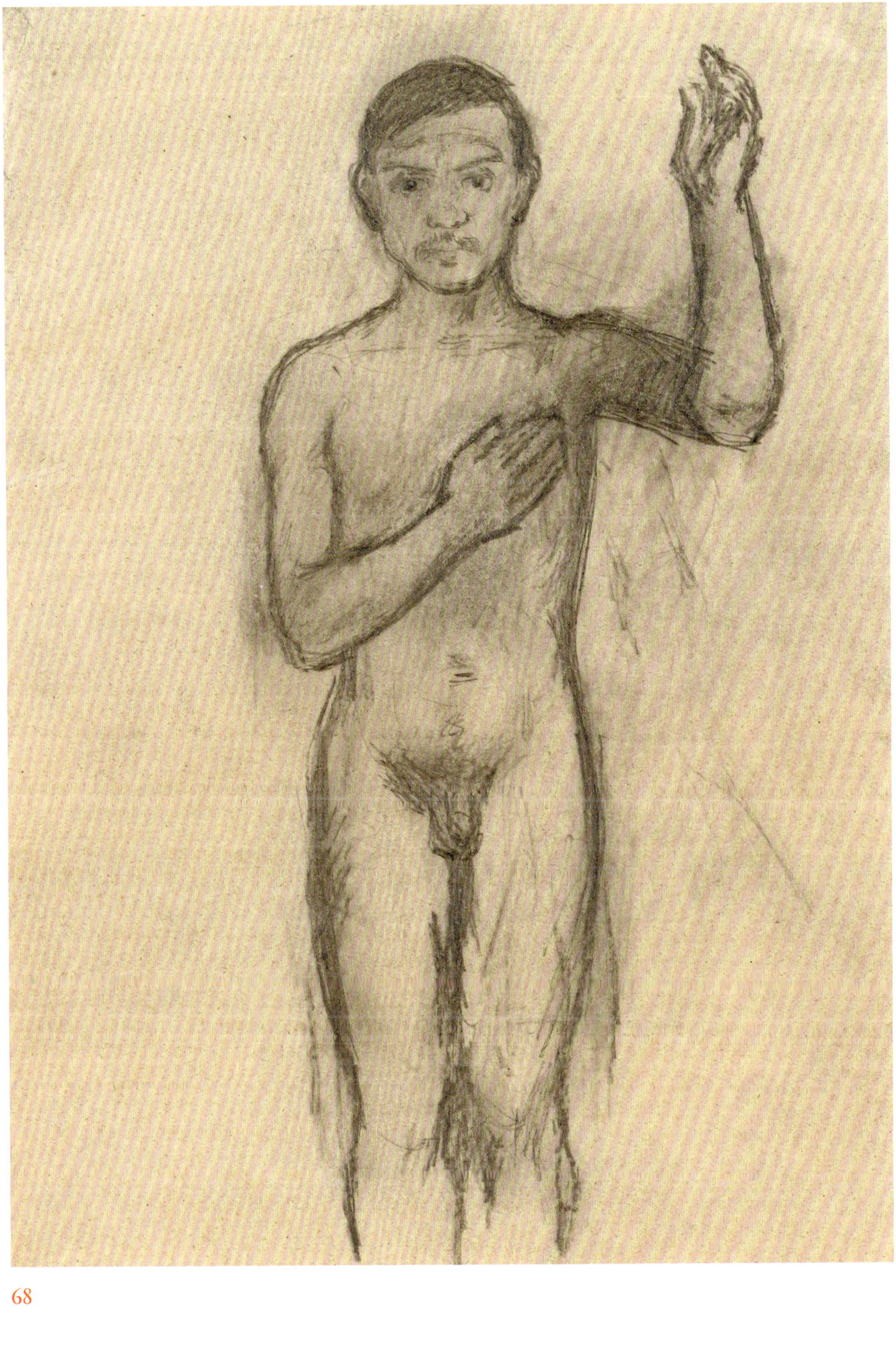

1902–1903

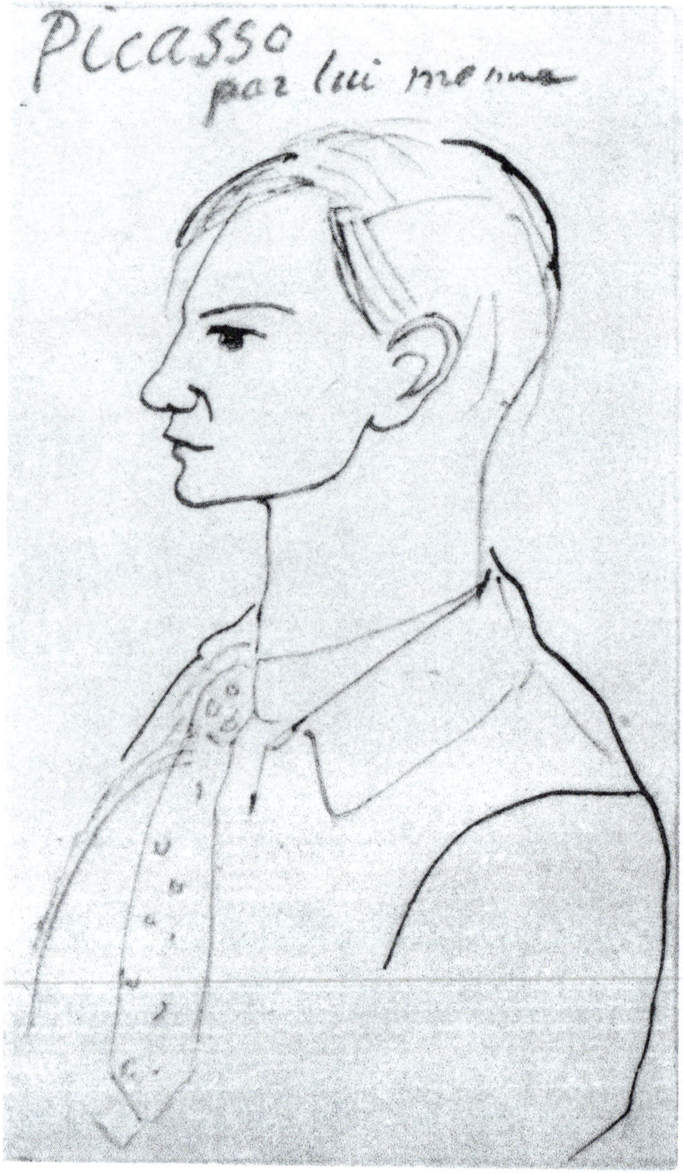

69

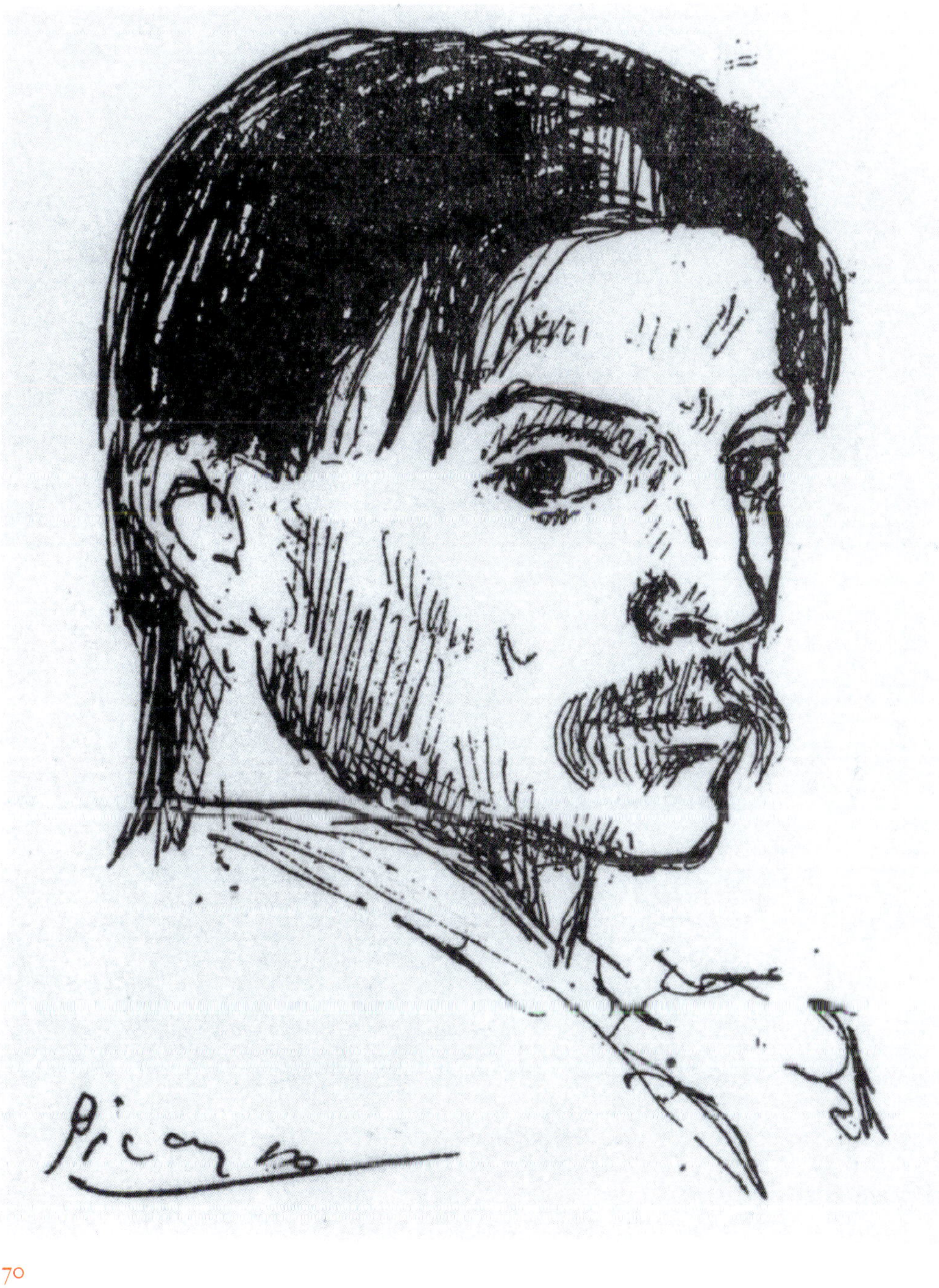
Picasso

1903

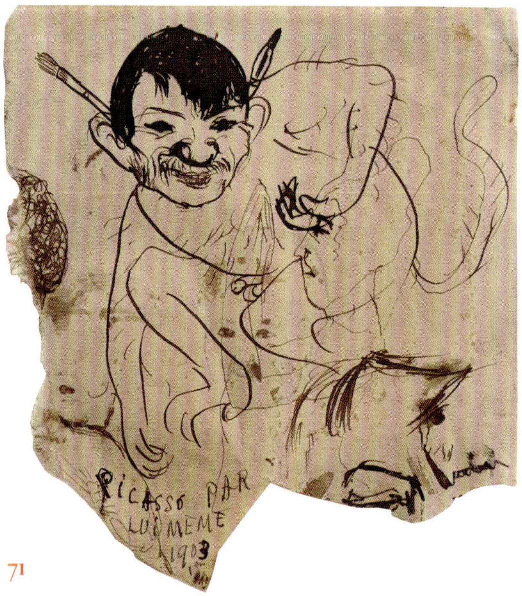

71

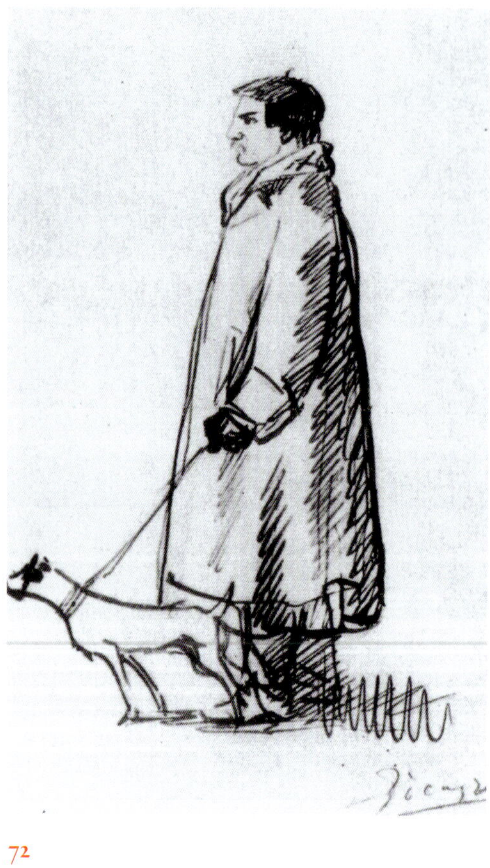

72

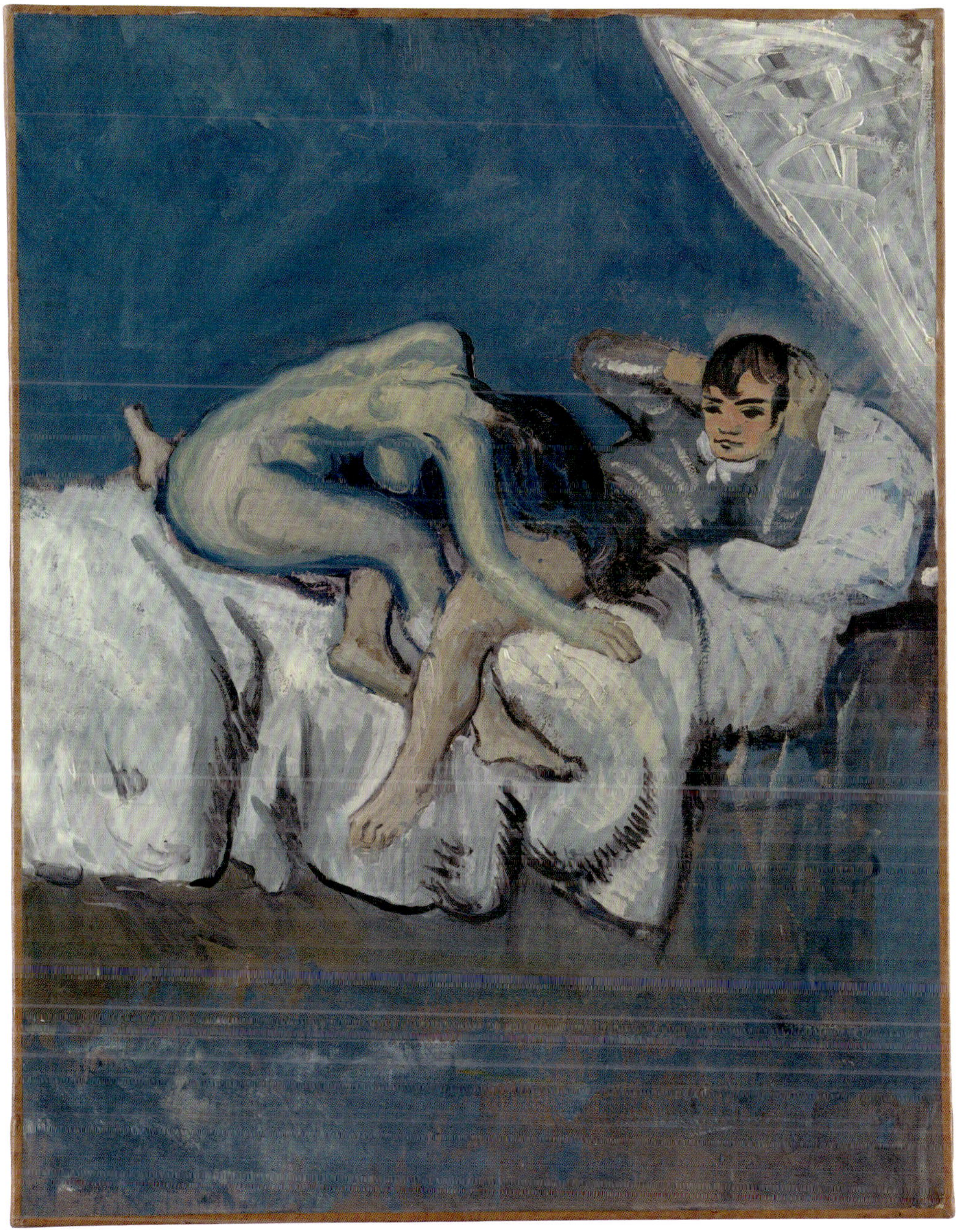

1903–1904

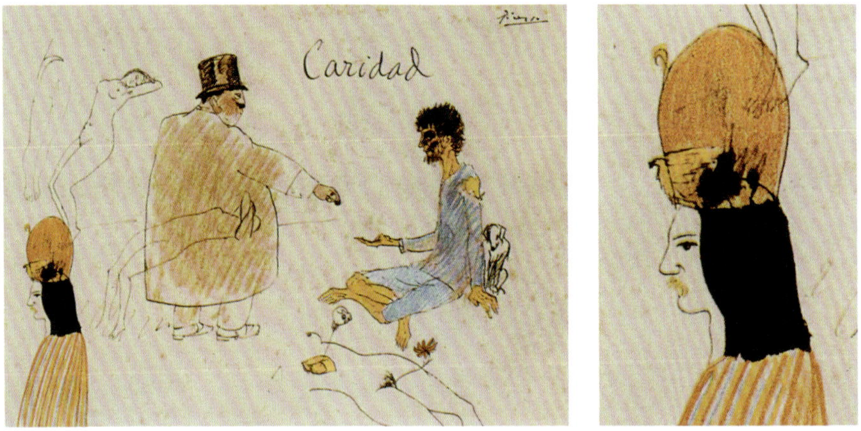

74

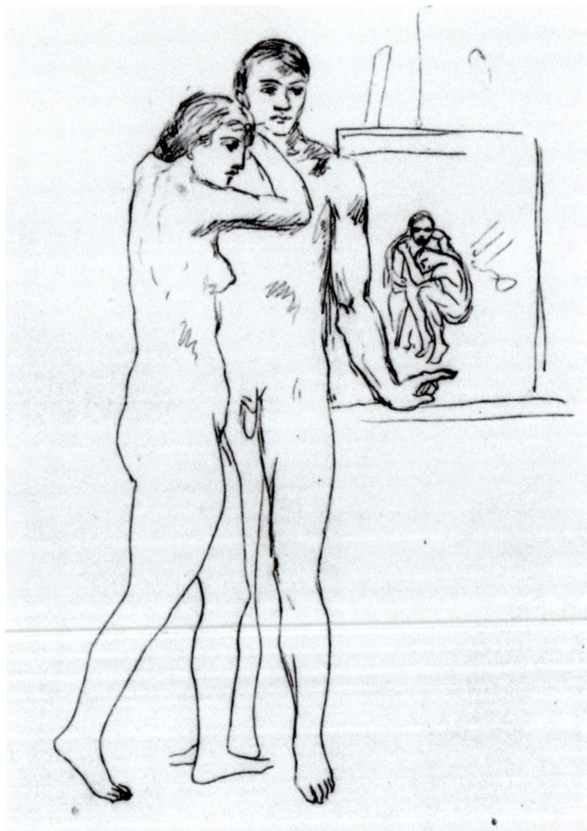

75

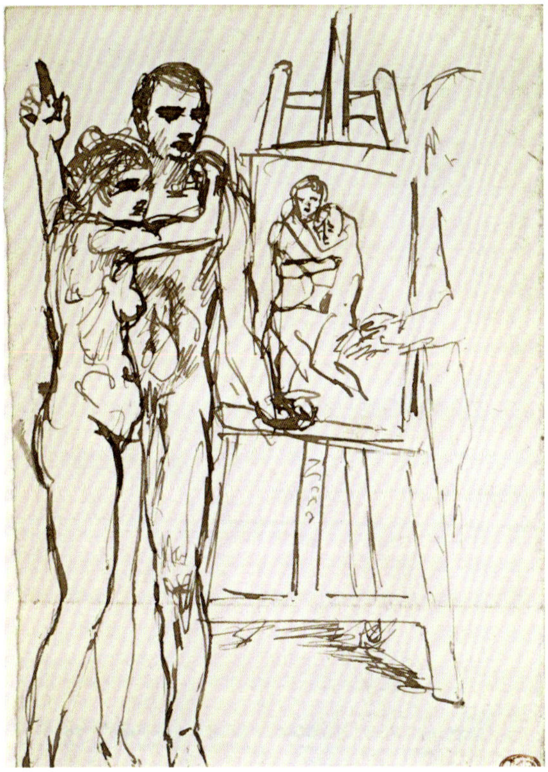

76

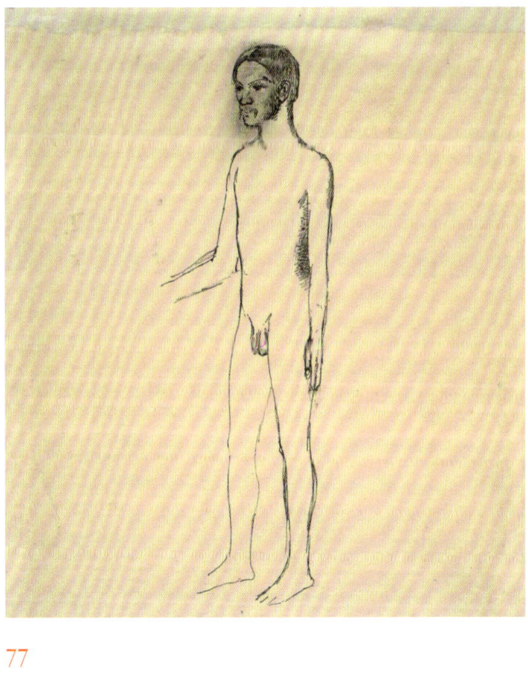

77

1903–1904

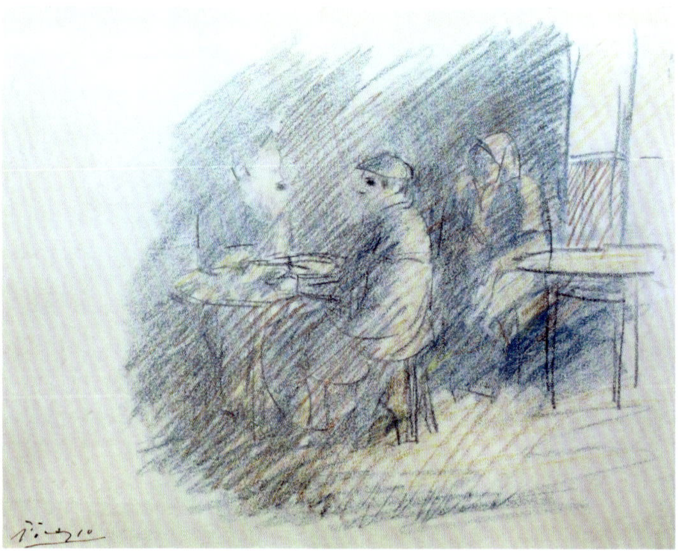

78

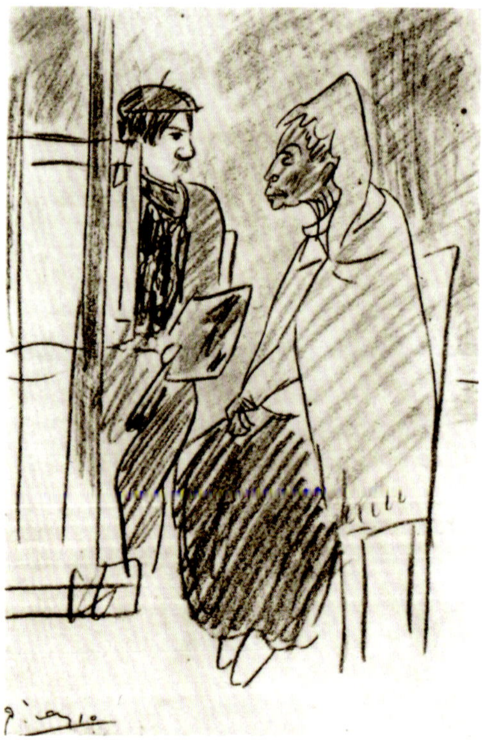

79

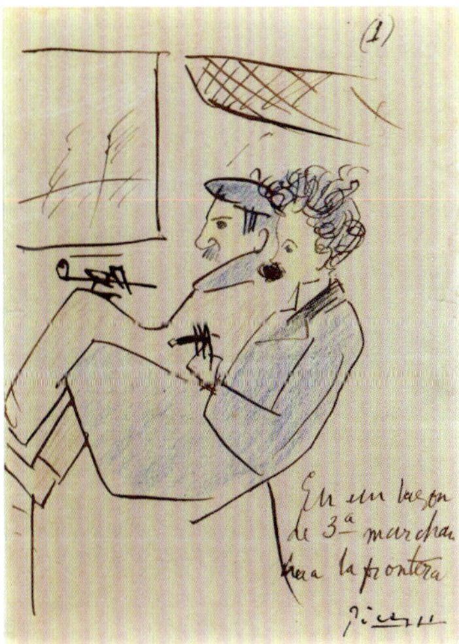
(1)
En un vagon
de 3ª marchan
hacia la frontera

80

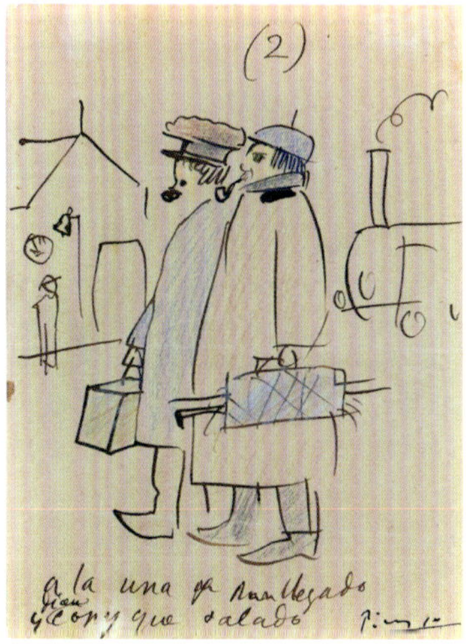
(2)
a la una ya han llegado

81

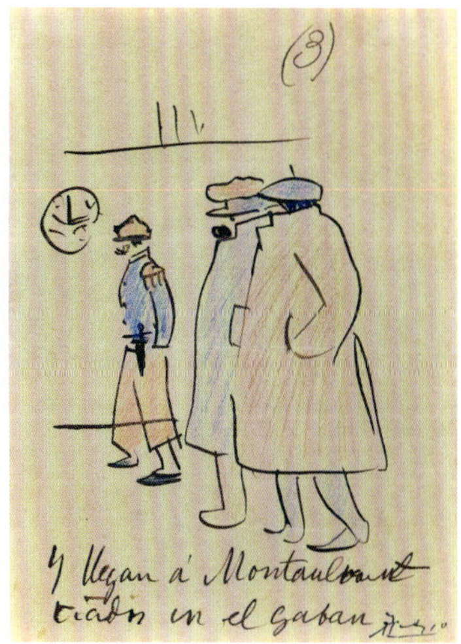
(3)
y llegan á Montauban

82

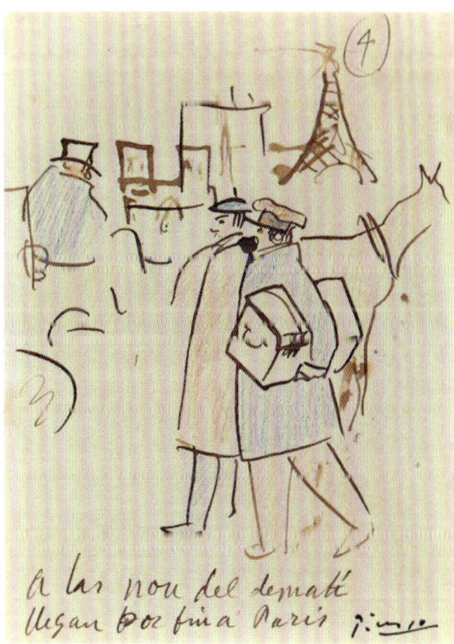
(4)
a las nou del dematí
llegan por fin á Paris

83

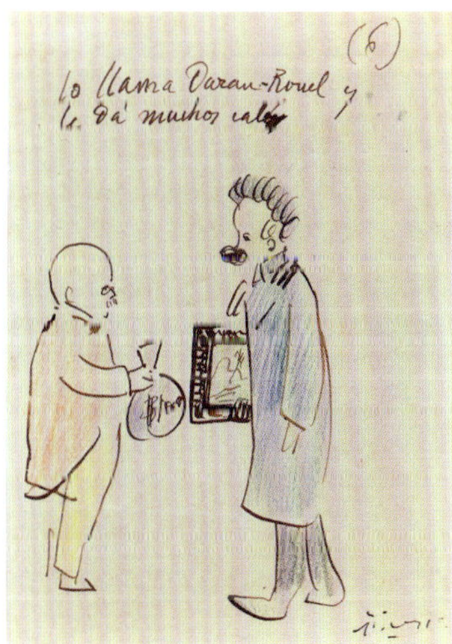
(6)
lo llama Durand-Ruel y

84

1904

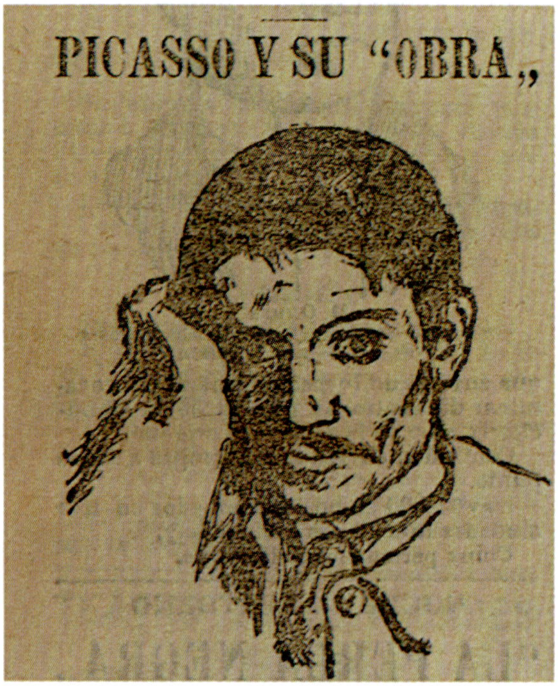

PICASSO Y SU "OBRA,,

85

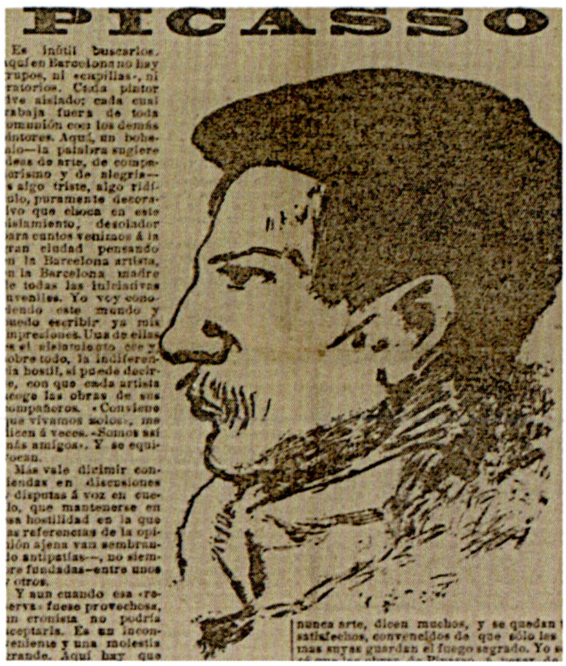

PICASSO

Es inútil buscarlos. aquí en Barcelona no hay grupos, ni «capillas», ni oratorios. Cada pintor vive aislado; cada cual trabaja fuera de toda comunión con los demás pintores. Aquí, un bohemio—la palabra sugiere ideas de arte, de compañerismo y de alegría—es algo triste, algo ridículo, puramente decorativo que choca en este aislamiento, desolador para cuantos venimos á la gran ciudad pensando en la Barcelona artista, en la Barcelona madre de todas las iniciativas juveniles. Yo voy conociendo este mundo y puedo escribir ya mis impresiones. Una de ellas es el aislamiento ese y, sobre todo, la indiferencia hostil, si puede decirse, con que cada artista acoge las obras de sus compañeros. «Conviene que vivamos solos», me dicen á veces. «Somos así más amigos». Y se equivocan.

Más vale dirimir contiendas en discusiones y disputas á voz en cuello, que mantenerse en esa hostilidad en la que las referencias de la opinión ajena van sembrando antipatías—, no siempre fundadas—entre unos y otros.

Y aun cuando esa «reserva» fuese provechosa, un cronista no podría aceptarla. Es un inconveniente y una molestia grande. Aquí hay que

nunca arte, dicen muchos, y se quedan satisfechos, convencidos de que sólo las mas suyas guardan el fuego sagrado. Yo s

86

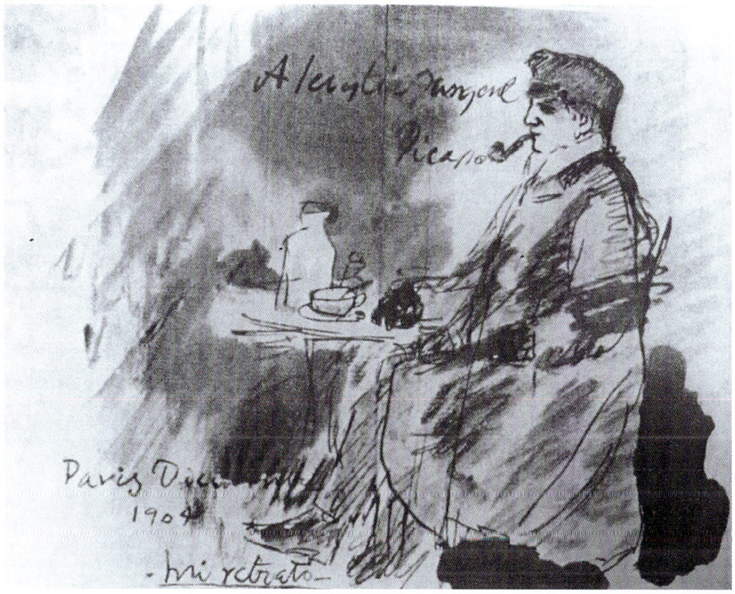

87

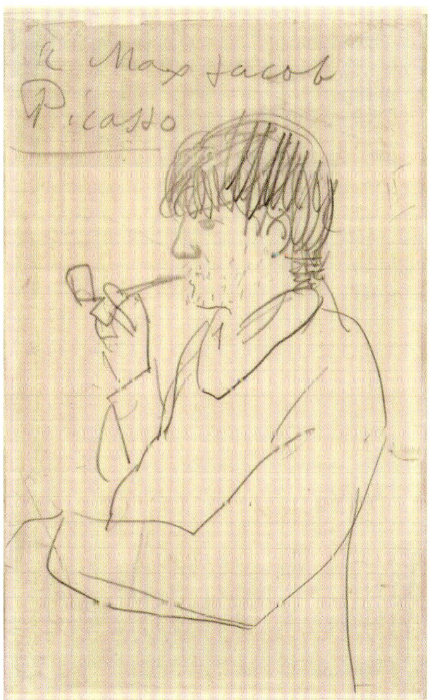

88

1904

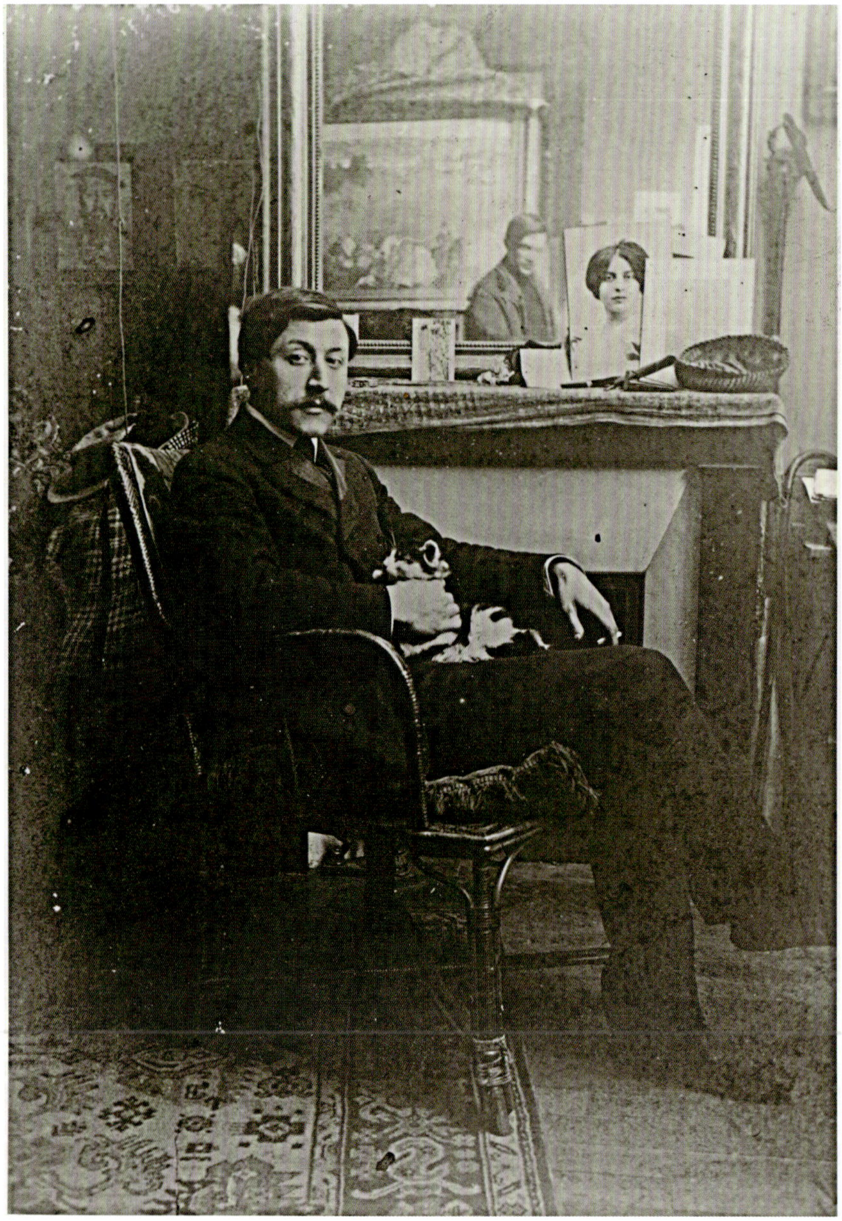

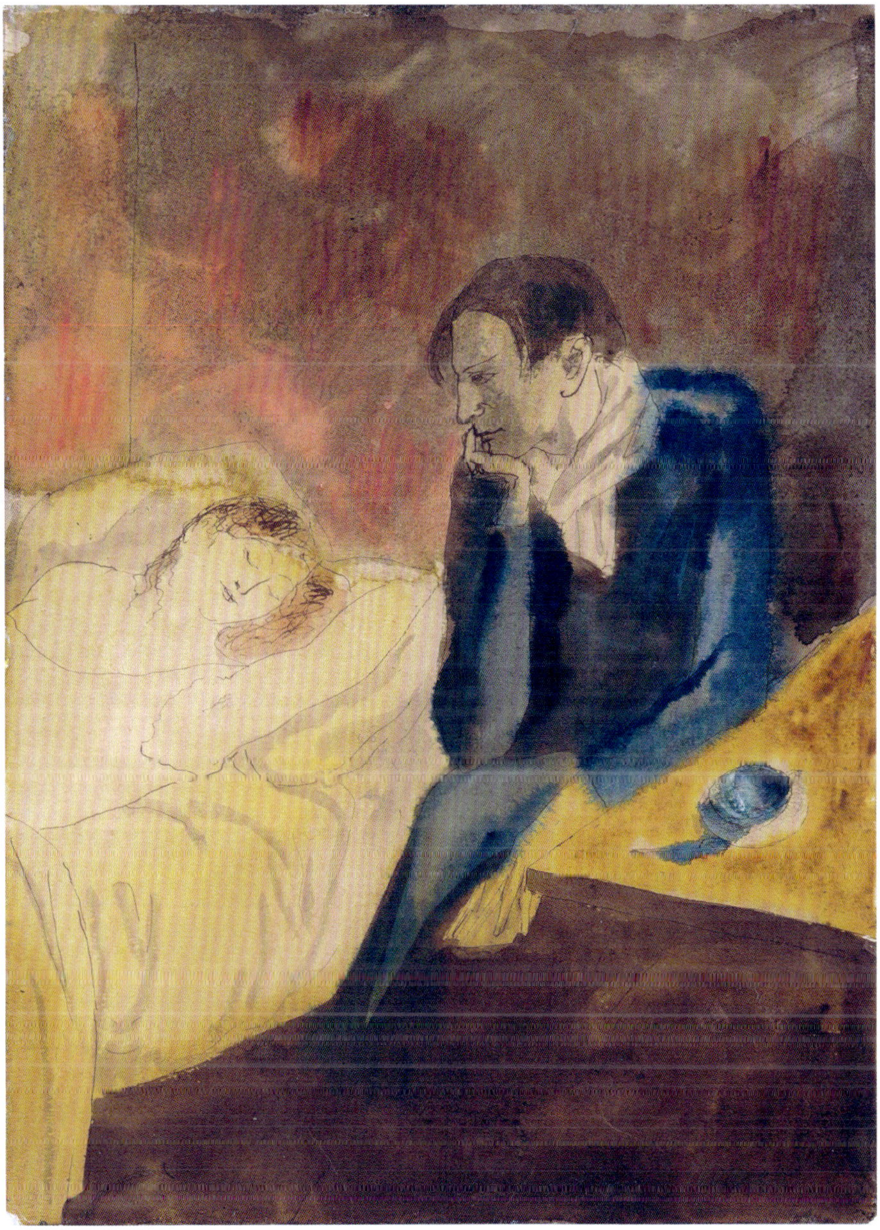

1904–1905

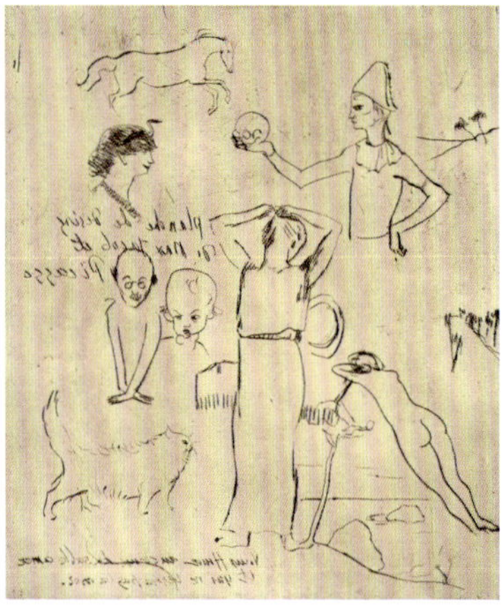

91

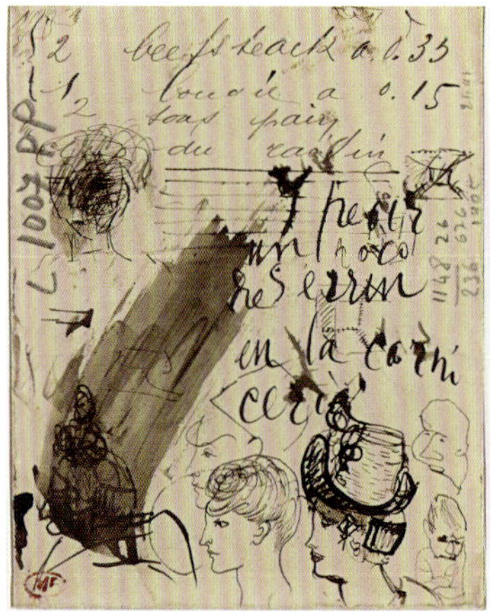

92

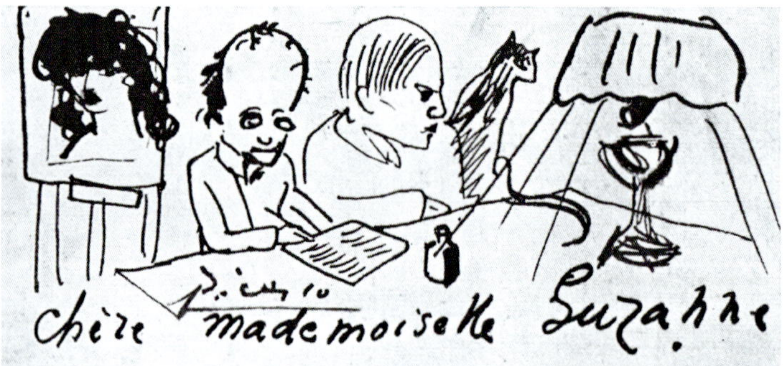

93

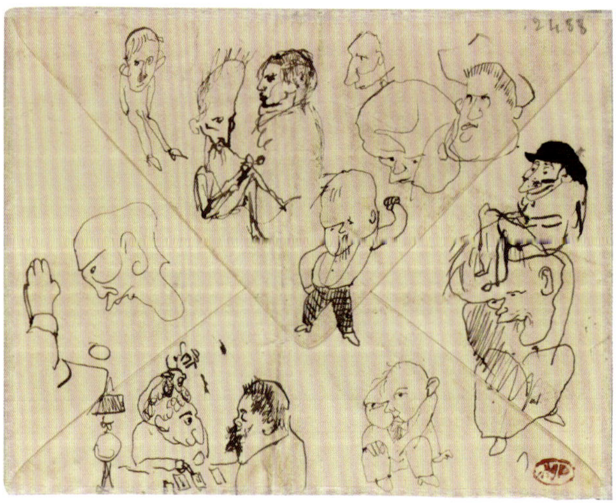

94

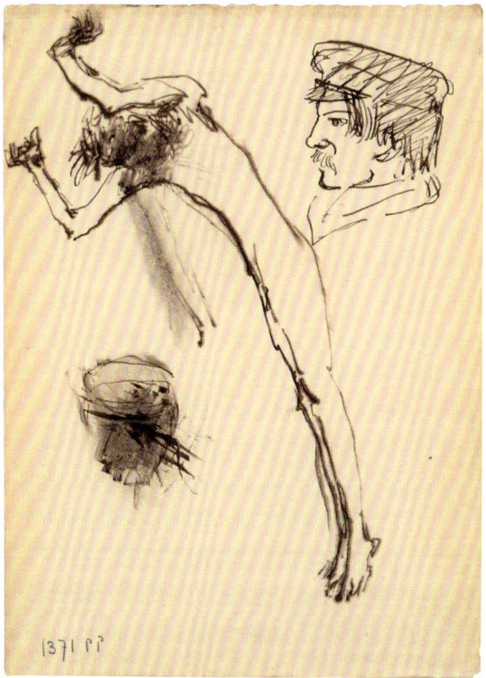

95

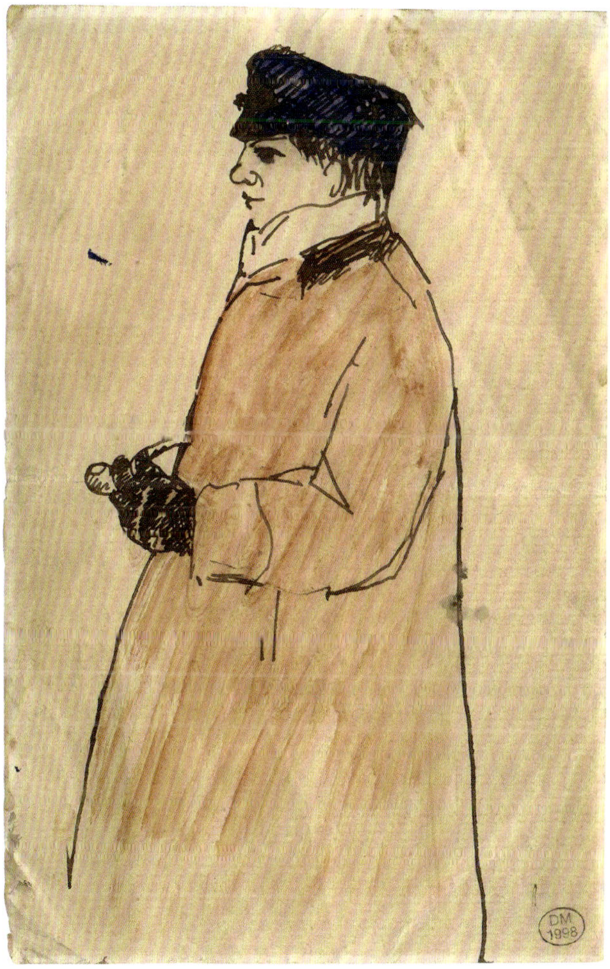

96

1905

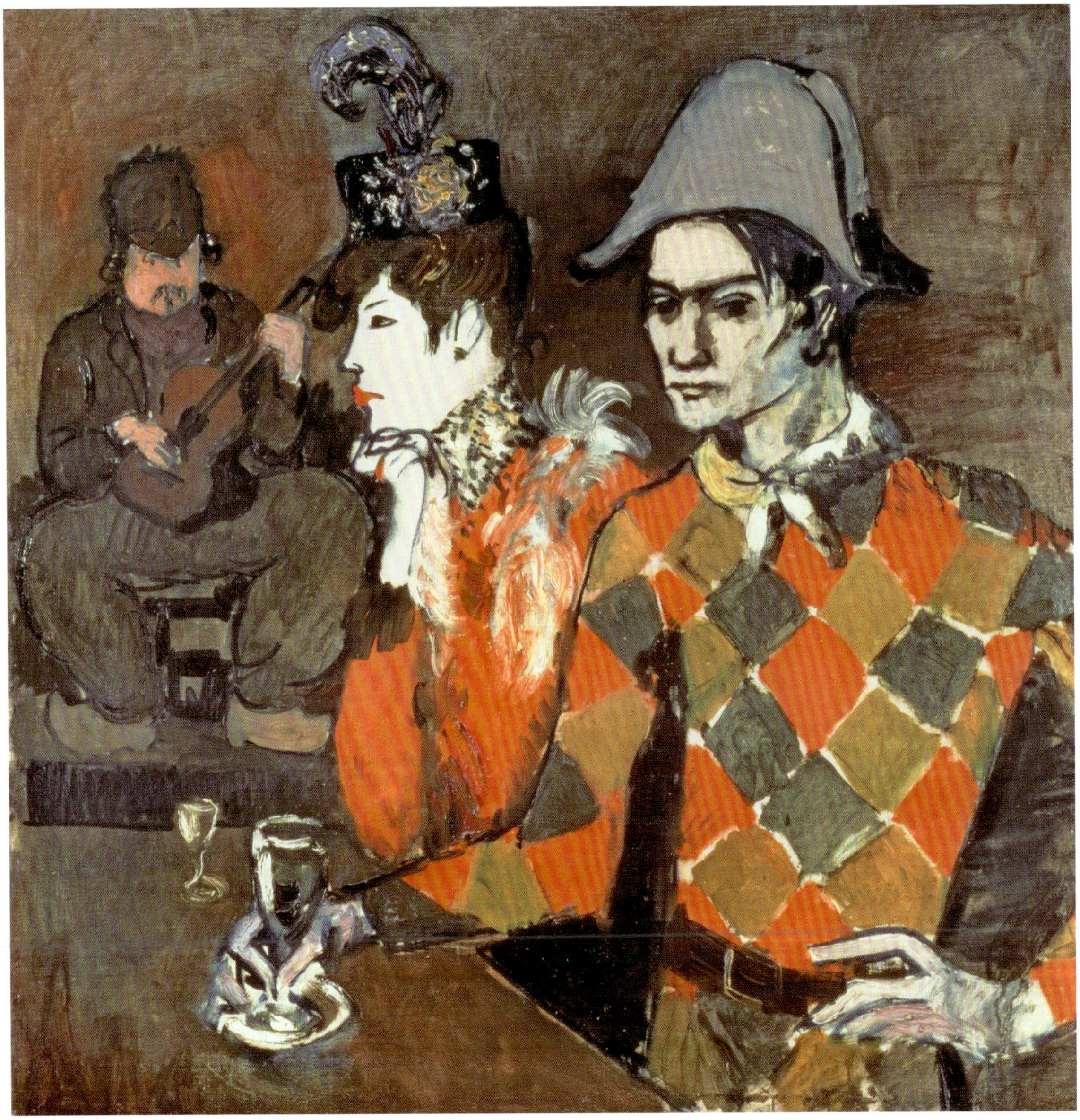

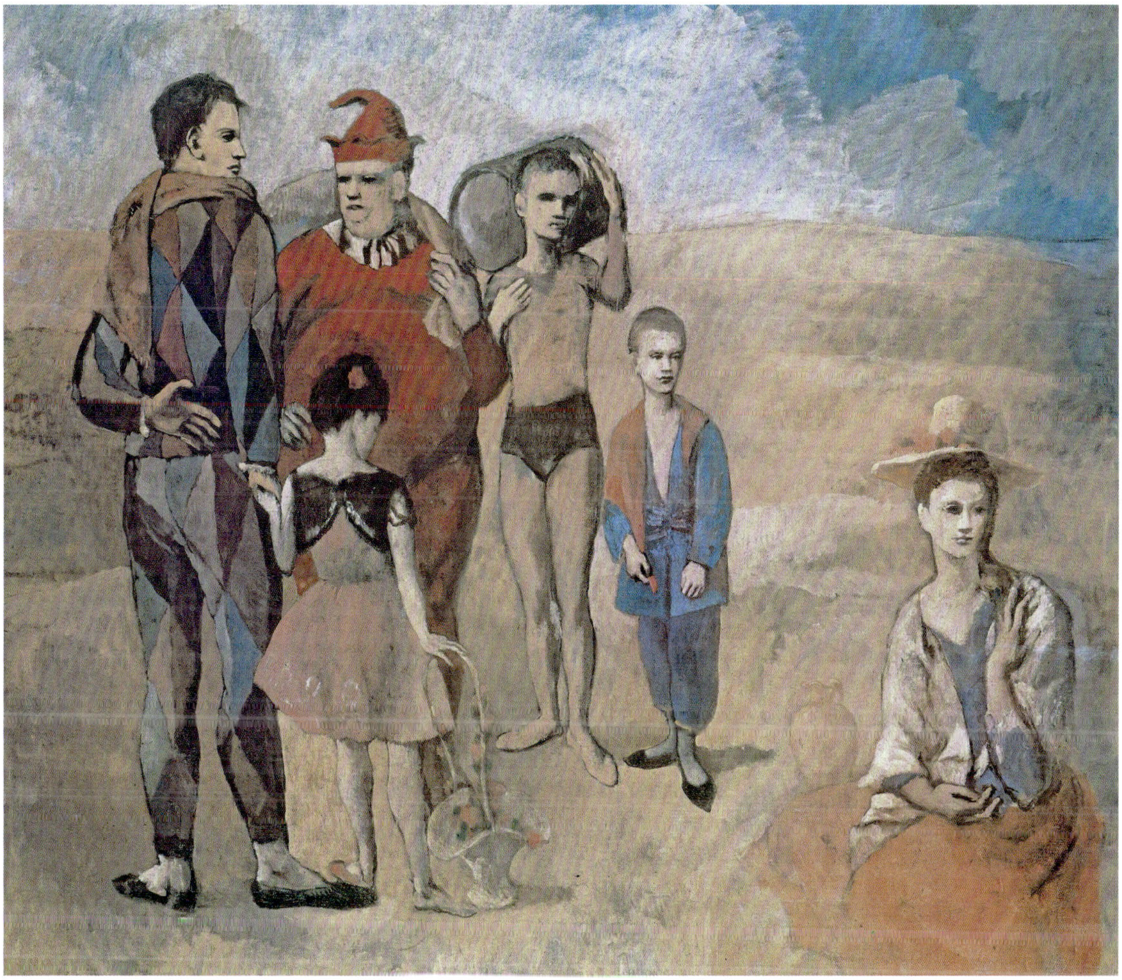

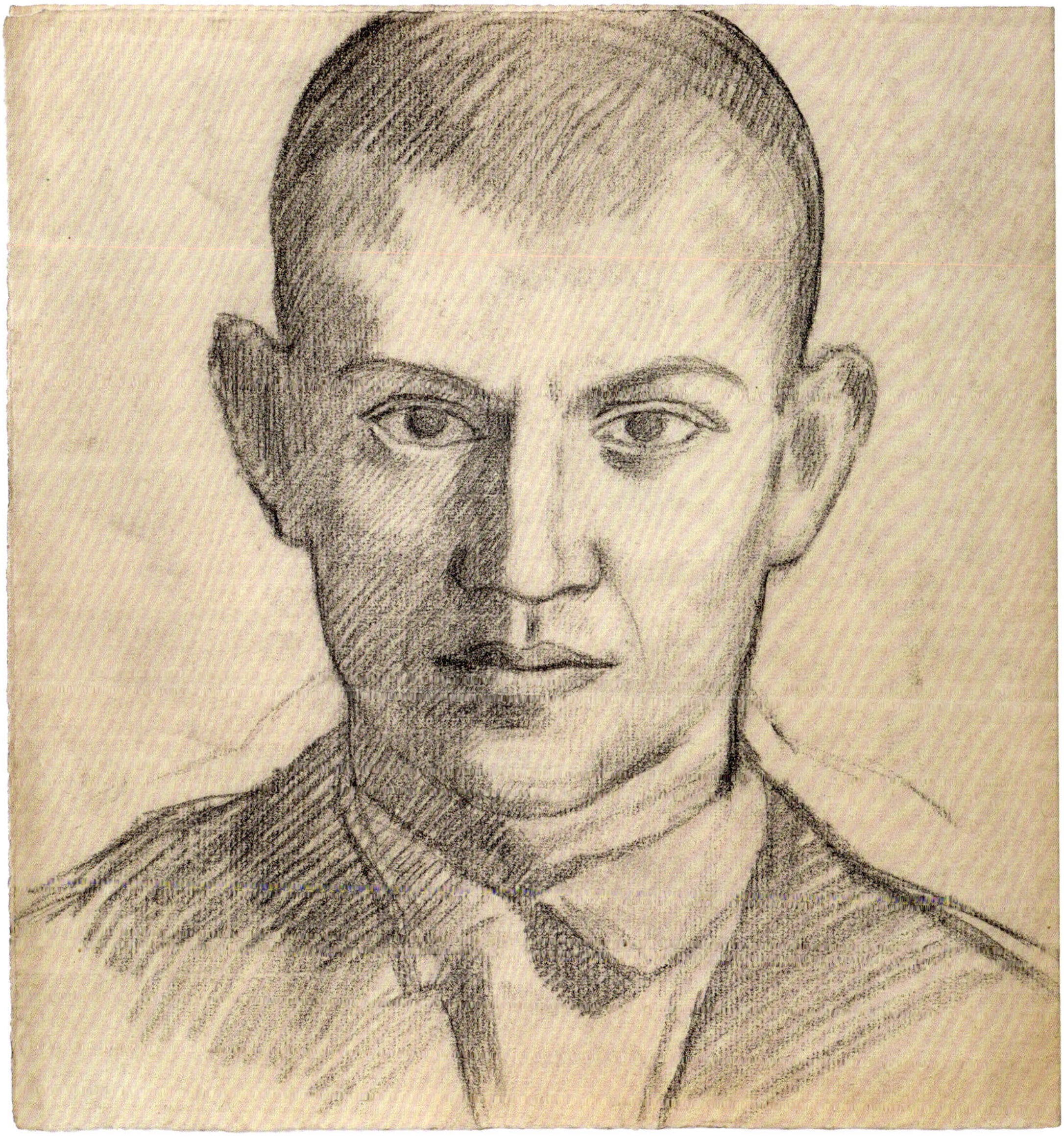

1906

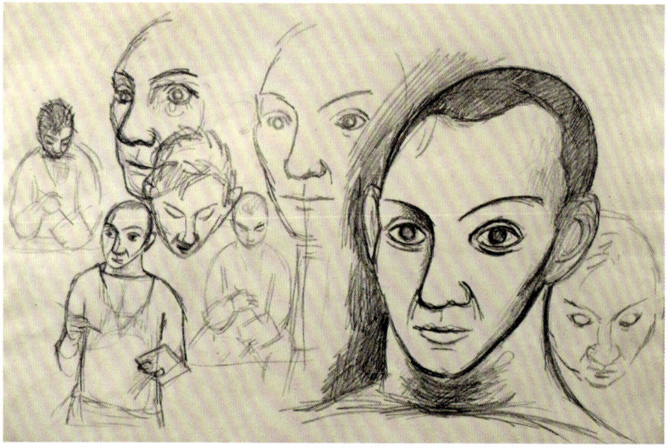

100

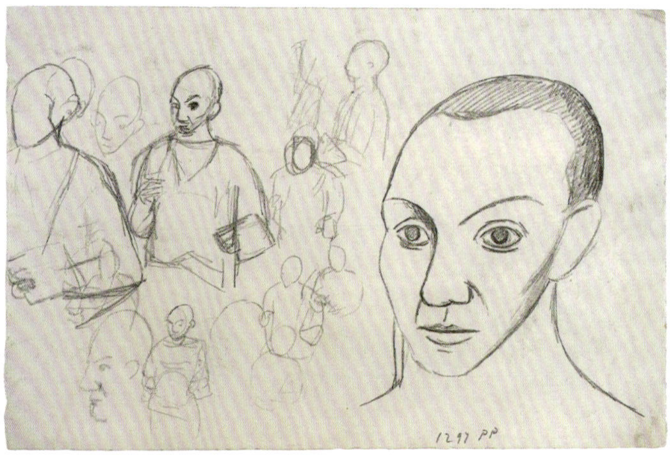

101

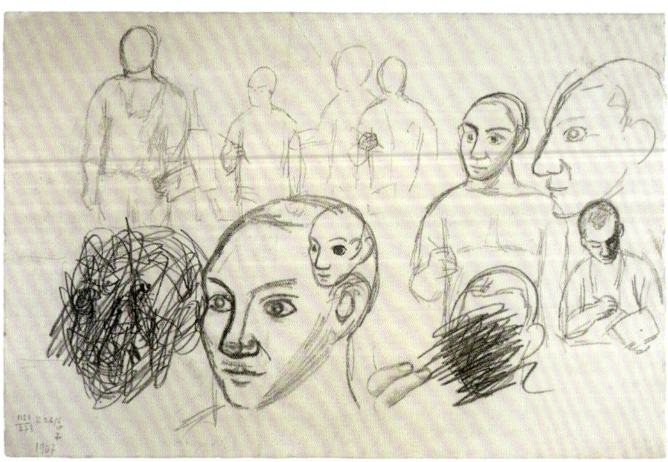

102

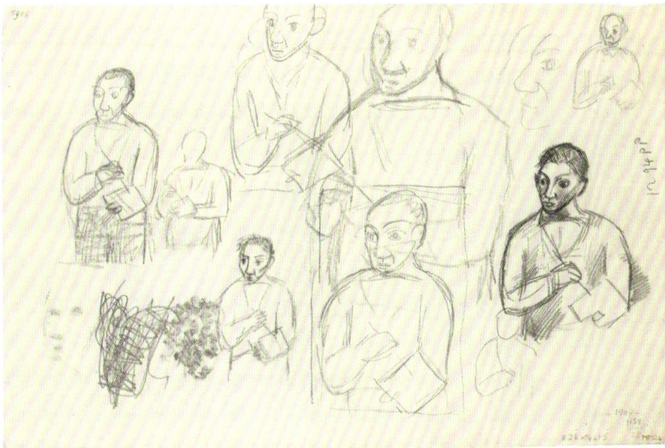

103

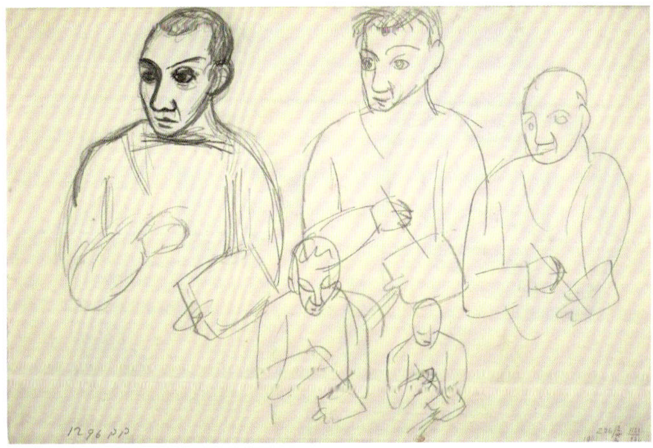

104

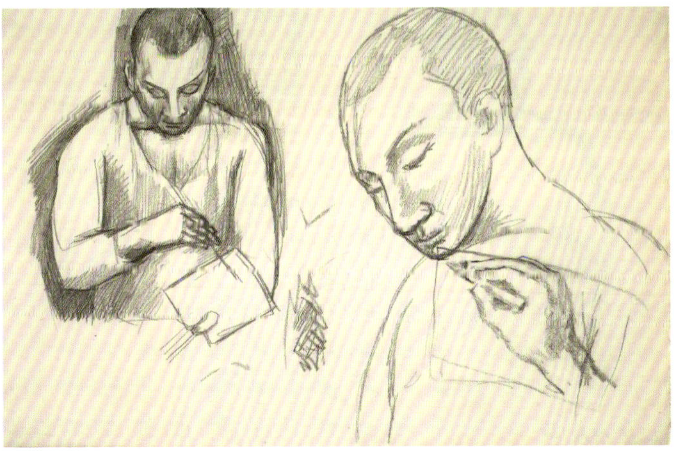

105

1906

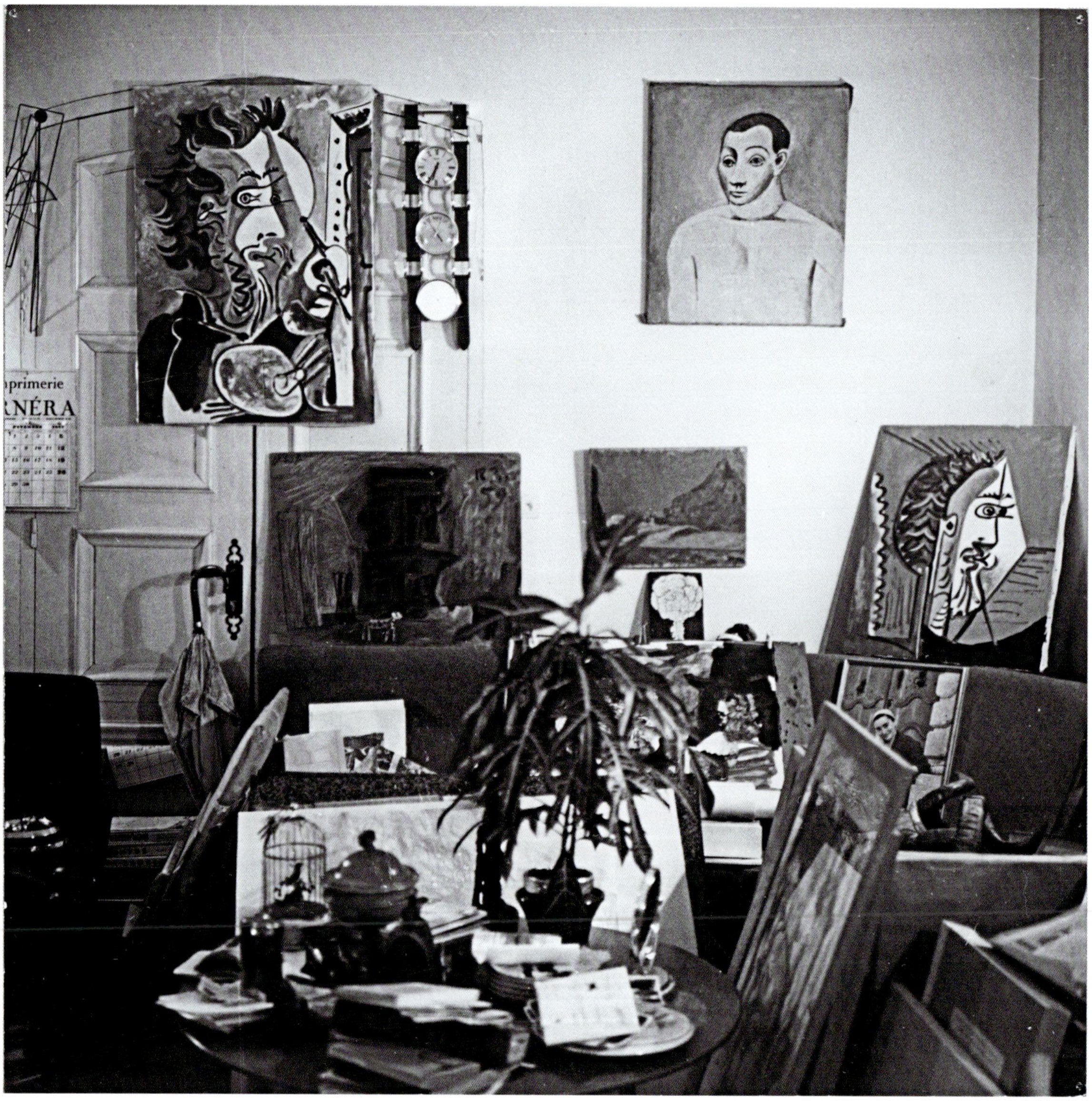

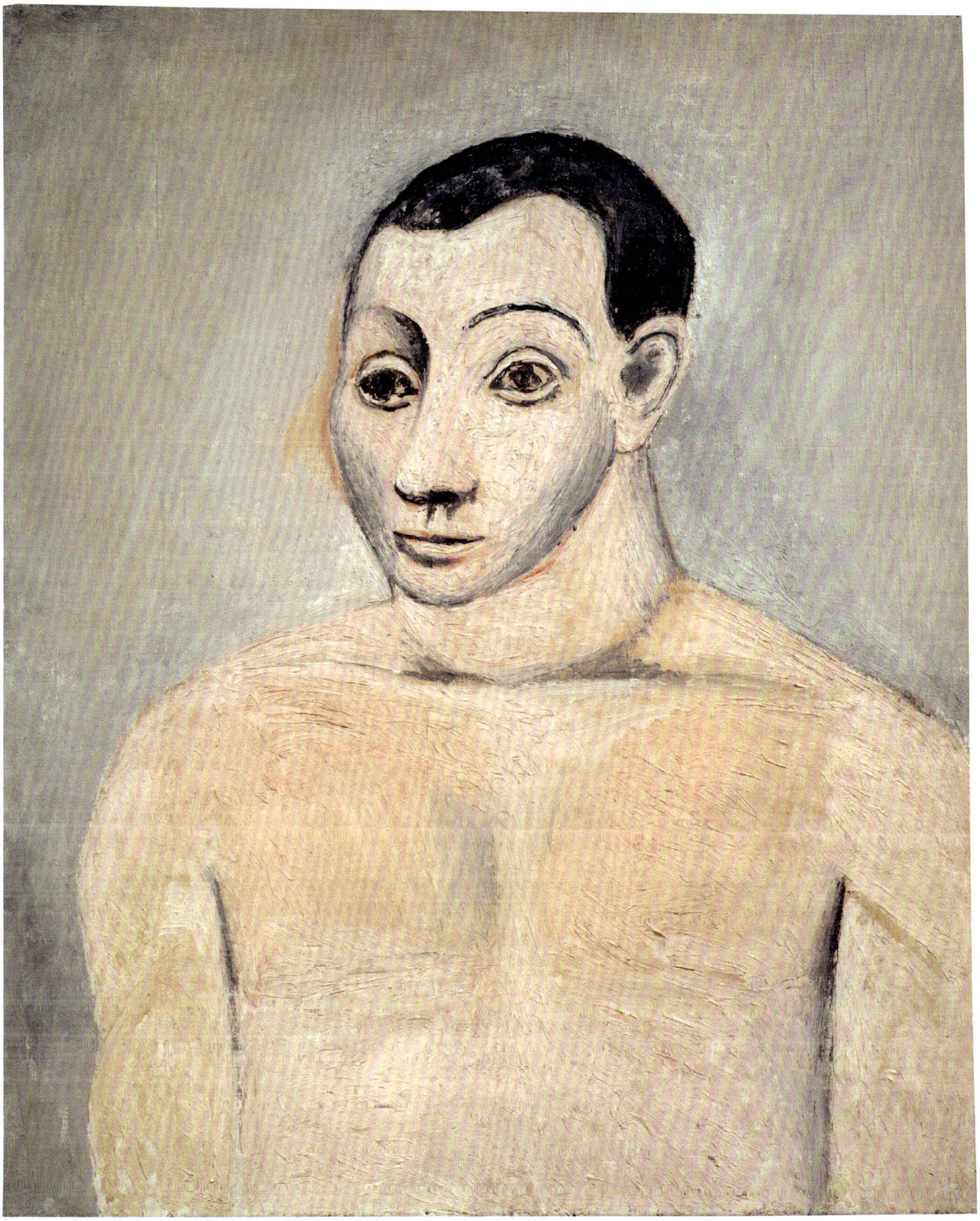

1906

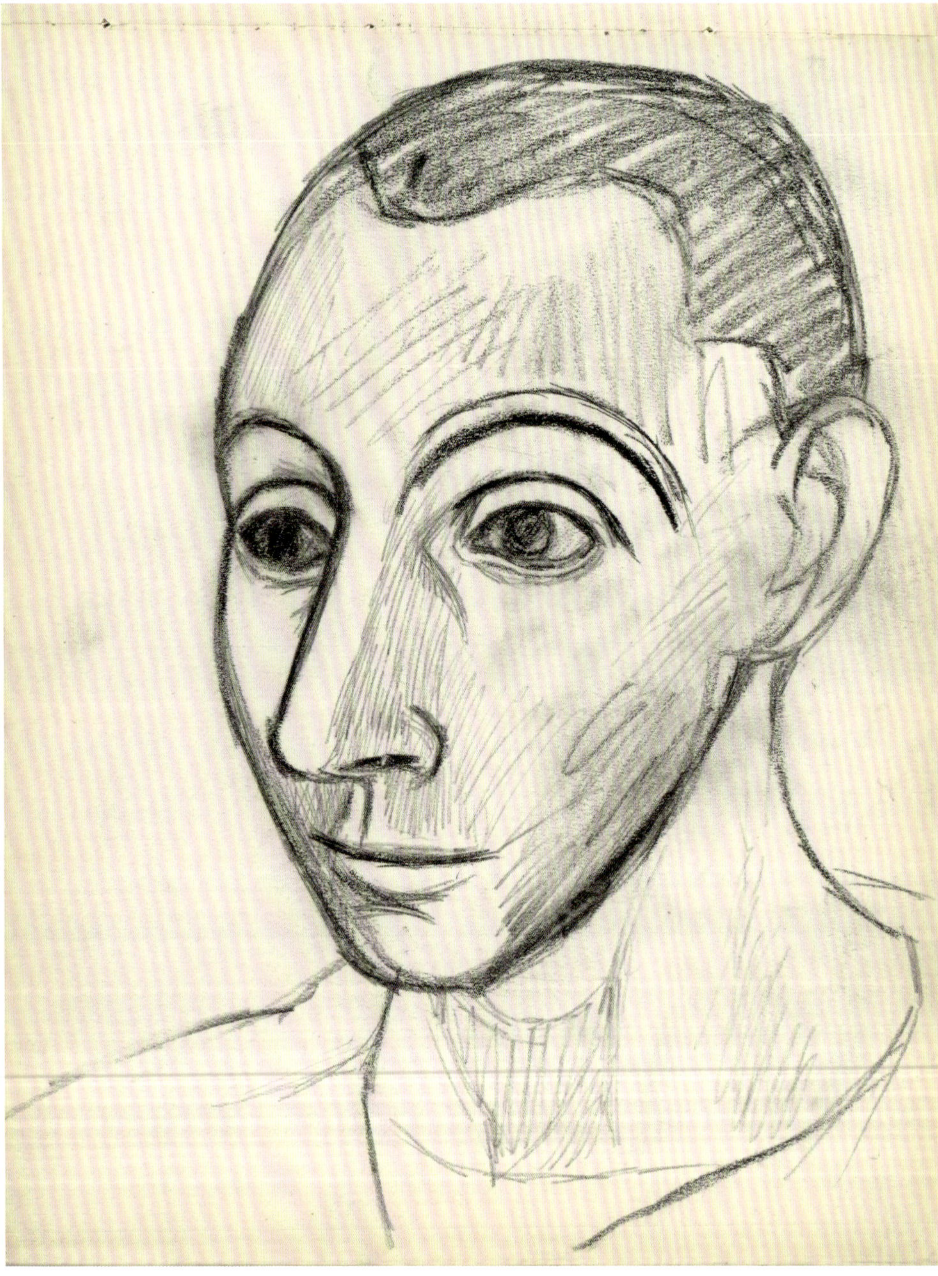

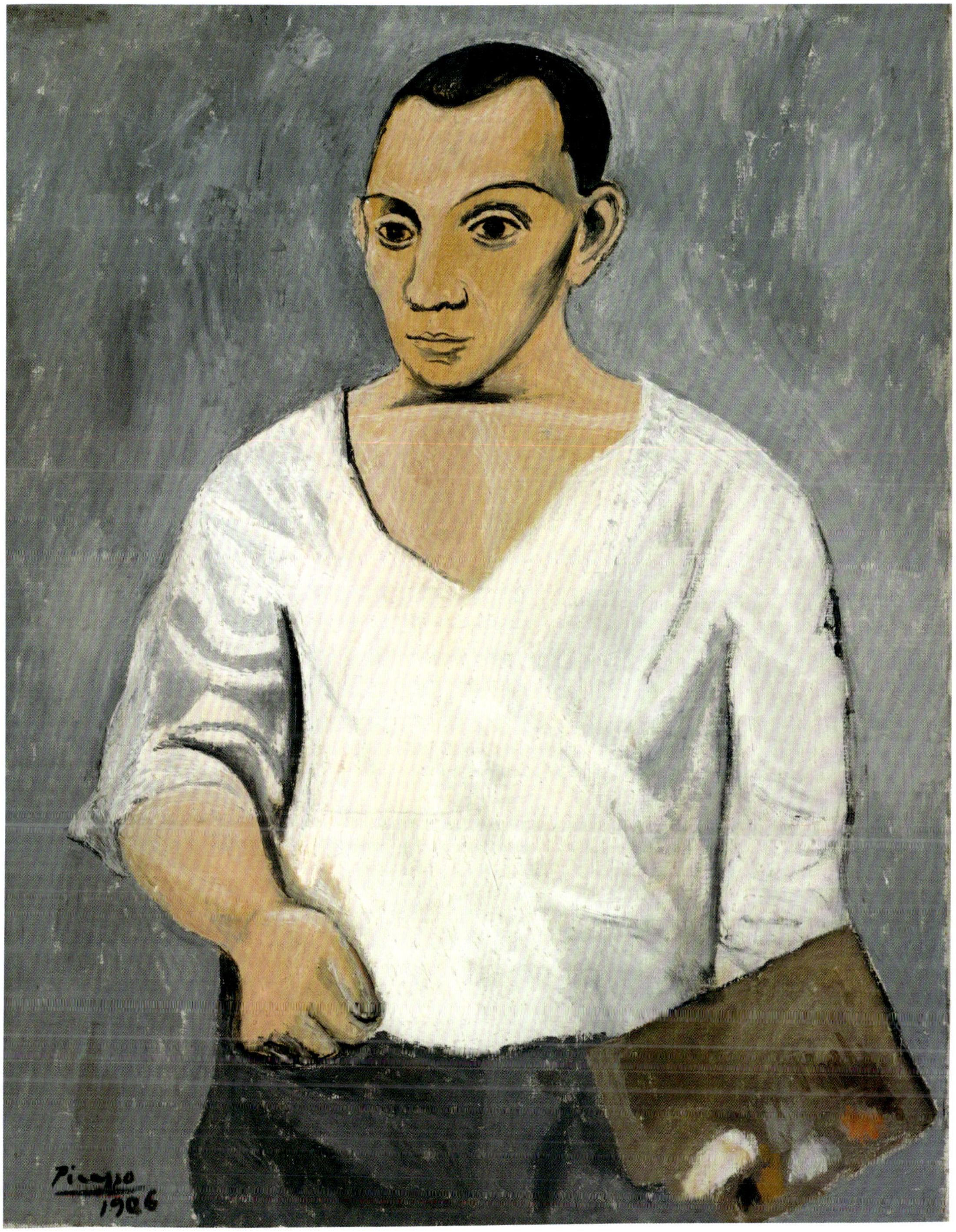

109

1906

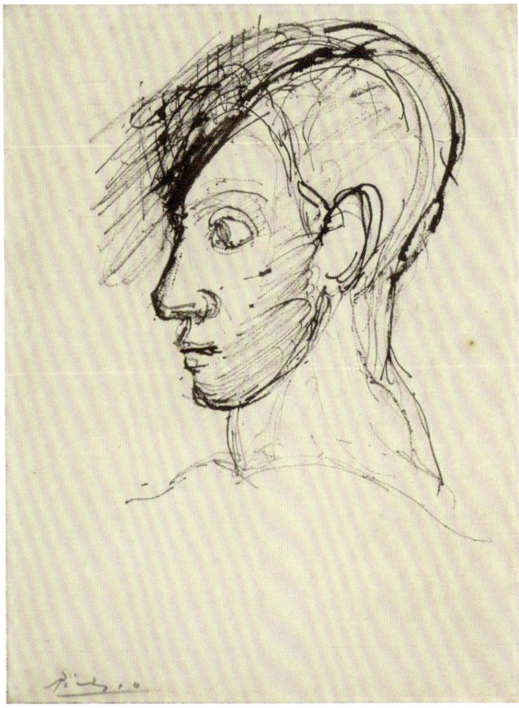

110

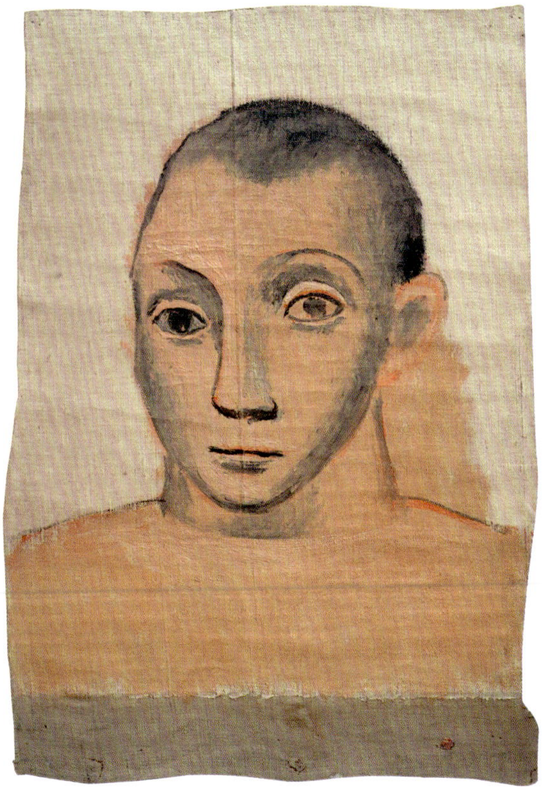

111

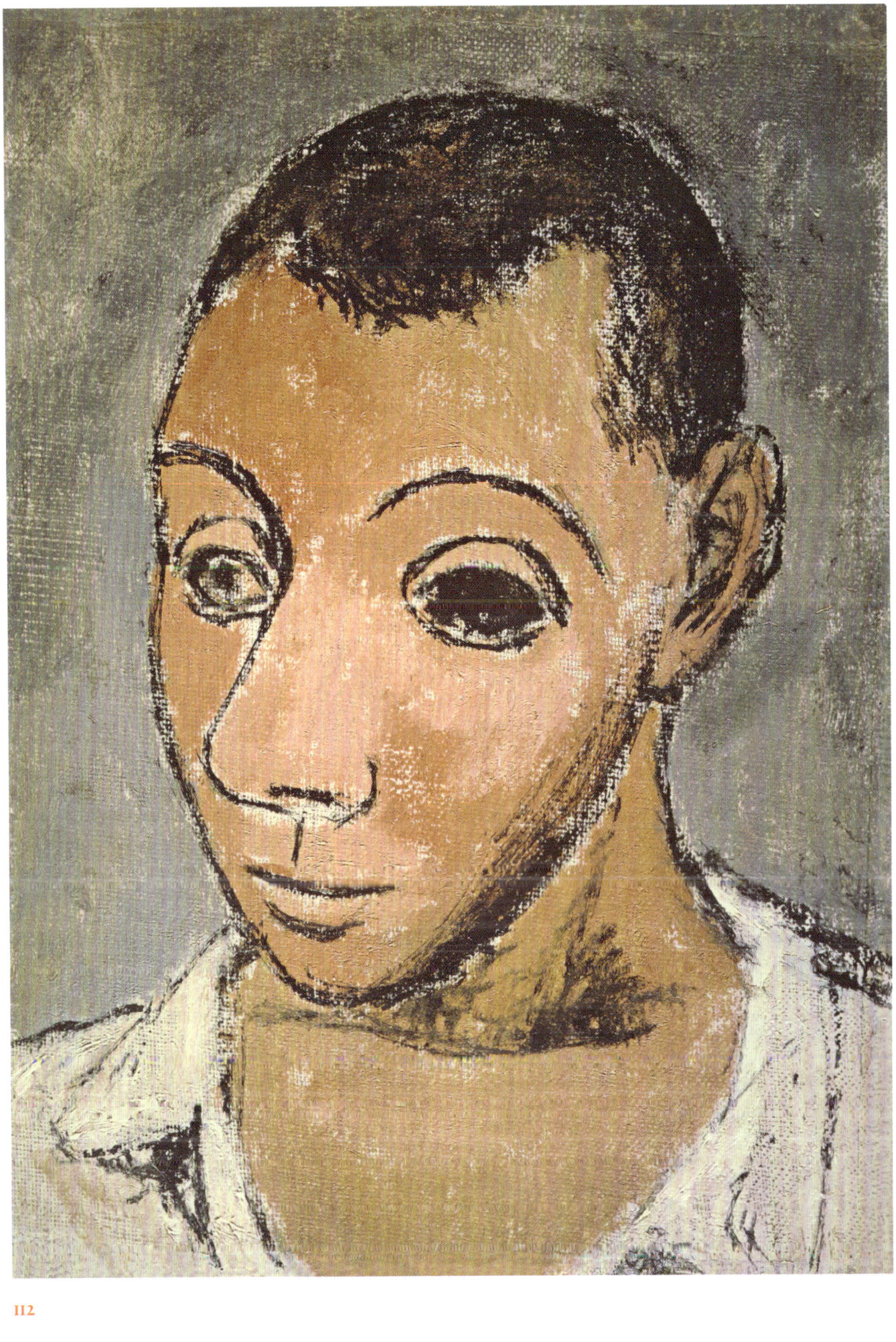

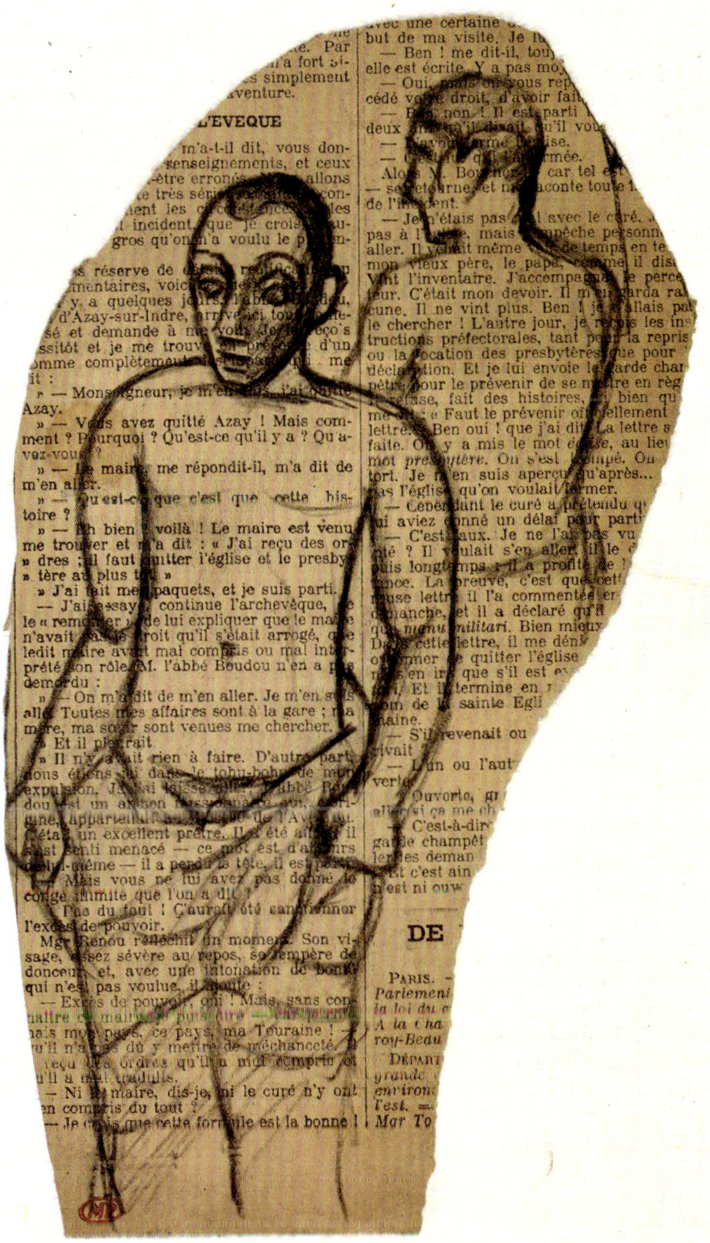
L'EVEQUE
DE

1907

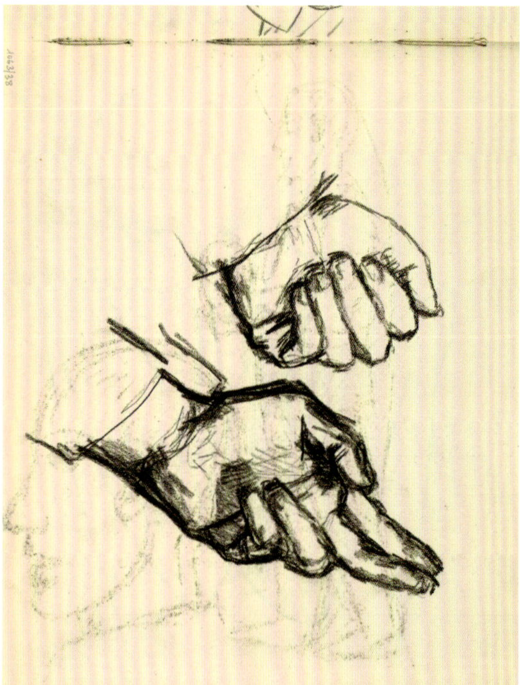

114

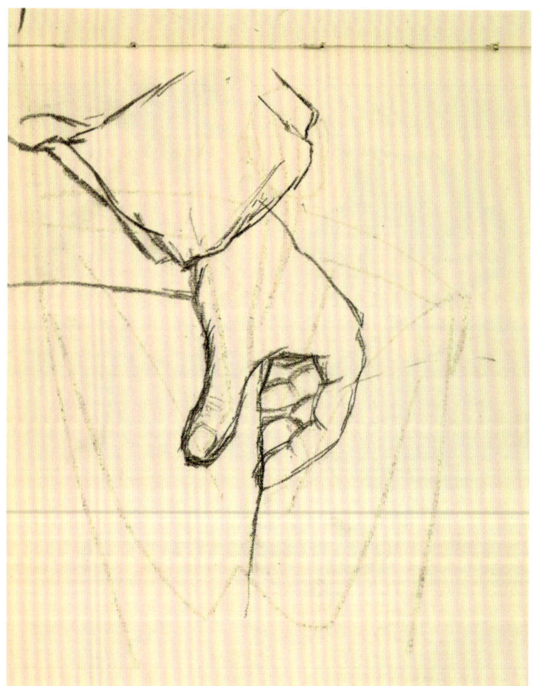

115

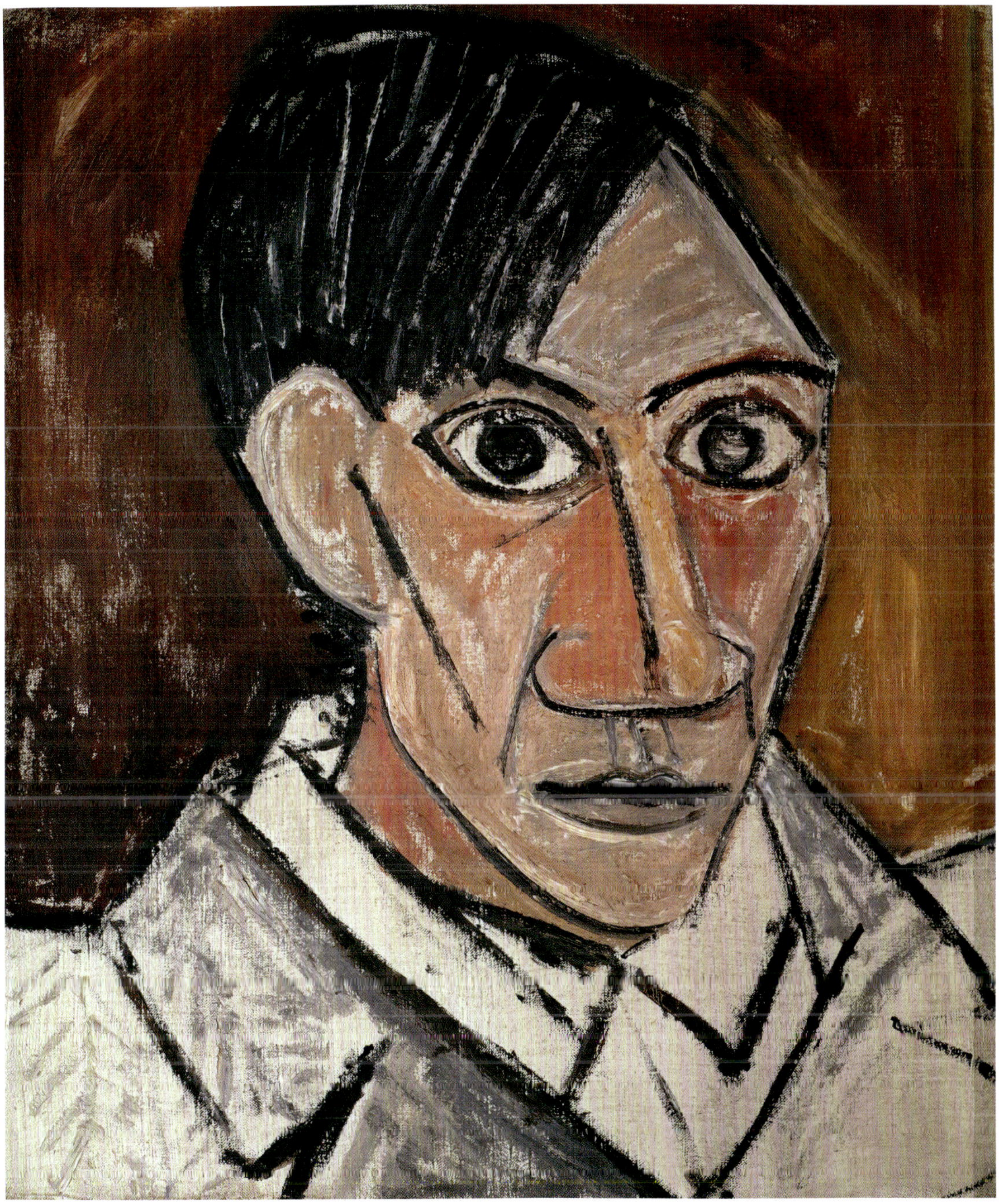

1908

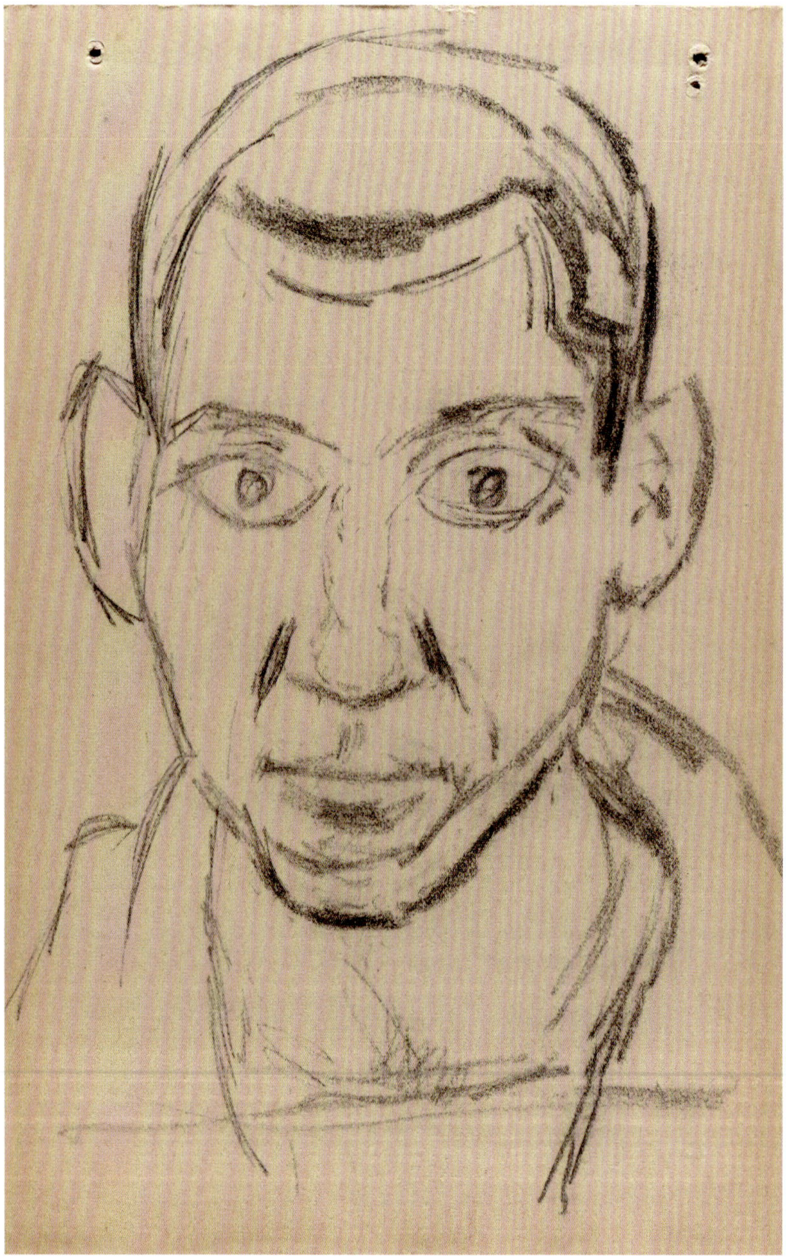

117

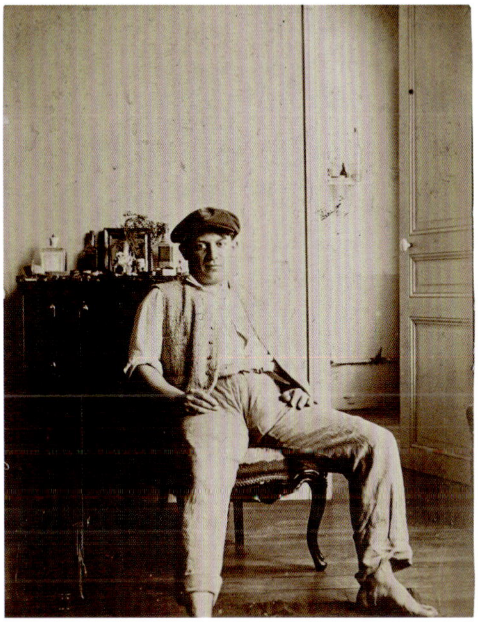

118

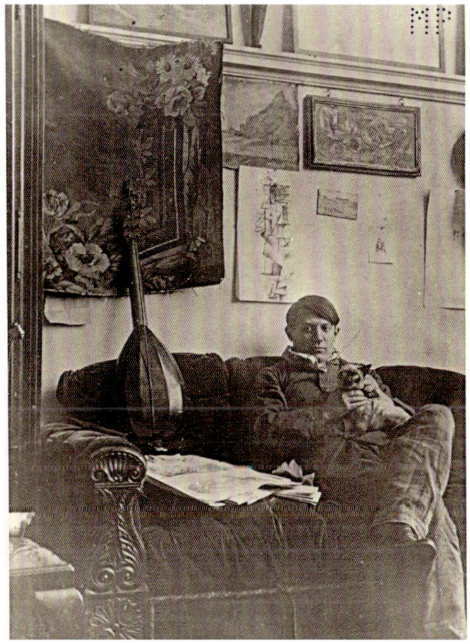

119

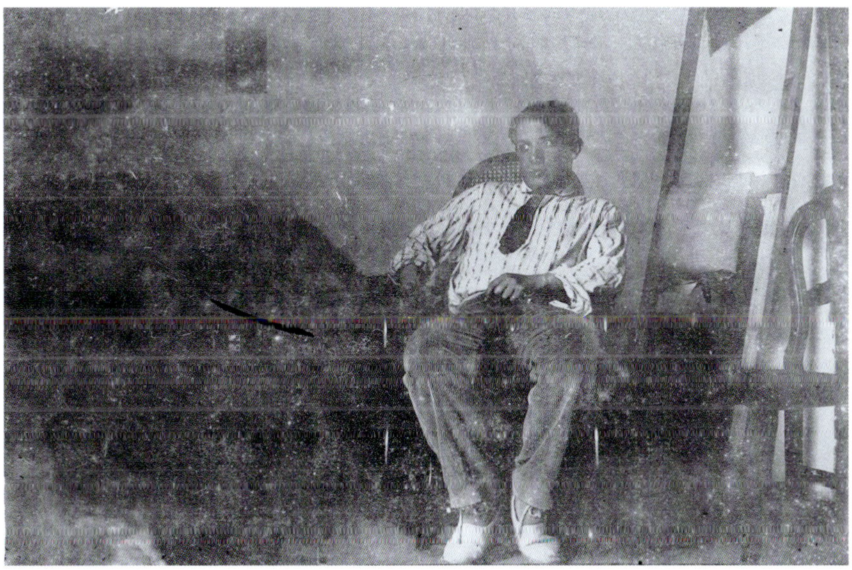

120

1915–1916

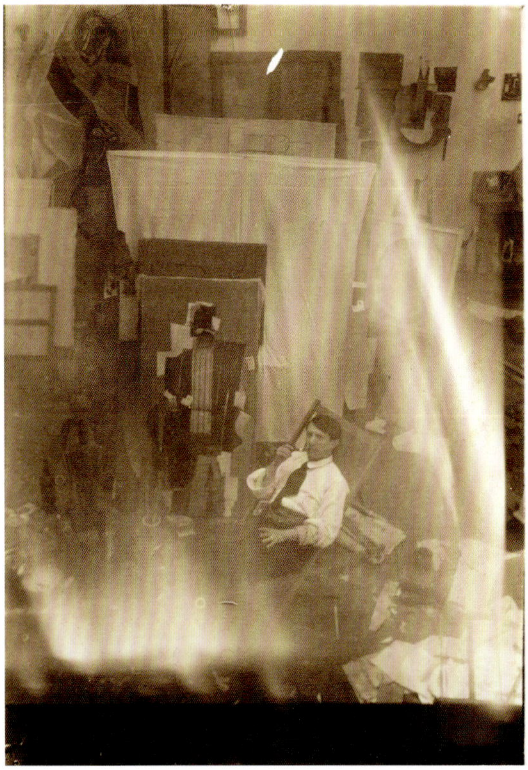

121

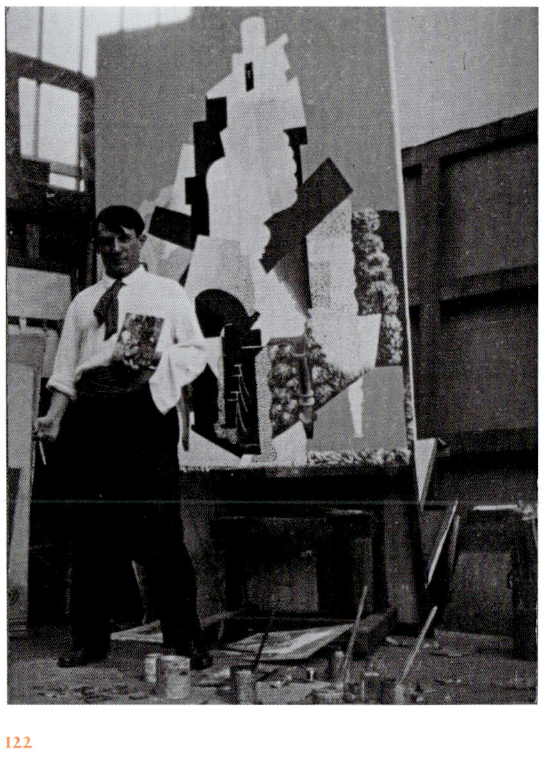

122

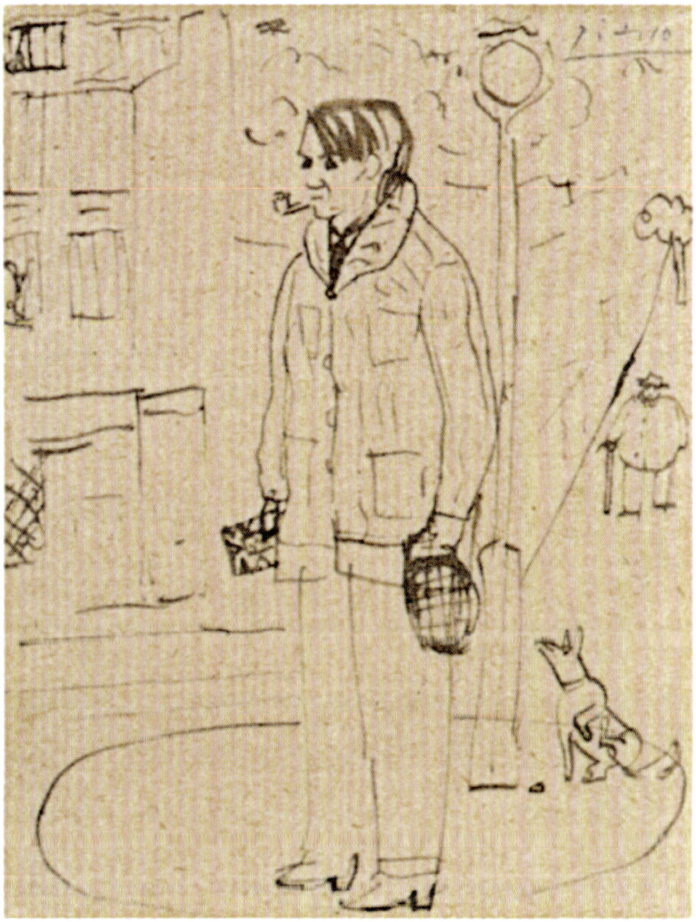

123

1915–1916

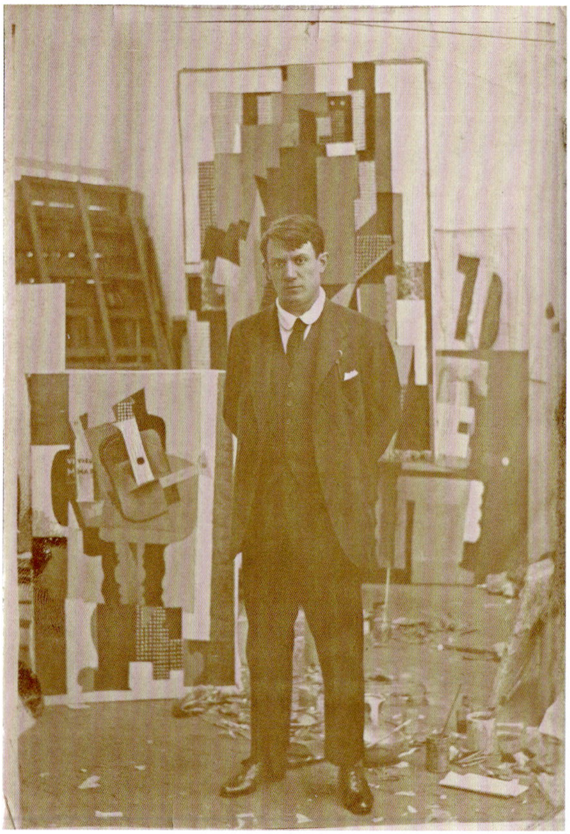

124

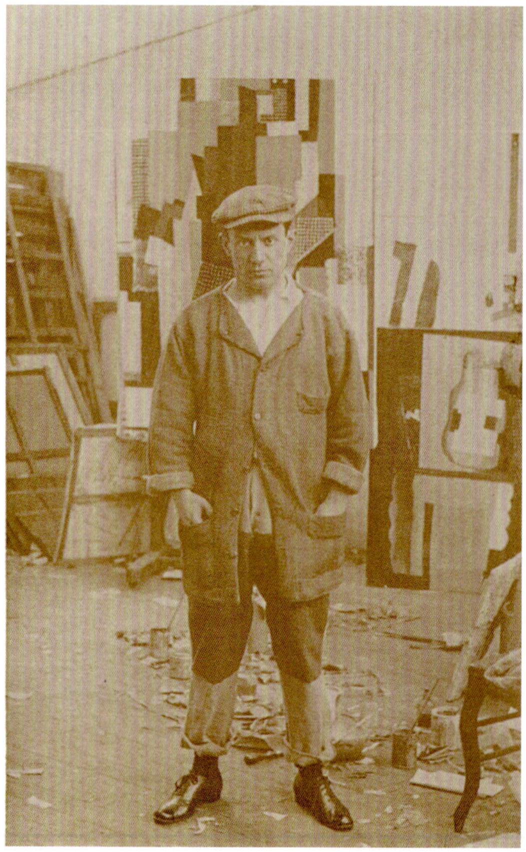

125

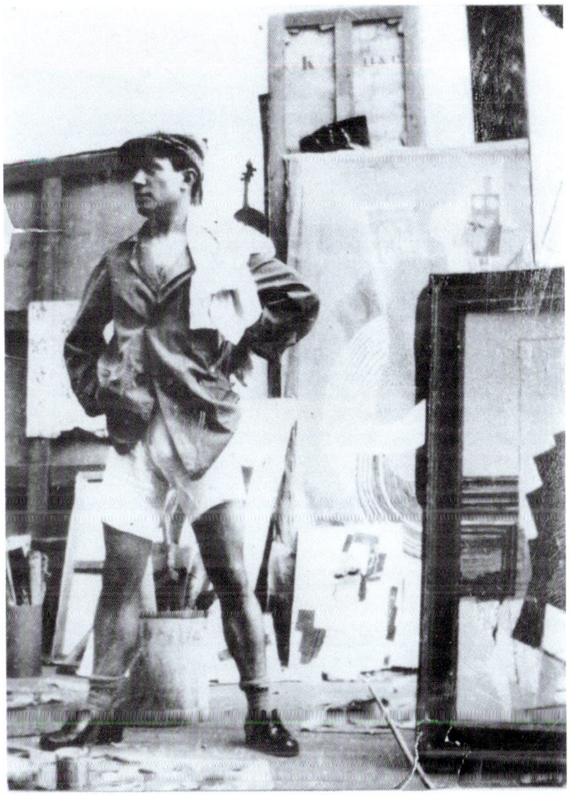

126

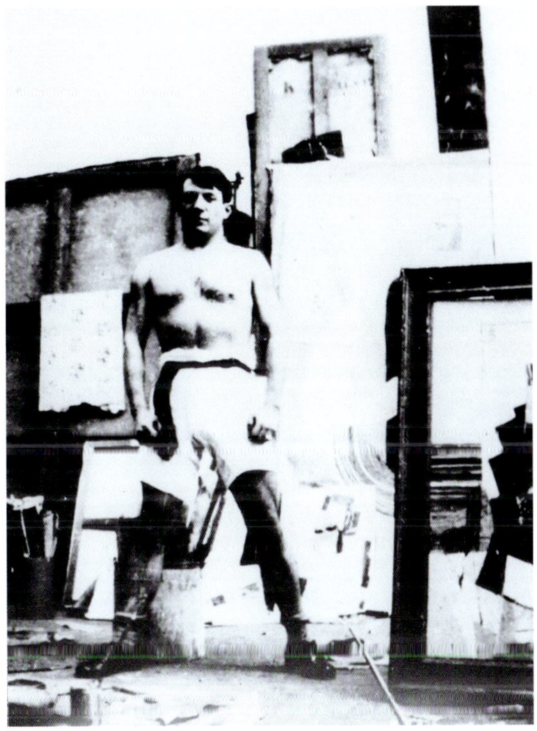

127

1917

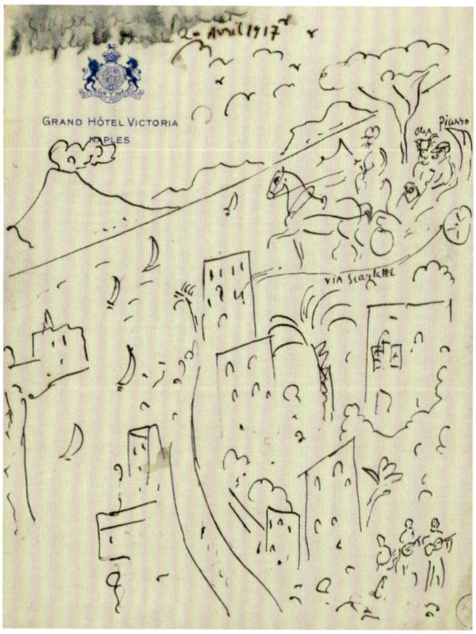

128

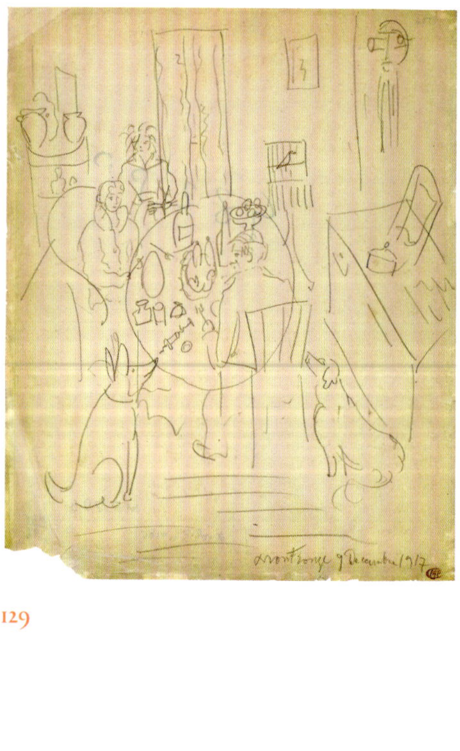

129

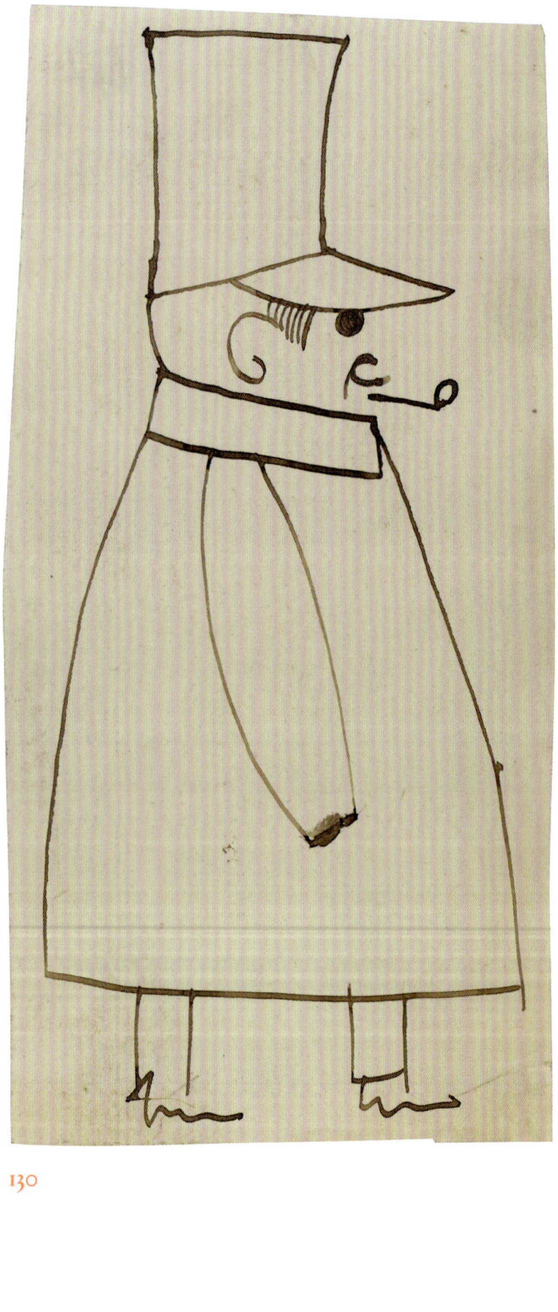

130

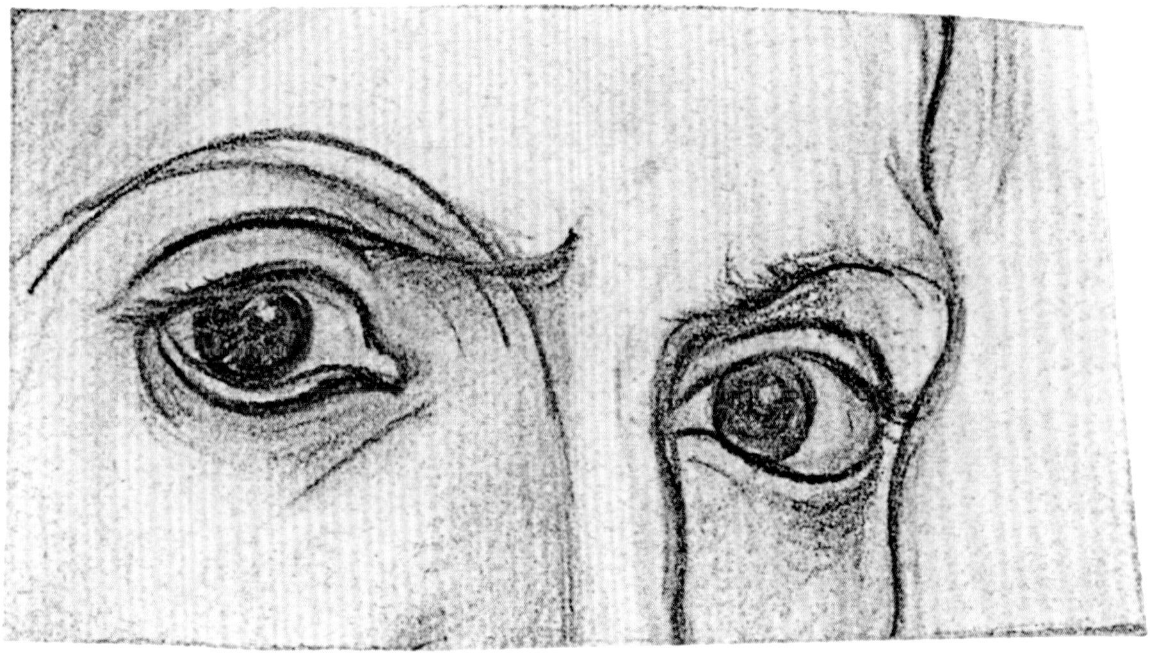

131

1917

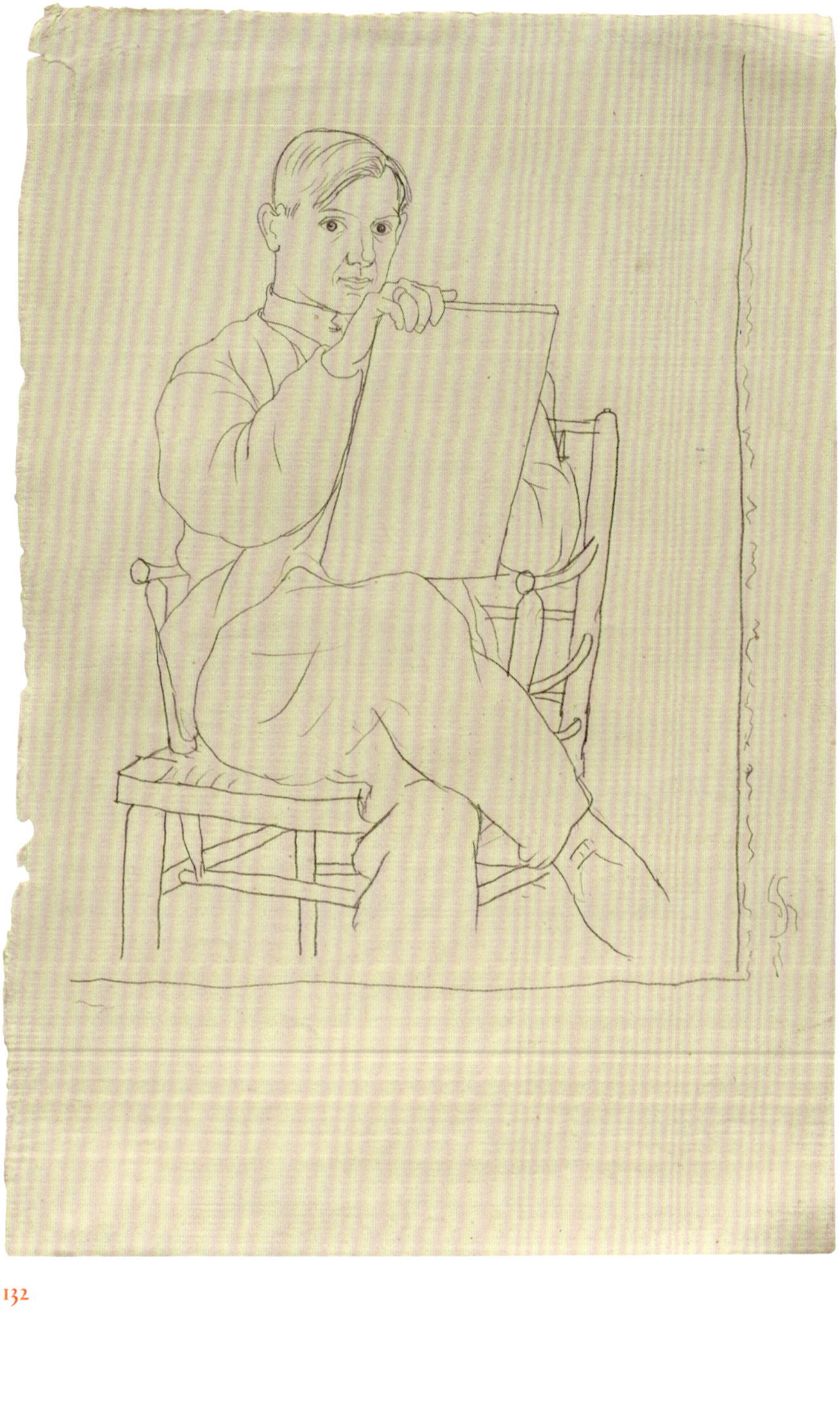

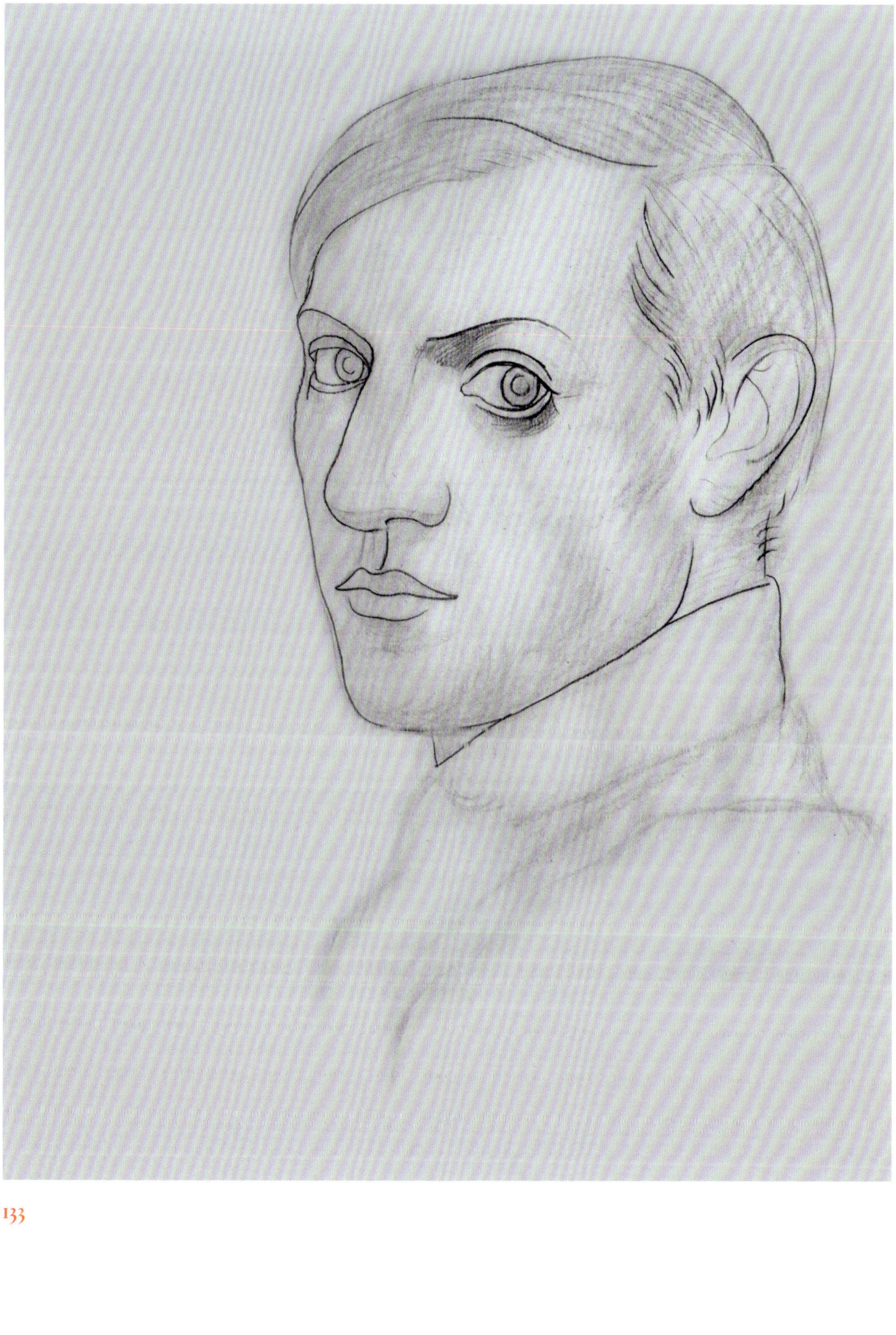

1918

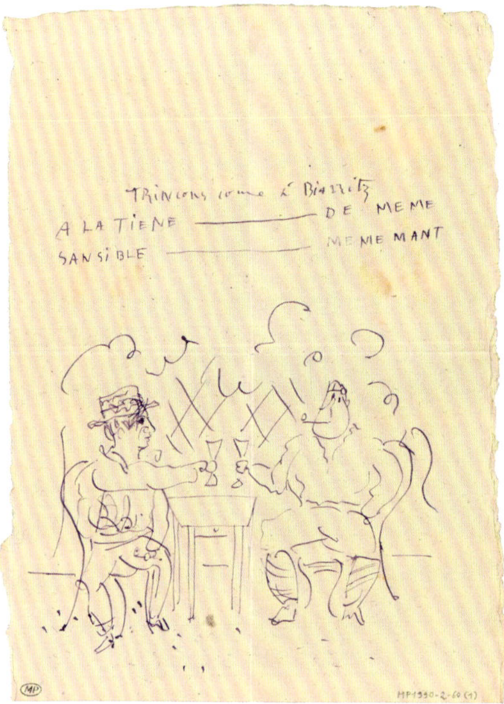
Trincons comme à Biarritz
A LA TIENE —— DE MEME
SANSIBLE —— MEMEMANT

134

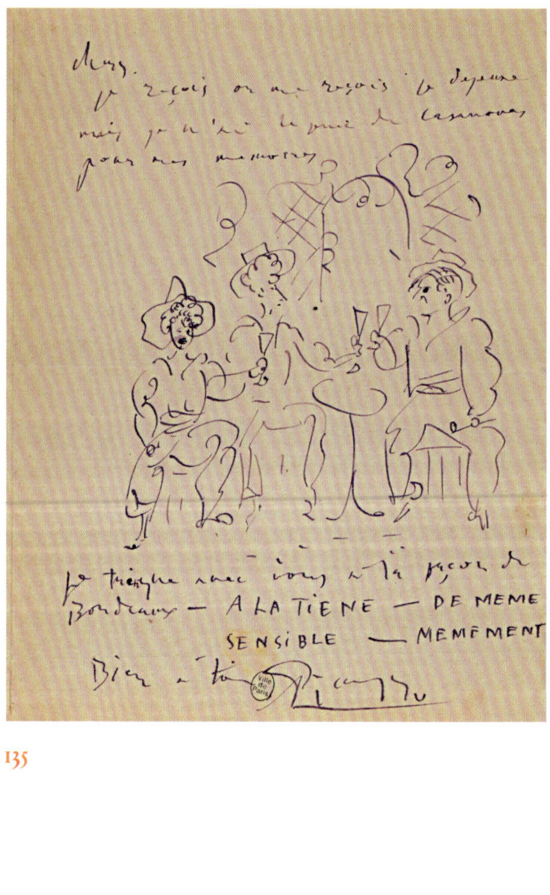
A LA TIENE — DE MEME
SENSIBLE — MEMEMENT

135

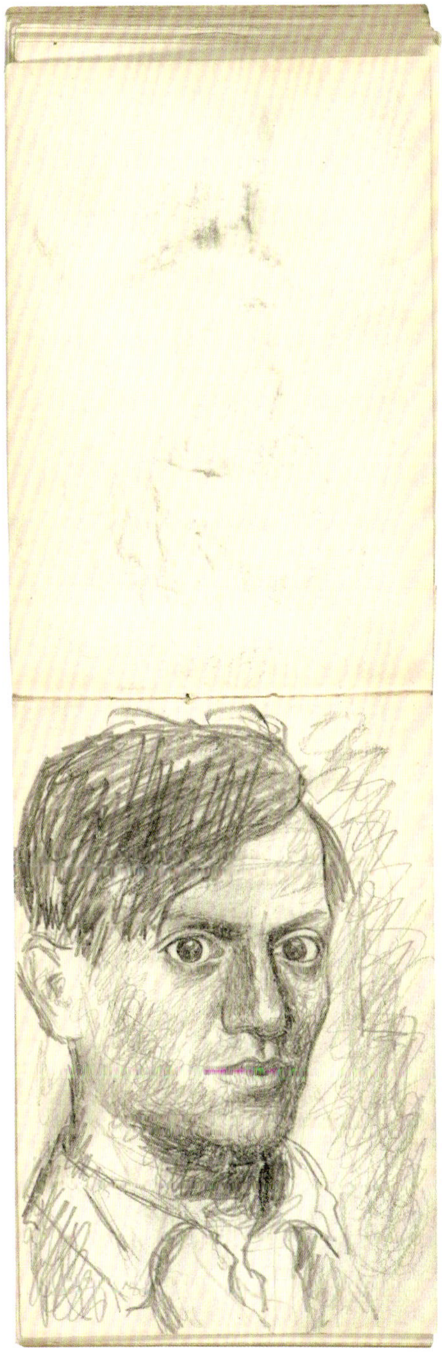

1918

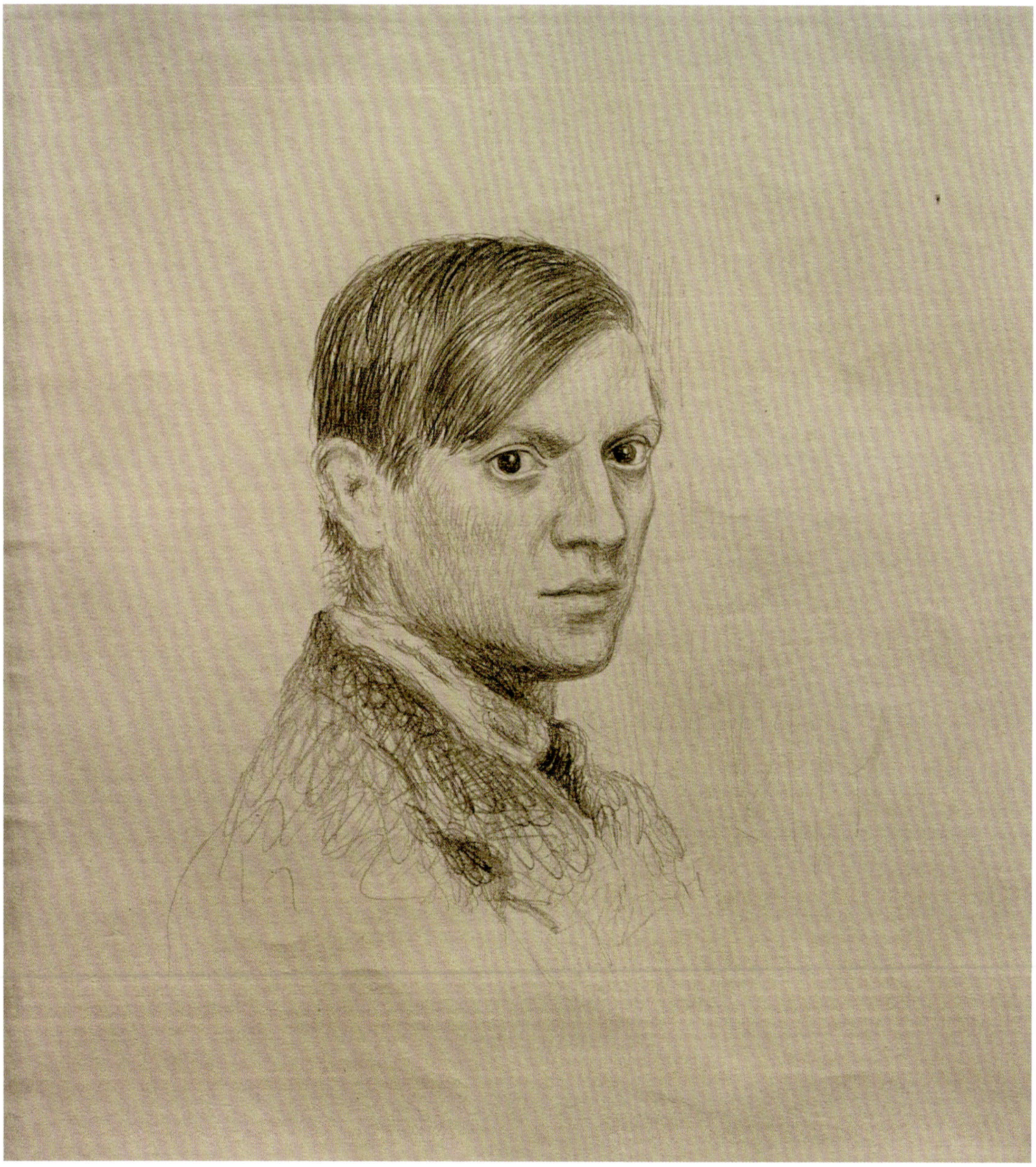

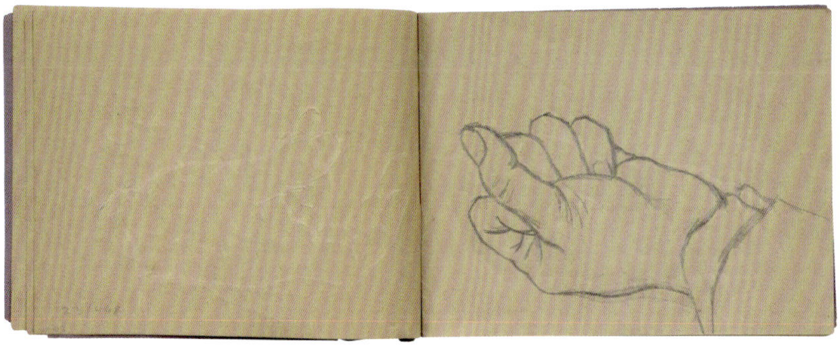

138

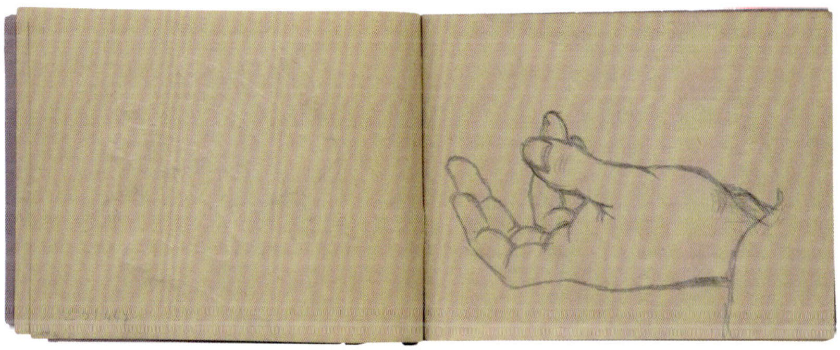

139

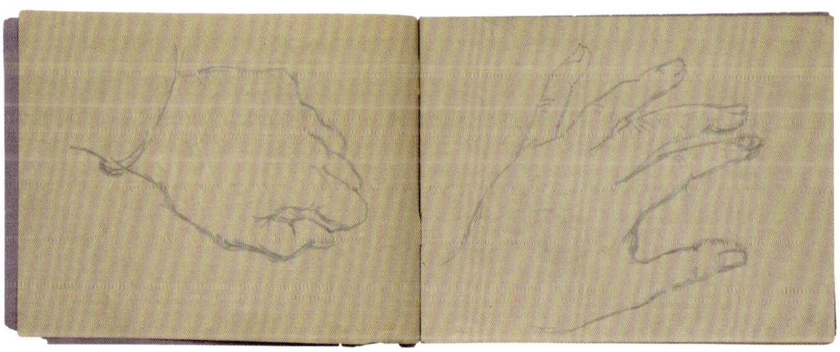

140

1919

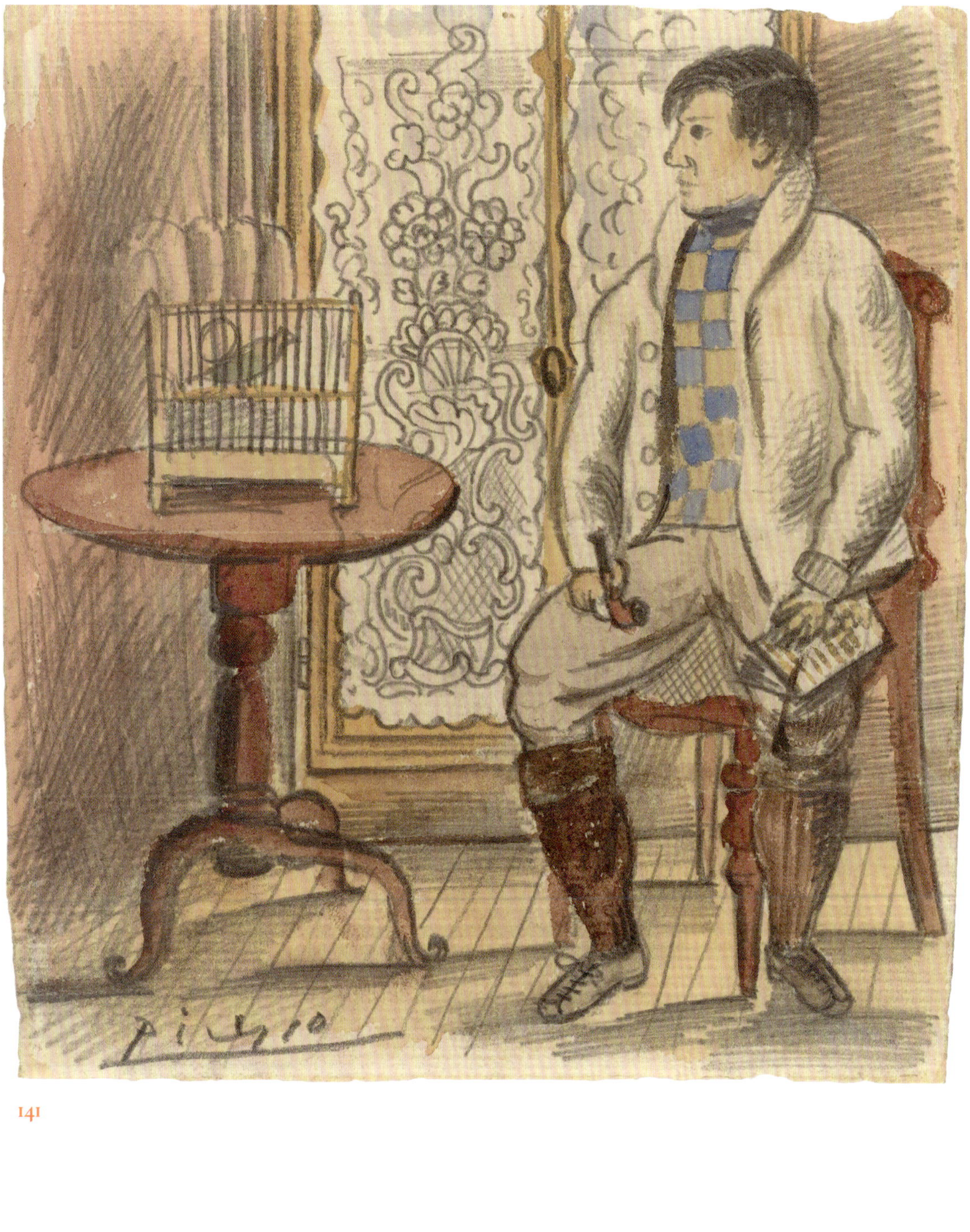

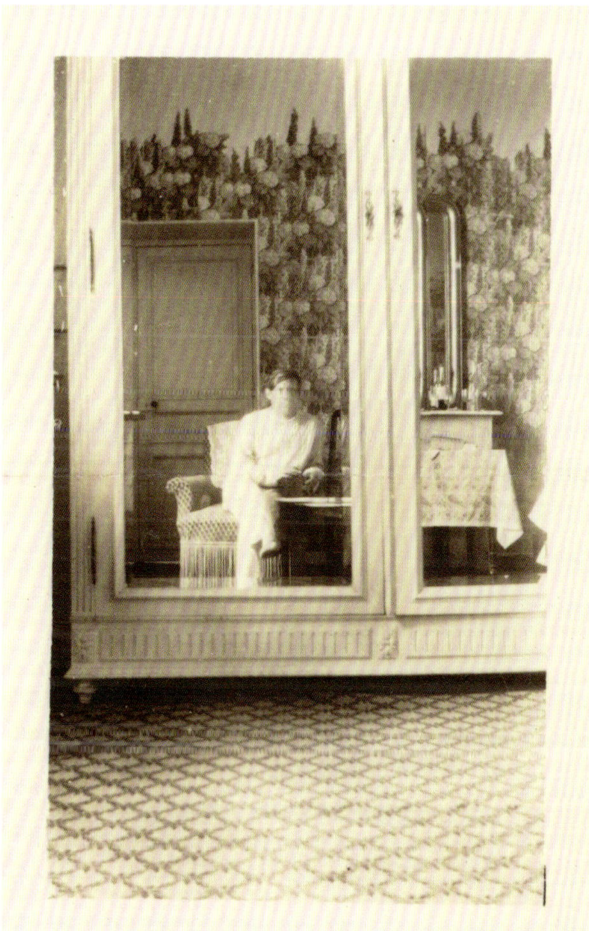

142

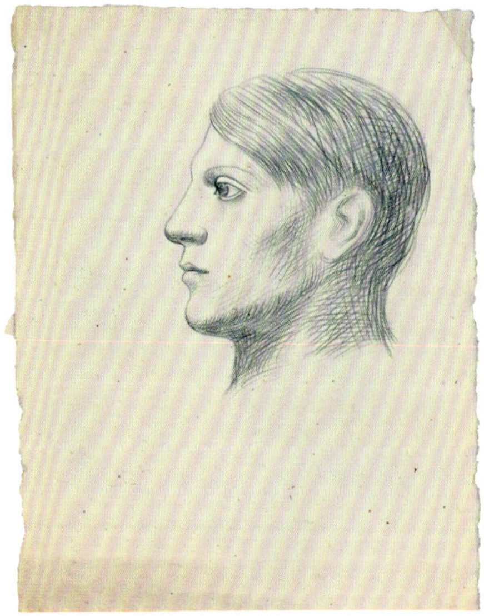

143

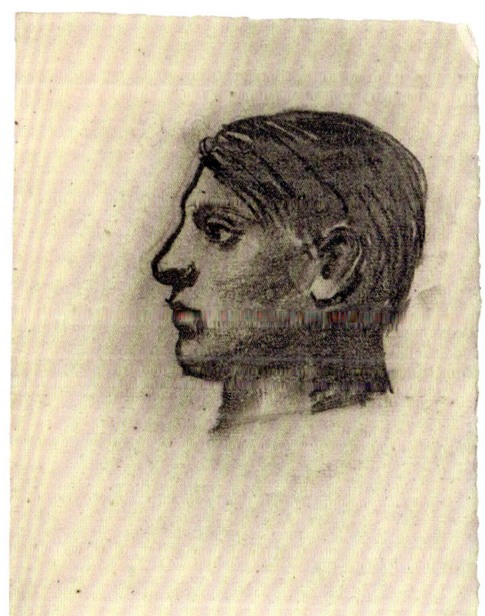

144

1927–1928

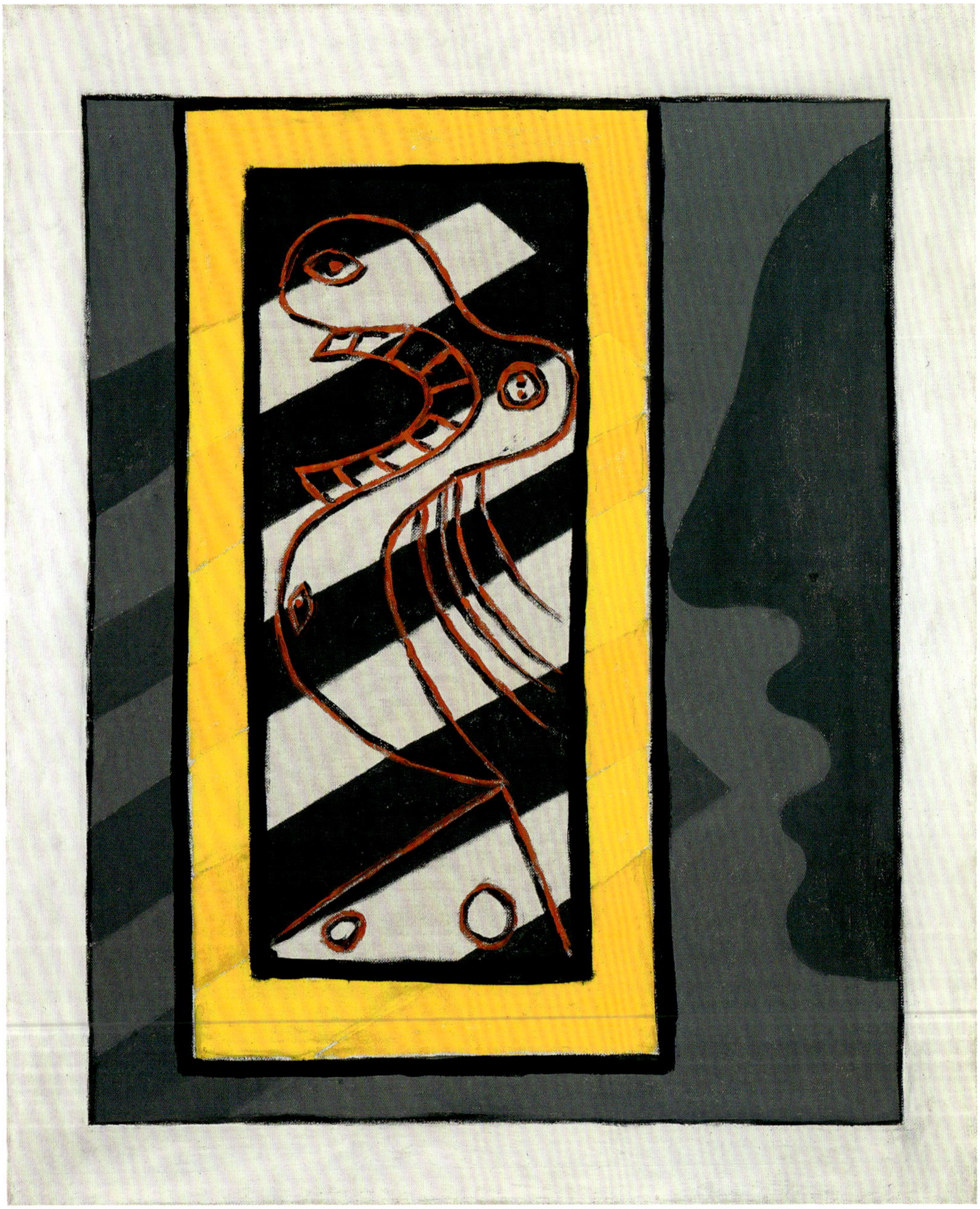

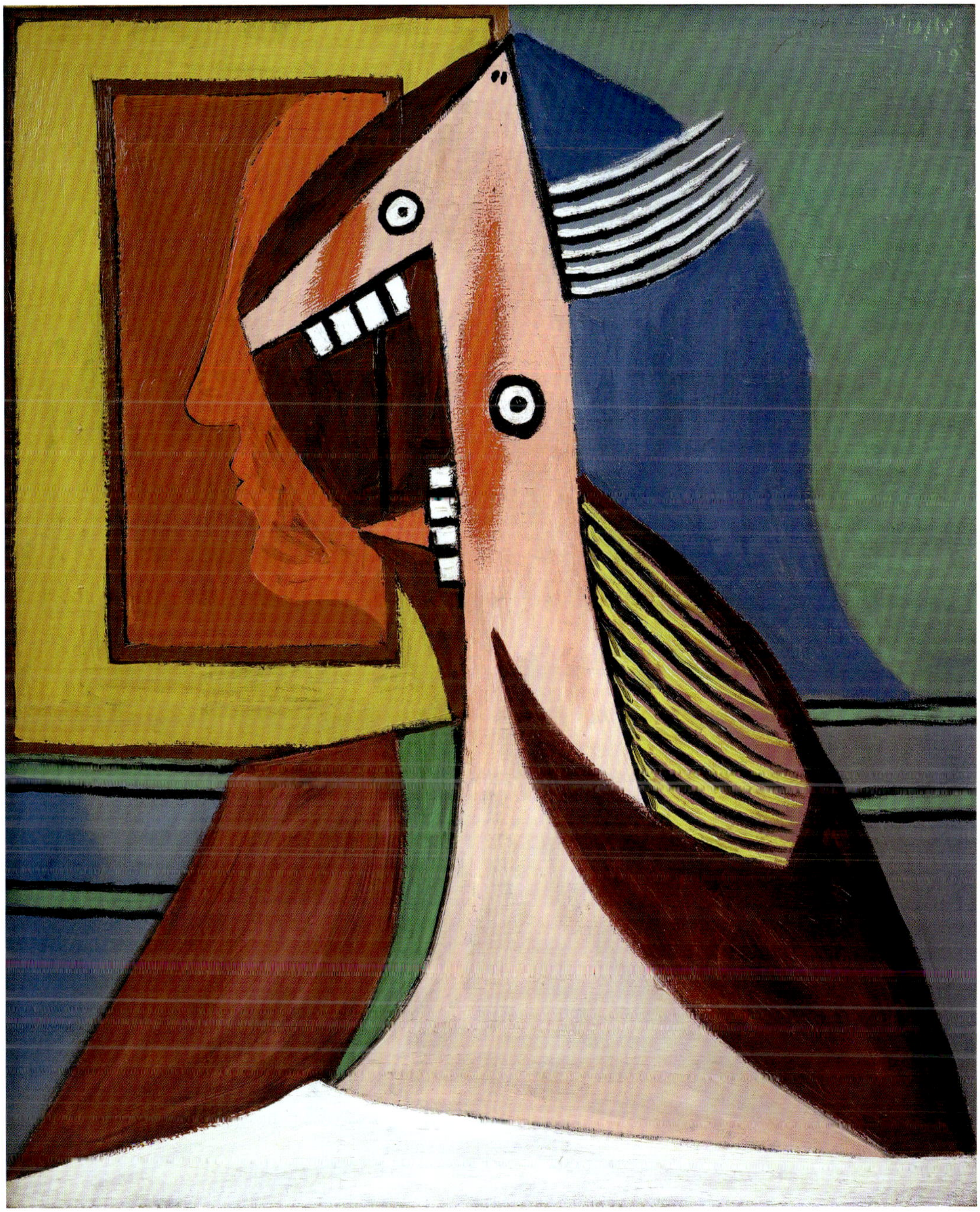

1938

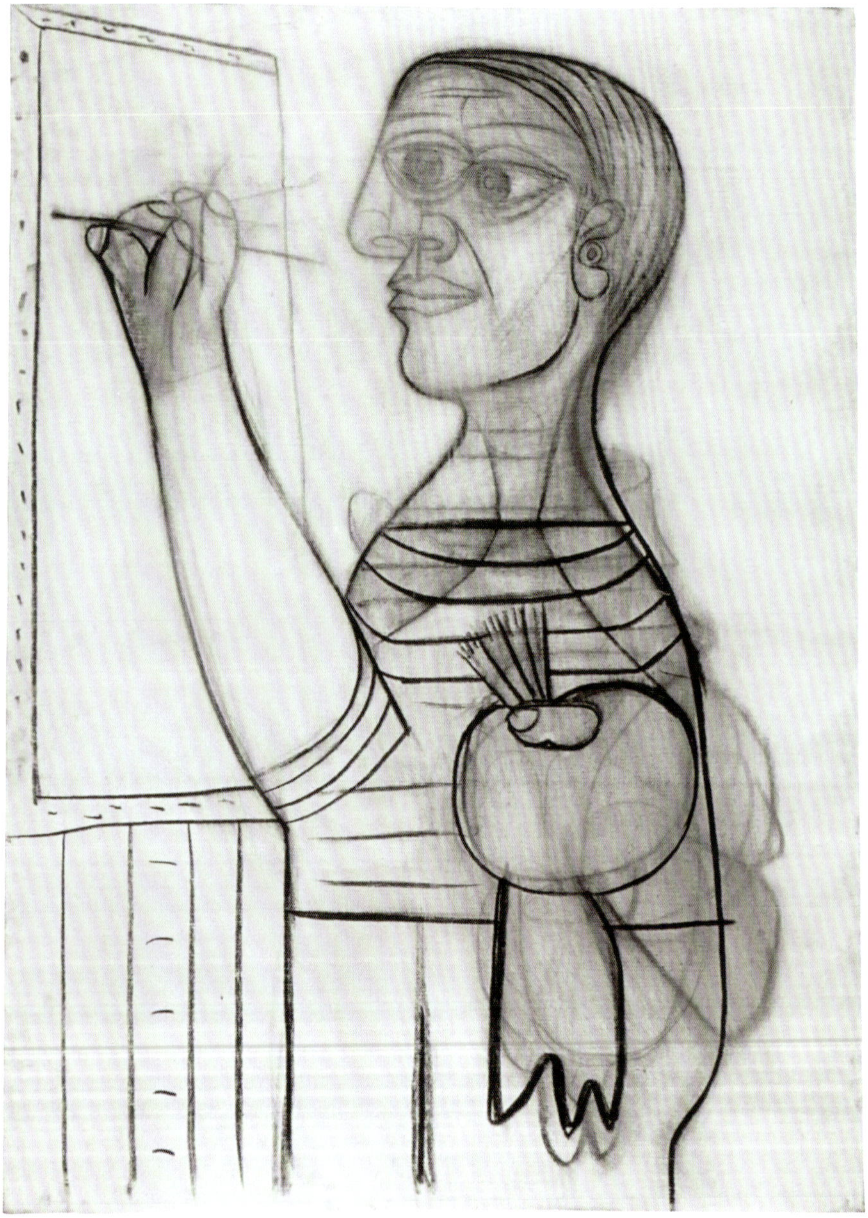

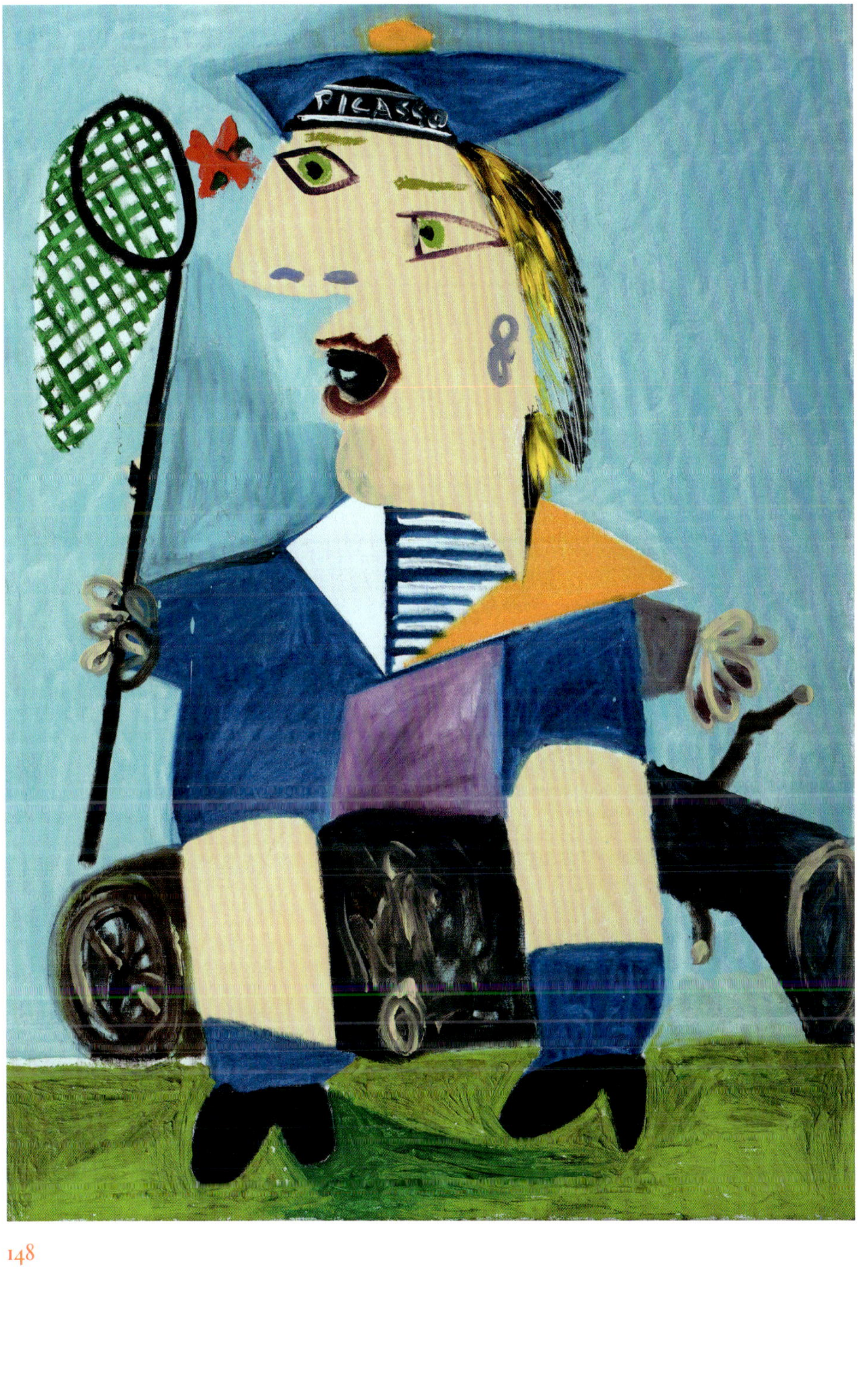
PICASSO

1940

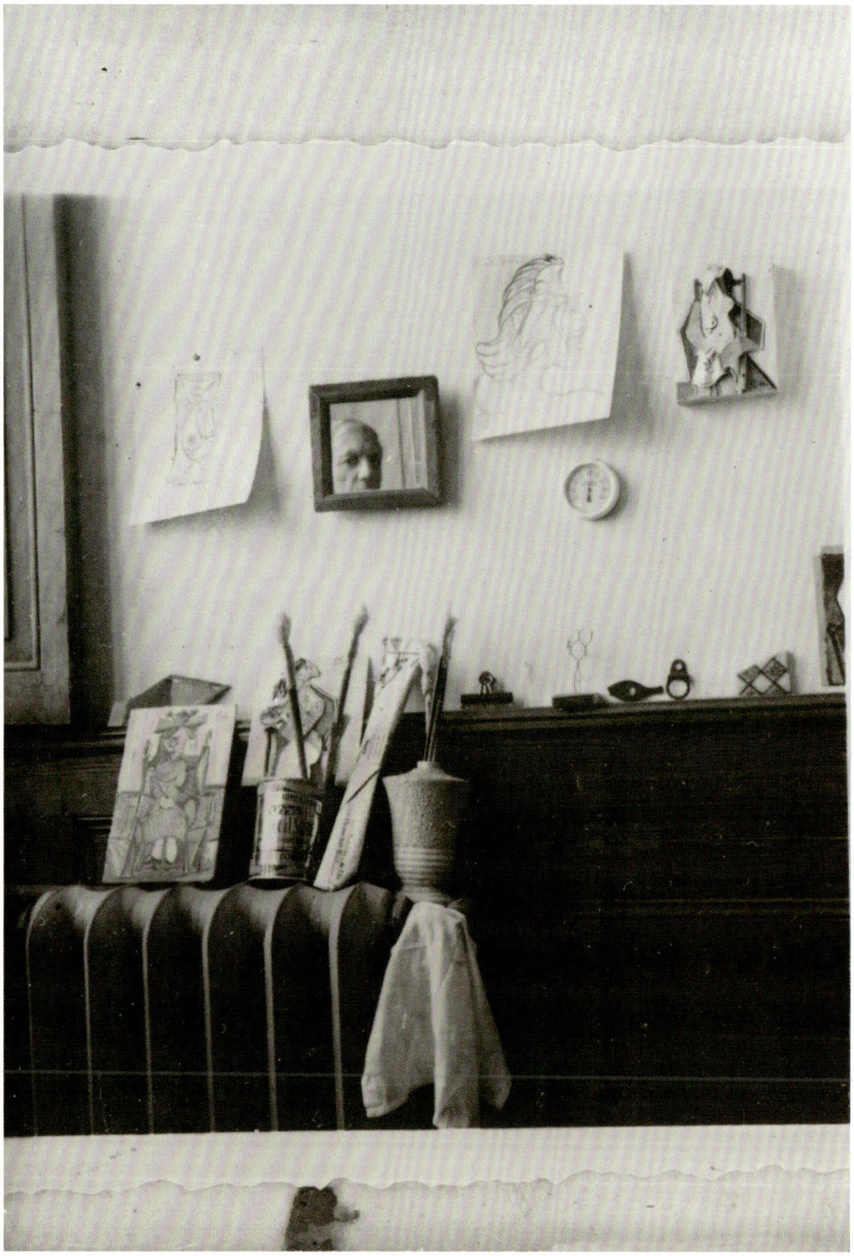

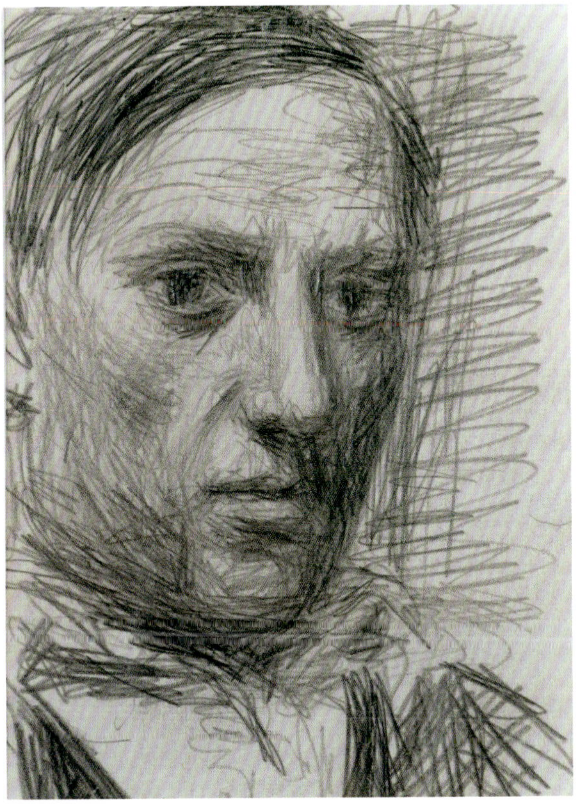

150

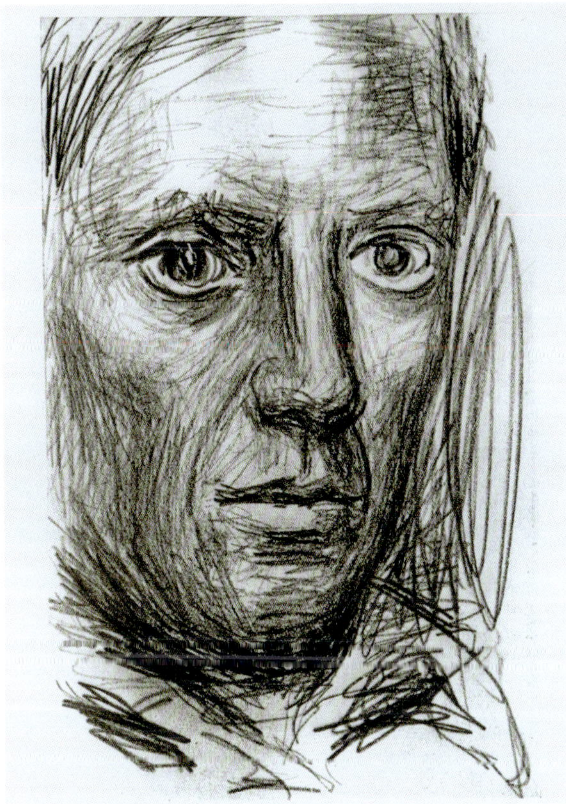

151

1941

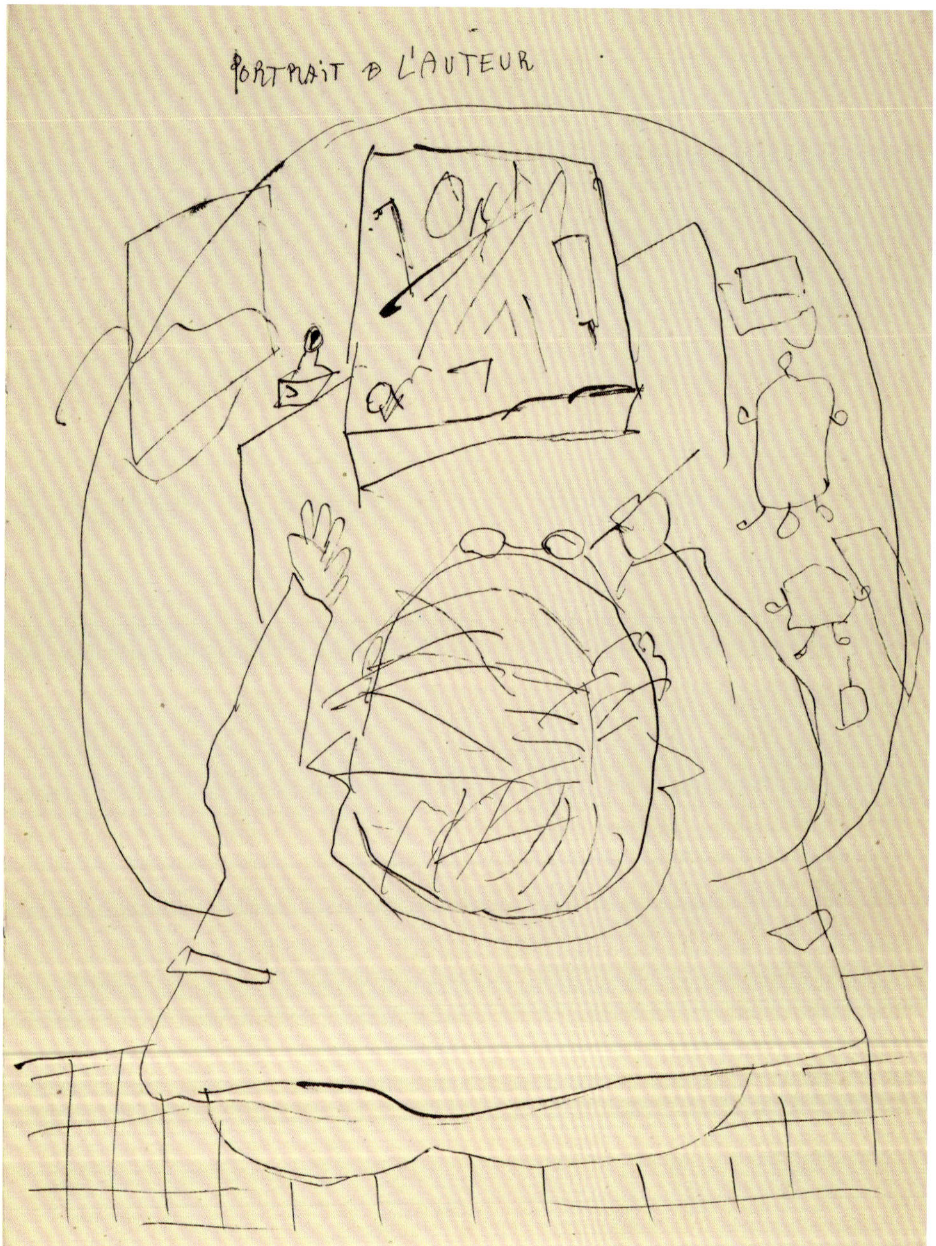

1942–1943

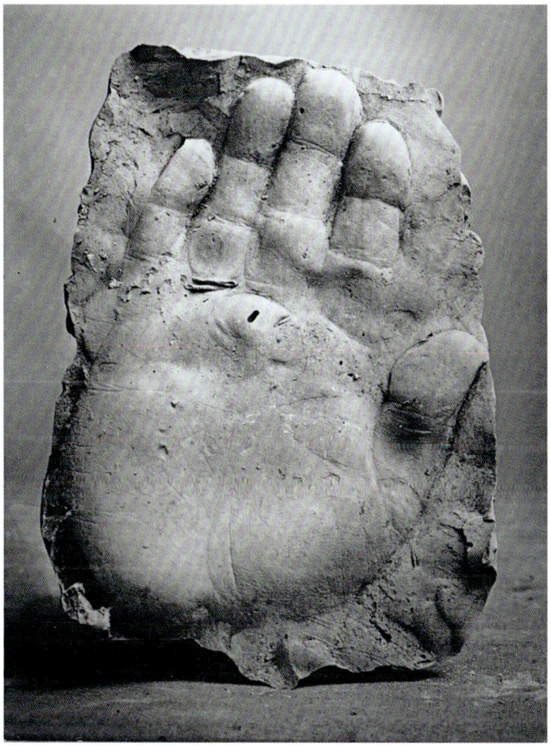

153

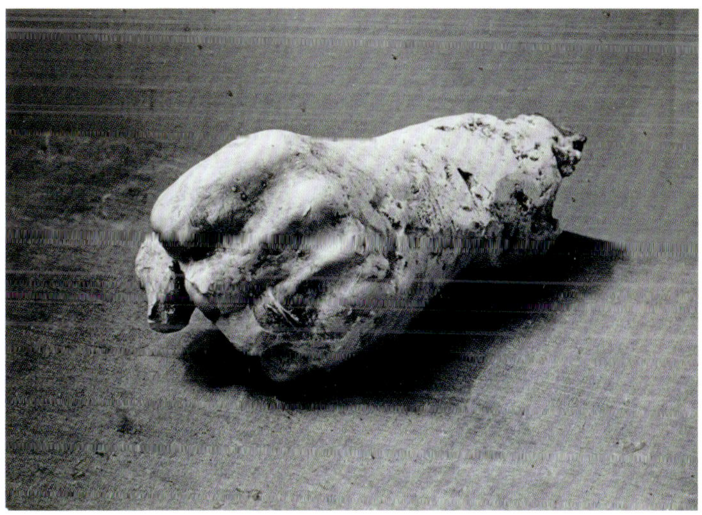

154

1943

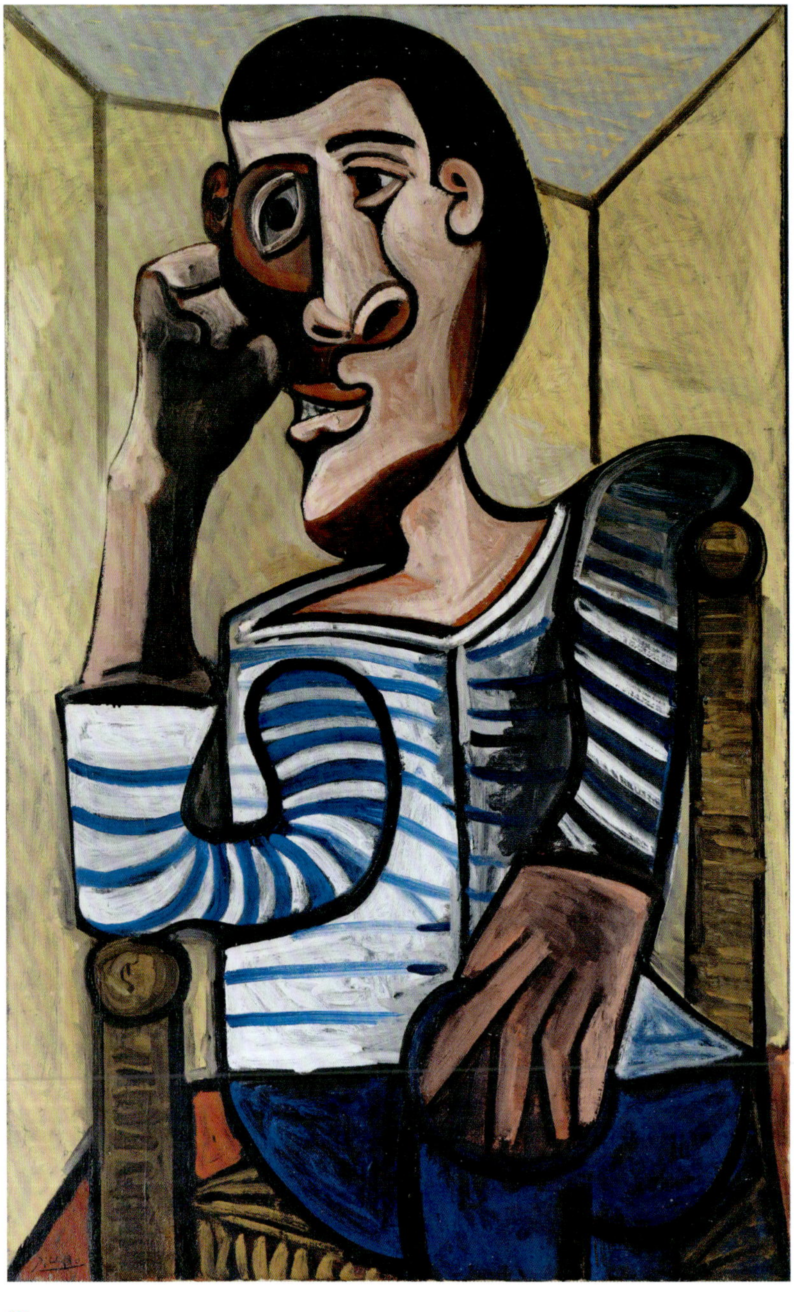

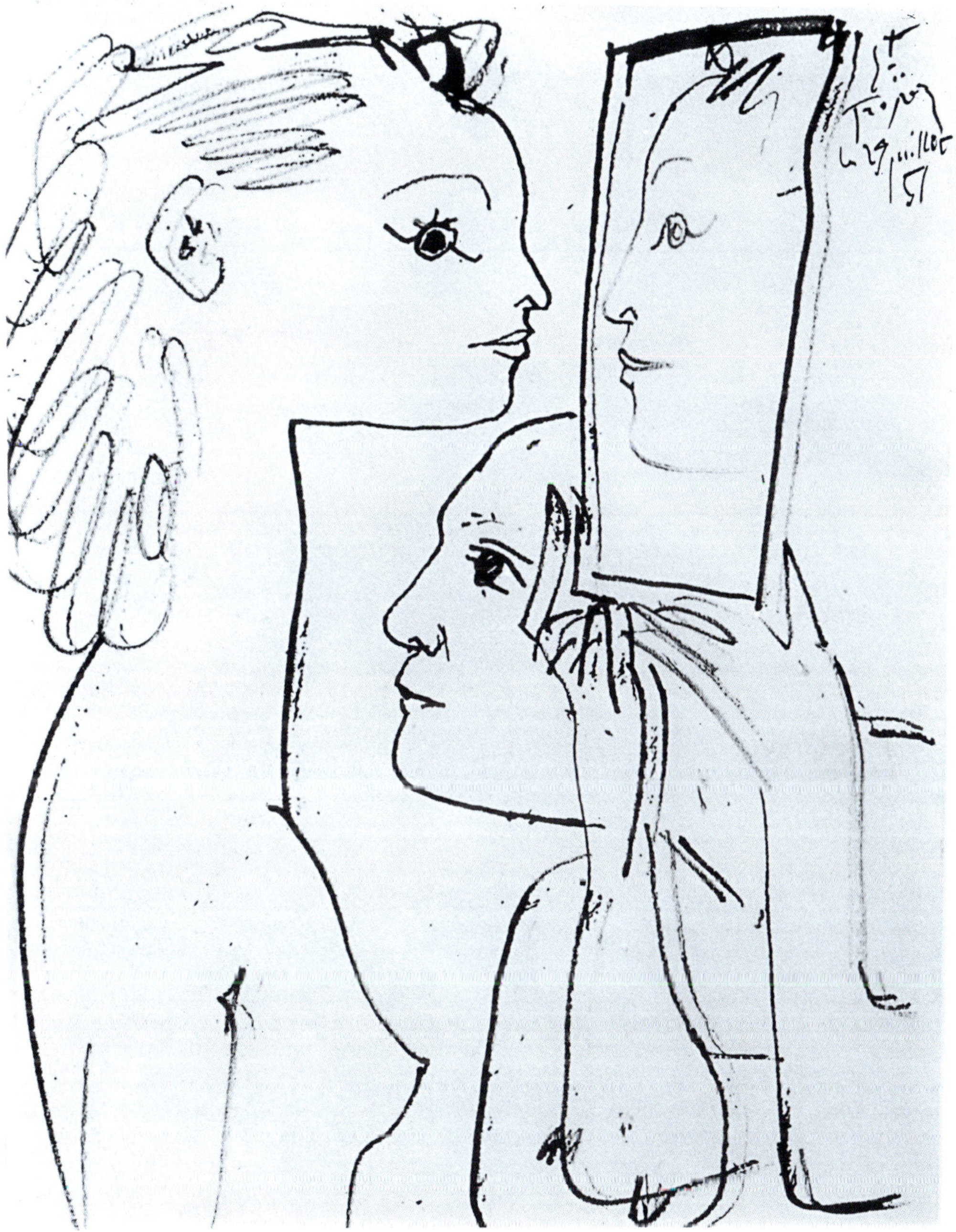
St
Tropez
le 29 juillet
51

1953

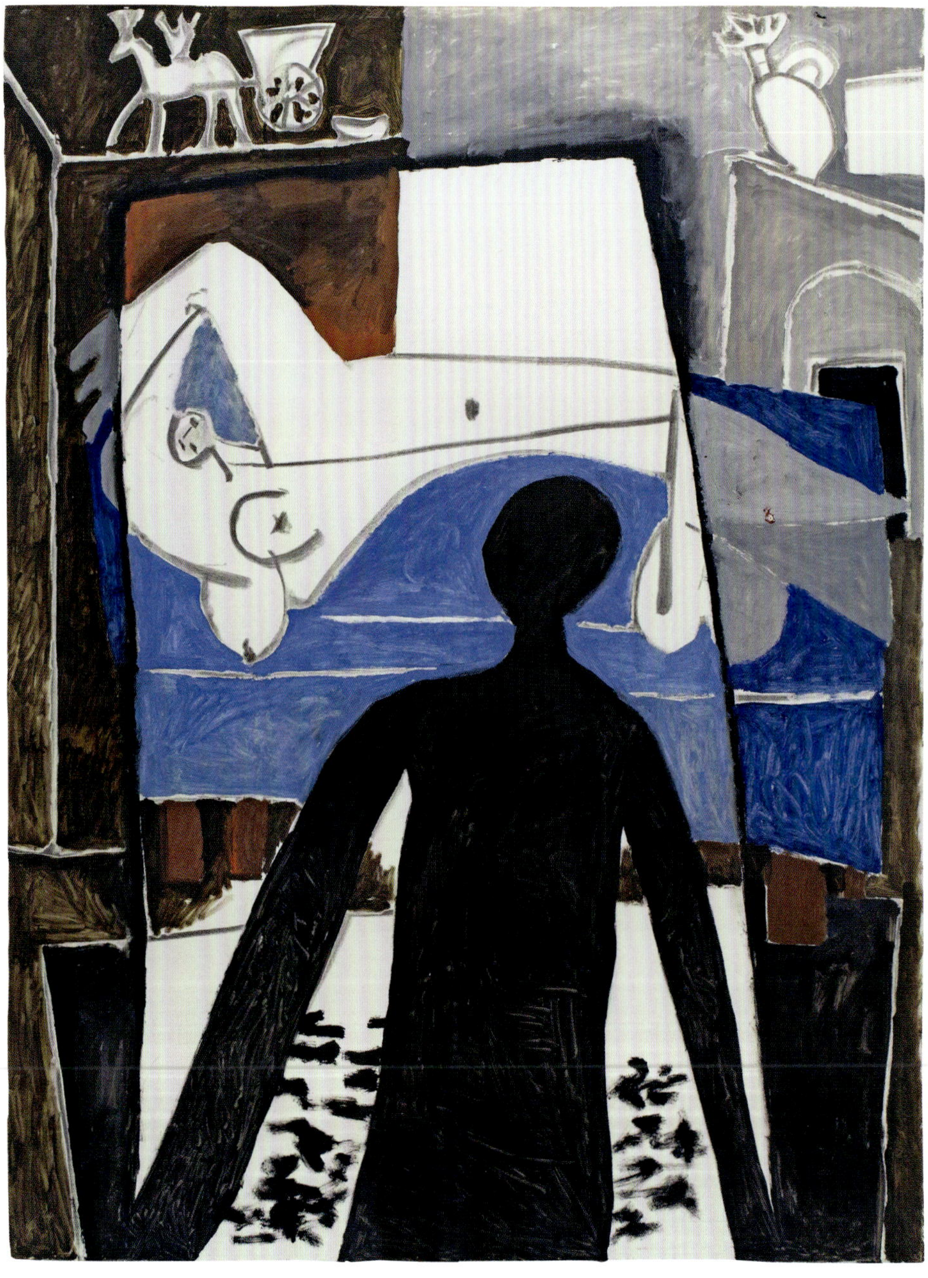

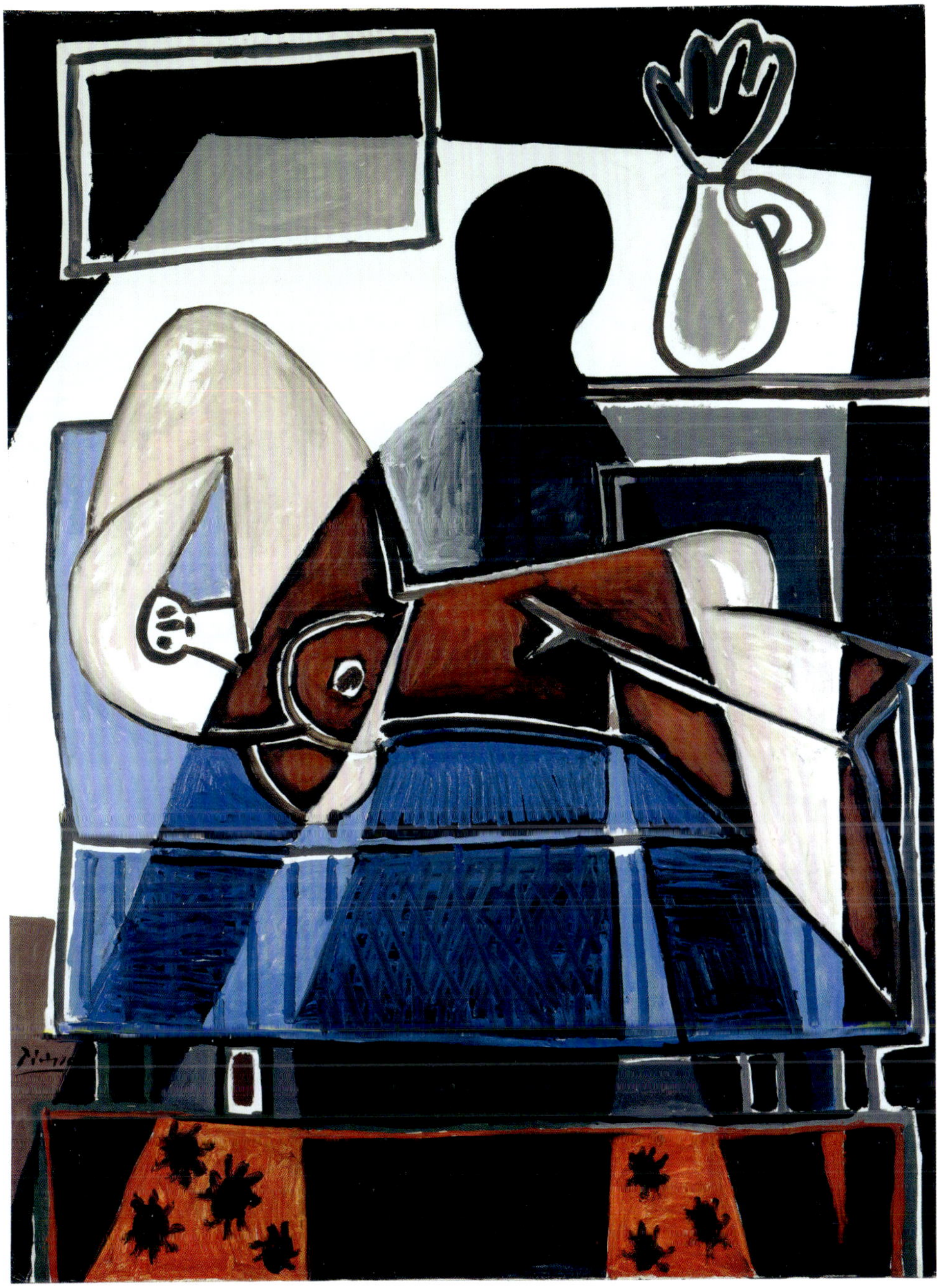

1955

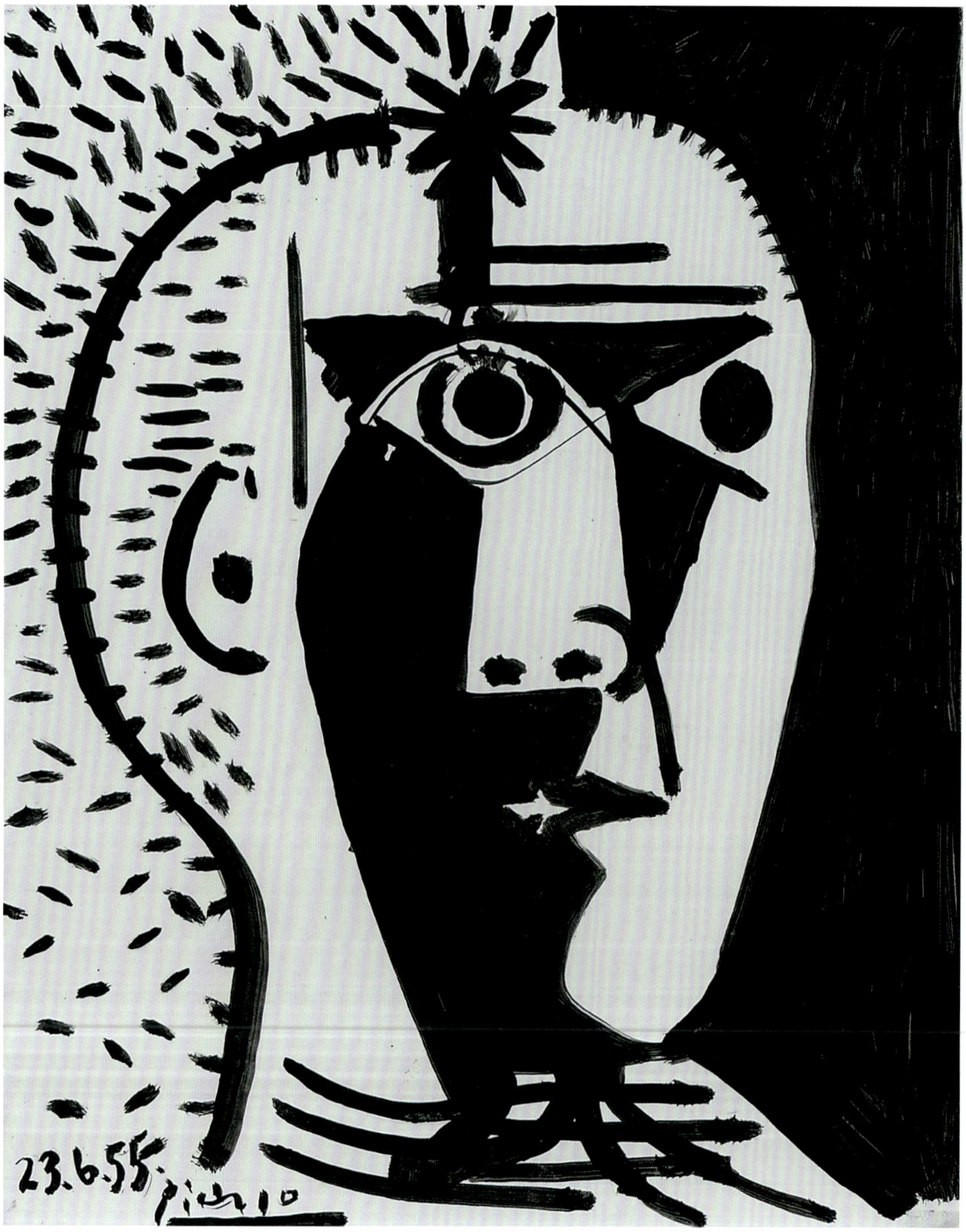

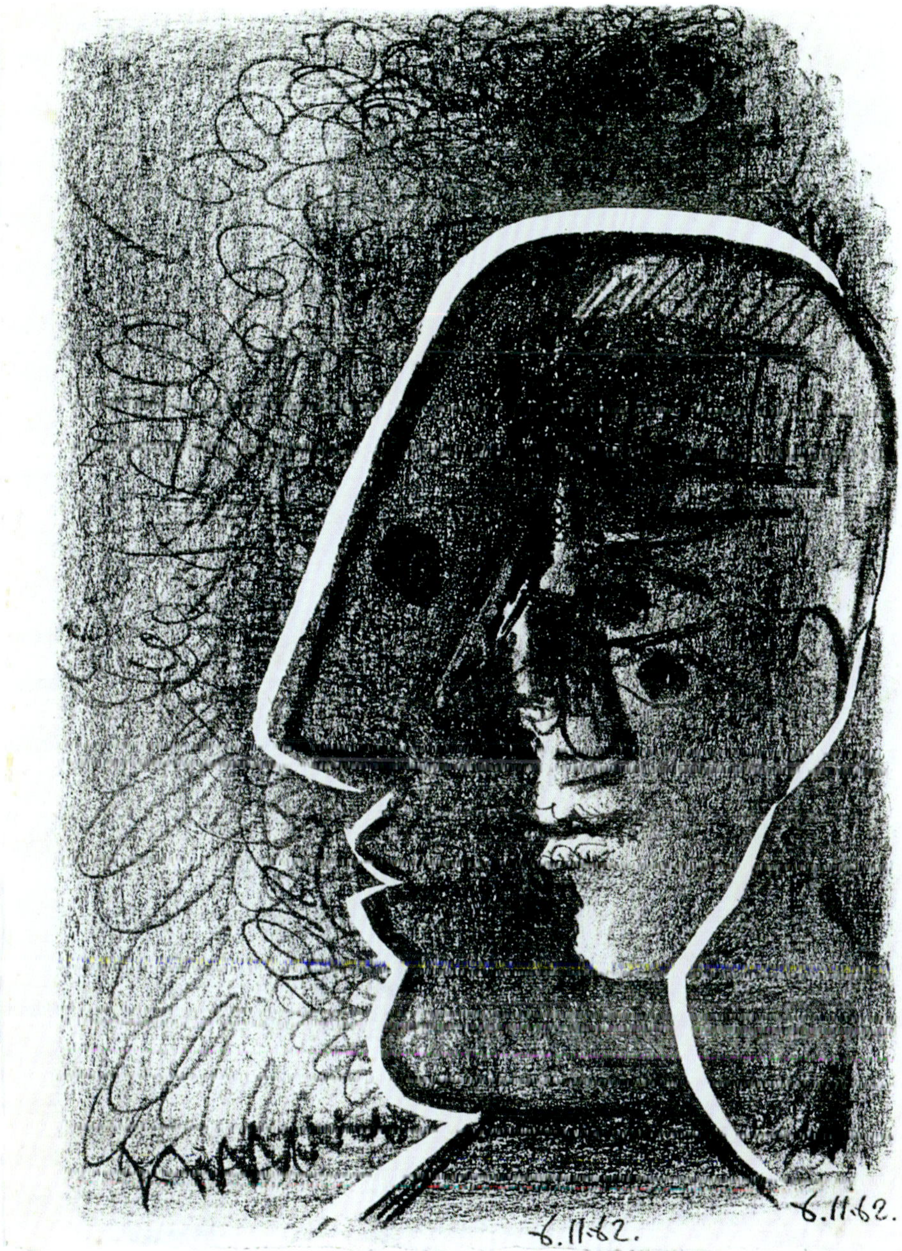
6.11.62.
6.11.62.

1966

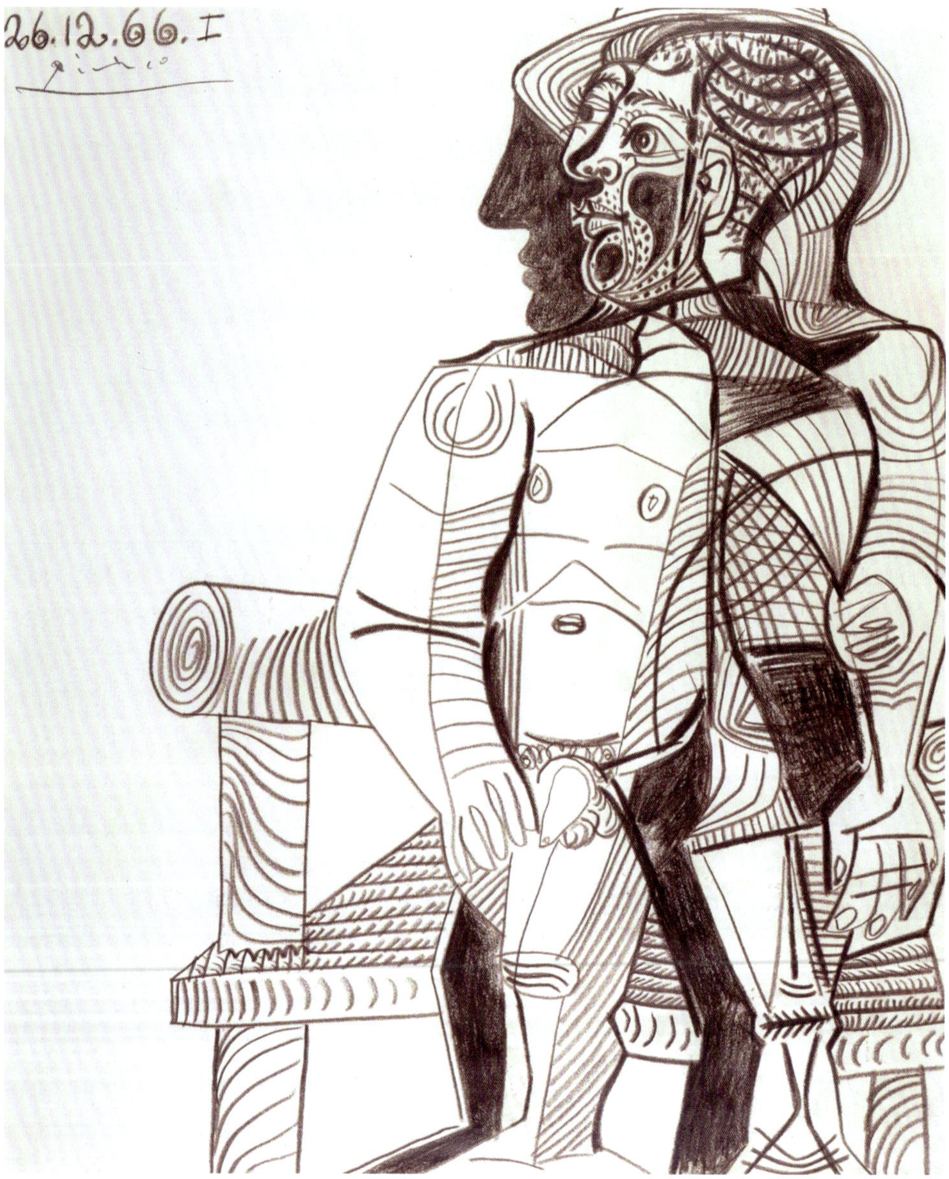

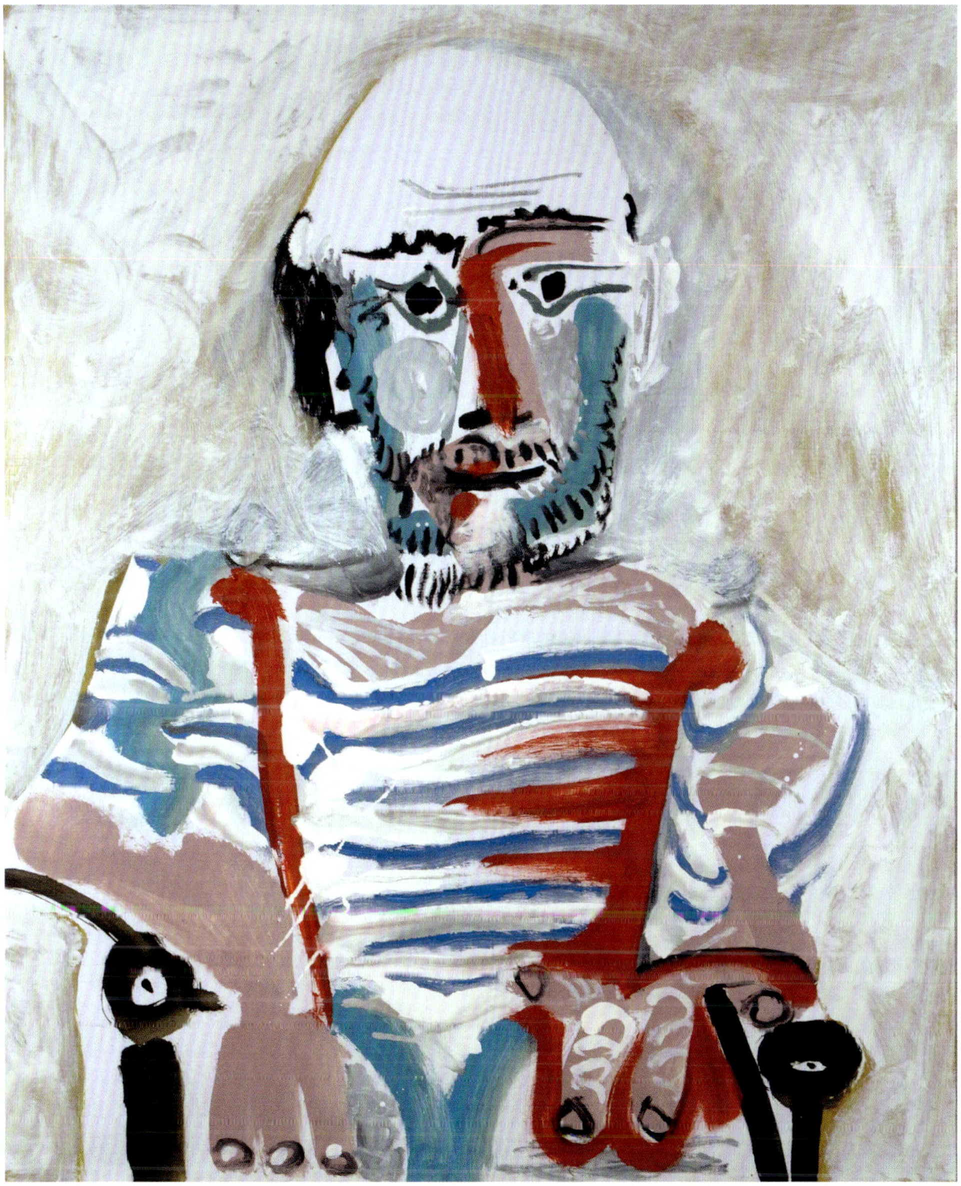

1968

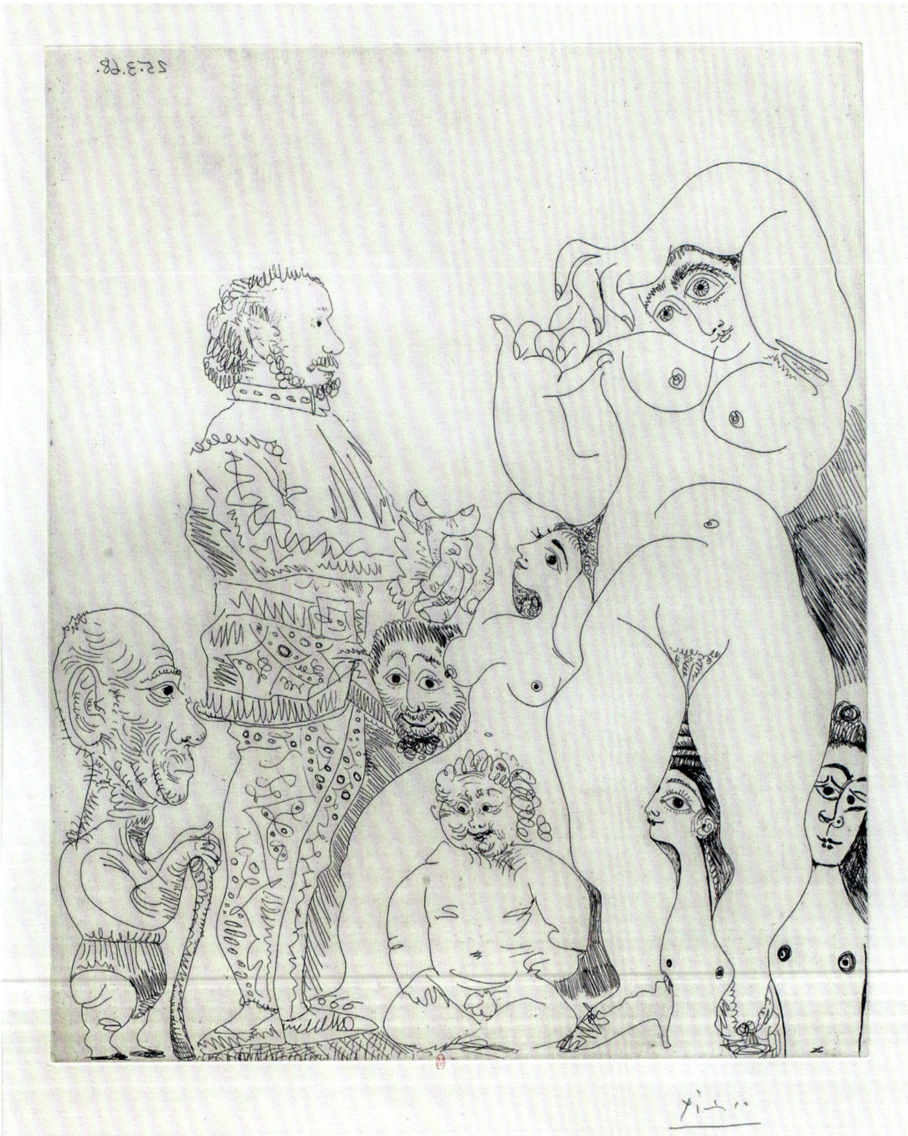

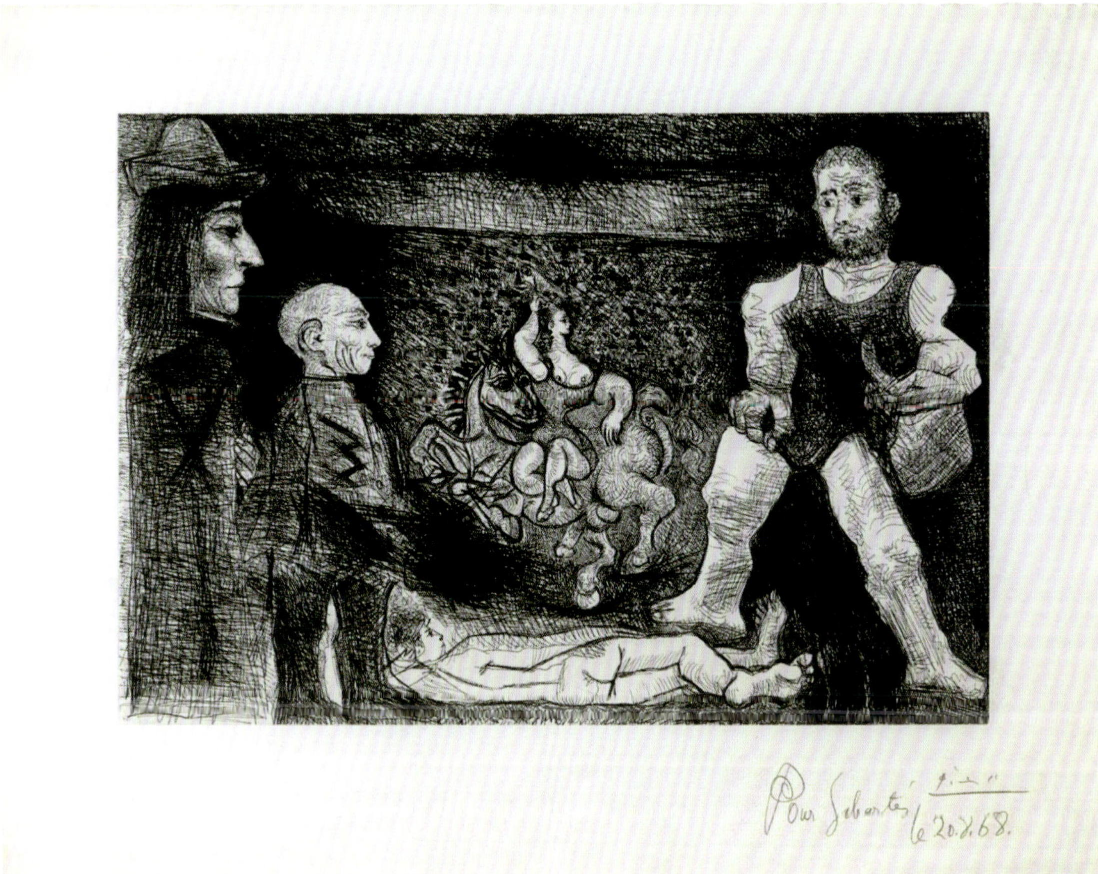
Pour Sabartés

1972

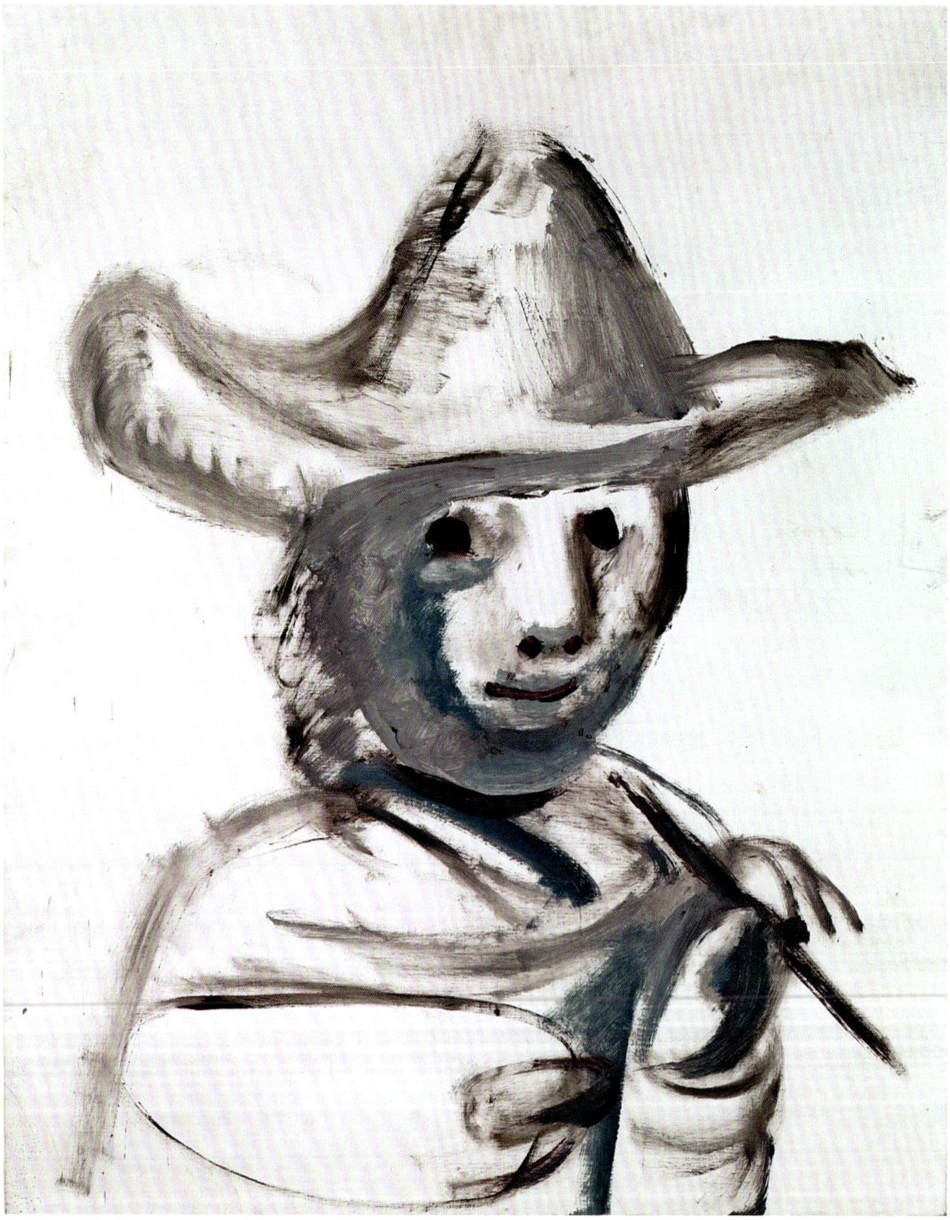

165

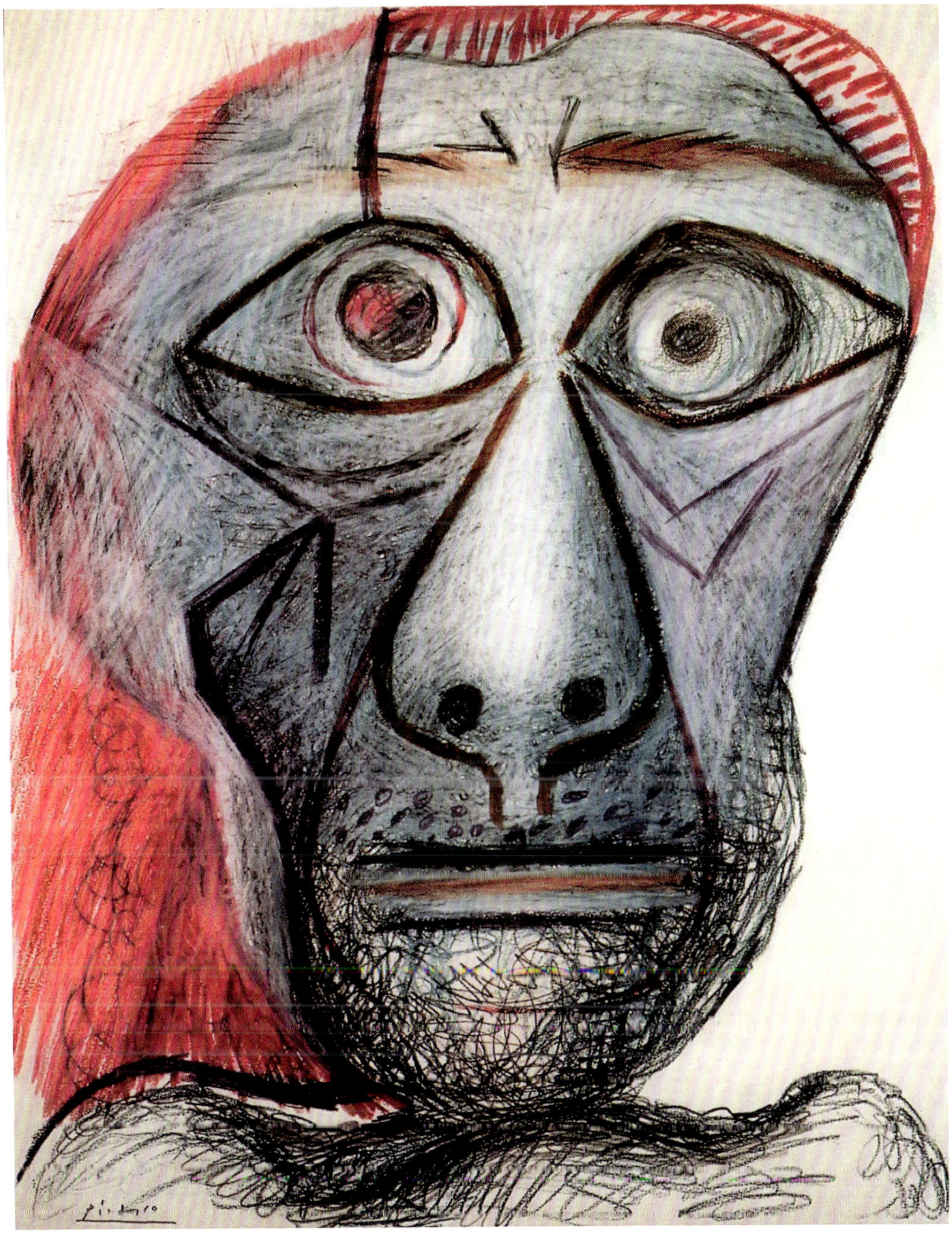

1972

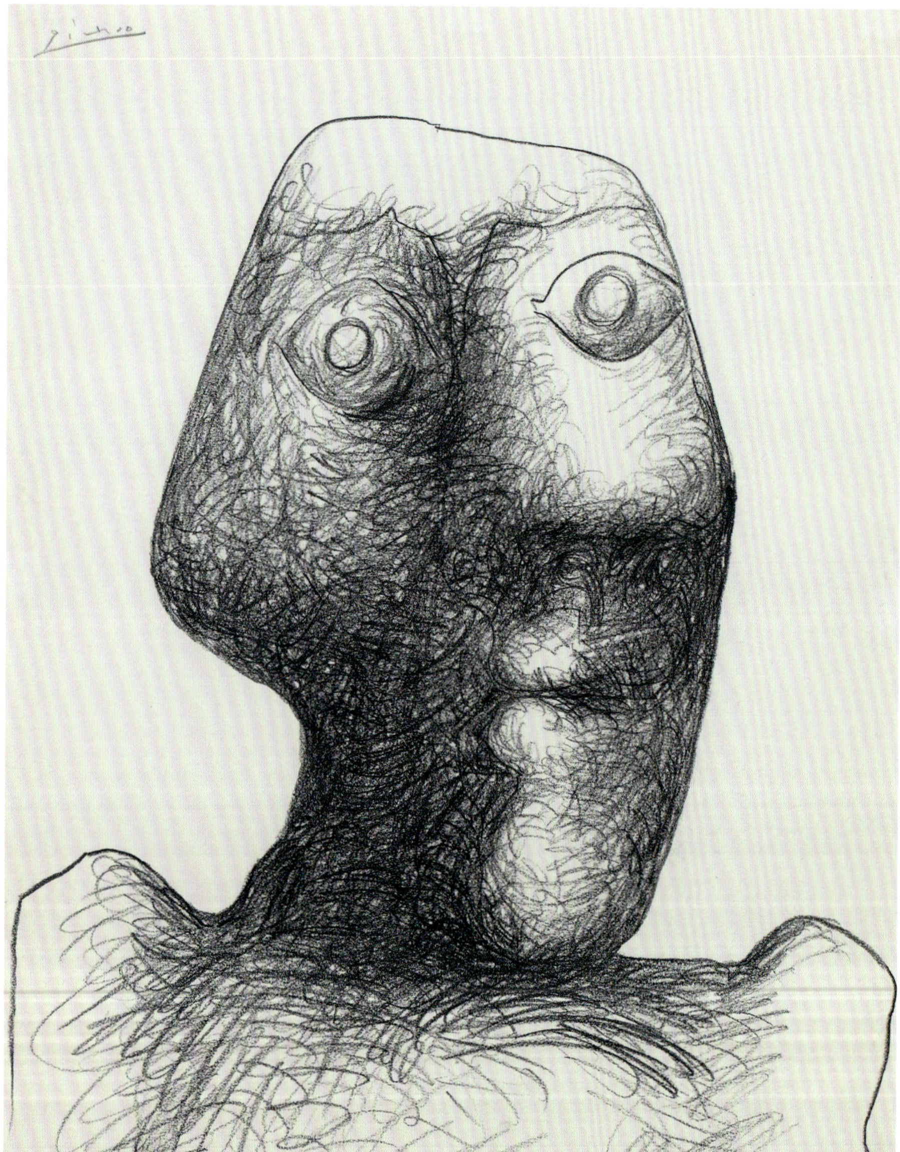

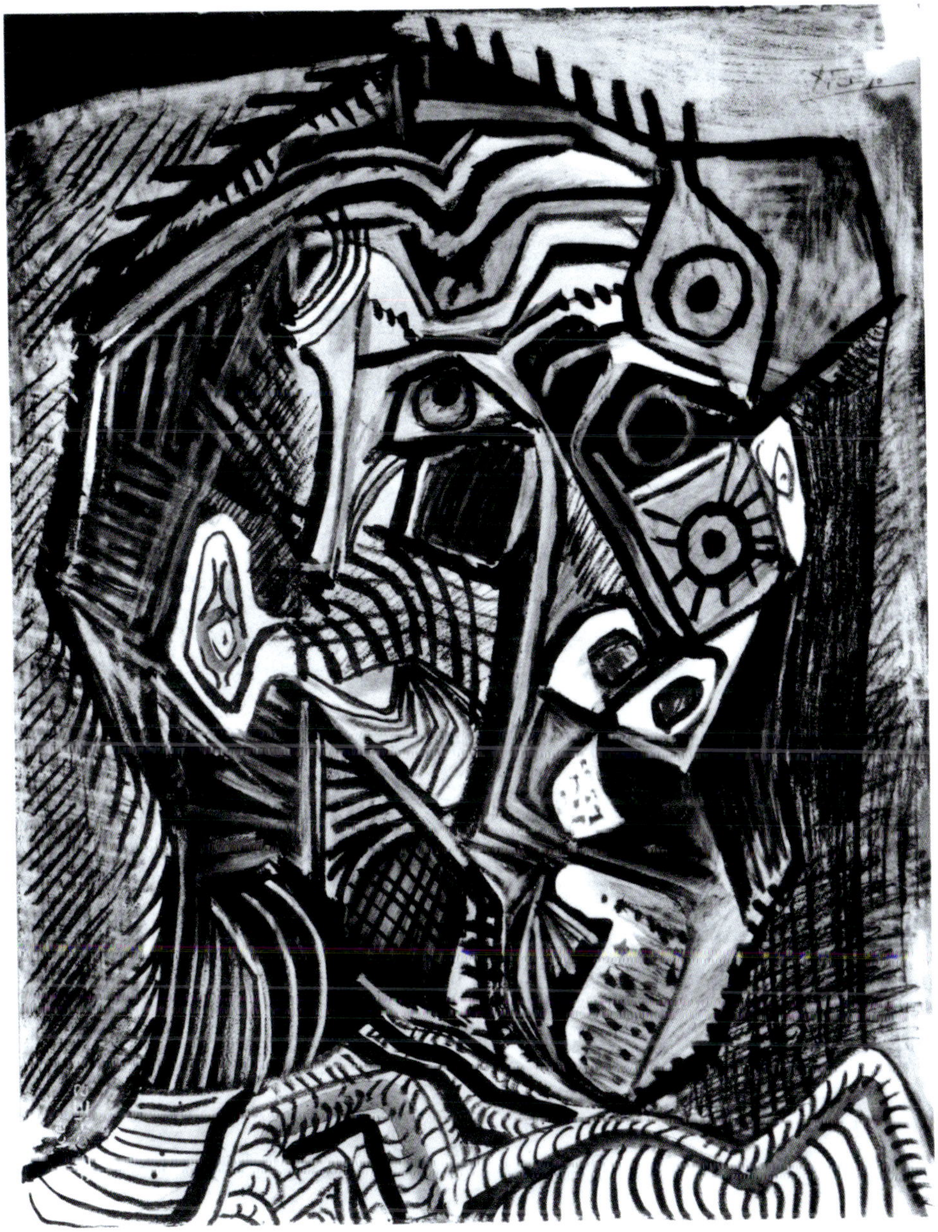

1972

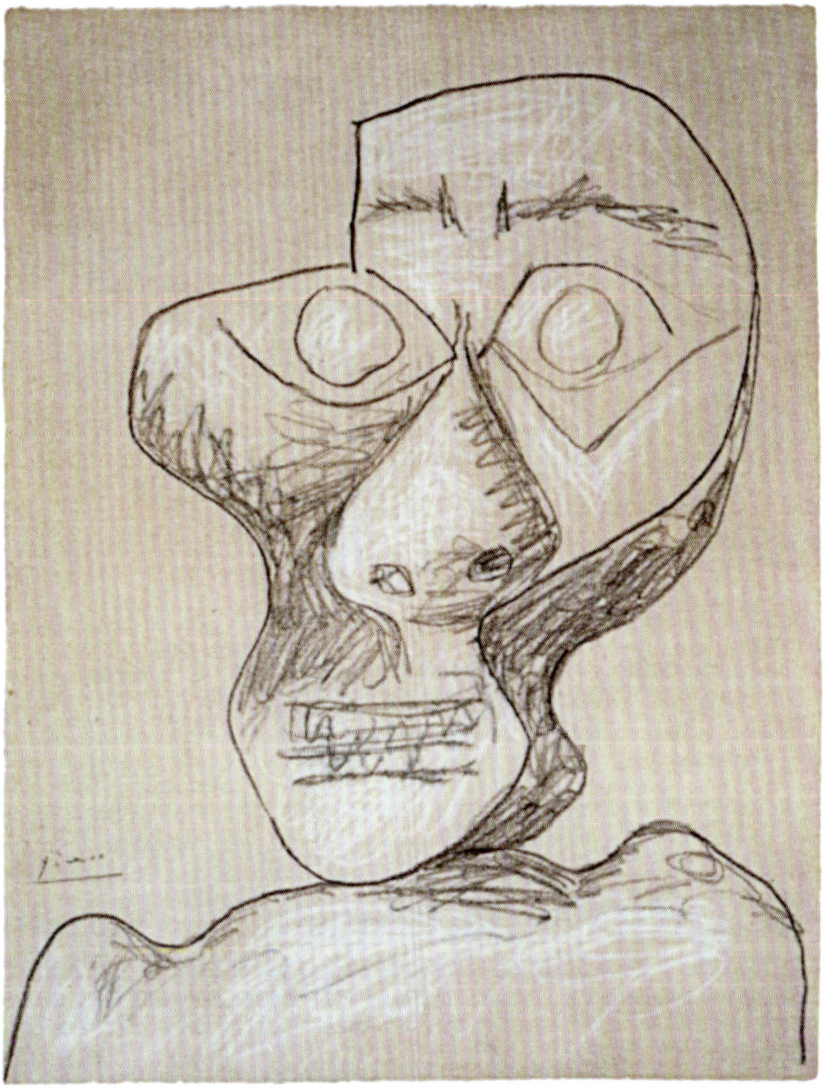

169

List of illustrations

Despite meticulous research, it has not been possible to establish the medium or dimensions of some of the works listed below, nor to determine the present location of certain ones.

1 Pablo Picasso, *Self-Portrait*, 1917, pencil on paper, 34 × 23.5 cm. Private collection.

2 Pablo Picasso, *Seated Child*, 1895, graphite pencil and fixative stains on paper, 19 × 12.6 cm. Barcelona, Museu Picasso.

3 Pablo Picasso, *Self-Portrait*, 1896, pen and ink on paper, 13.5 × 10.5 cm. Private collection.

4 Pablo Picasso, *Self-Portrait Painting*, *c.*1896, pen and ink on laid paper, 31 × 24.7 cm. Barcelona, Museu Picasso.

5 Pablo Picasso, *Self-Portraits and Caricature of Mariano Benlliure*, *c.*1896, pen and ink on laid paper, 31 × 24.7 cm, Barcelona, Museu Picasso.

6 Pablo Picasso, *Self-Portrait*, 1896, oil on canvas, 46.5 × 31.5 cm. Barcelona, Museu Picasso.

7 Pablo Picasso, *Self-Portrait*, 1896, oil on canvas, 22.1 × 13.7 cm. Barcelona, Museu Picasso.

8 Pablo Picasso, *Self-Portrait*, 1896, oil on canvas, 32.9 × 24 cm. Barcelona, Museu Picasso.

9 Pablo Picasso, *Self-Portrait*, 1897, charcoal and brown pencil on paper, 22 × 13 cm. Private collection.

10 Pablo Picasso, *Self-Portrait*, 1897, Conté crayon on paper, 31.6 × 21.8 cm. Barcelona, Museu Picasso.

11 Pablo Picasso, *Perplexed Picasso*, 1897, Conté crayon on paper, 32 × 24.7 cm. Private collection.

12 *Self-Portrait* (page of studies), 1897, Conté crayon on paper, 23.5 × 33 cm. Private collection.

13 Pablo Picasso, *The Artist Drawing and Study of Hands*, 1897–9, charcoal on paper, 33.2 × 23.4 cm. Paris, Musée national Picasso.

14 Pablo Picasso, *Self-Portrait, Study of an Ear and Hands*, 1898, Conté crayon and sanguine on paper, 10.5 × 5.8 cm. Barcelona, Museu Picasso.

15 Pablo Picasso, *Self-Portrait*, 1899, charcoal on paper, 42 × 51.3 cm. Private collection.

16 Pablo Picasso, *Self-Portrait*, 1899, Conté crayon on paper. Private collection.

17 Pablo Picasso, 1899, *Self-Portrait*, pencil on paper, 39.5 × 27.5 cm. Madrid, Fundación Almine y Bernard Ruiz-Picasso para el Arte.

18 Pablo Picasso, *Self-Portrait and Sketch of Fuerte*, 1899, ink and pencil on paper, 32 × 22 cm. Barcelona, Museu Picasso.

19 Pablo Picasso, *Self-Portrait*, 1899–1900, Conté crayon, charcoal and metallic paint on paper, 20.2 × 15.3 cm. Barcelona, Museu Picasso.

20 Pablo Picasso, *Chiaroscuro Self-Portrait, and Other Sketches*, 1899–1900, Conté crayon, brush and ink, and wash on laid paper, 48 × 43 cm. Barcelona, Museu Picasso.

21 Pablo Picasso, *Picasso and Manuel Pallarès, Self-Portrait and Studies*, 1899–1900, pencil and pen and ink on paper, 33.2 × 24.4 cm. Paris, Musée national Picasso.

22 Pablo Picasso, *Self-Portrait*, 1899–1900, watercolour and pen and ink on paper, 20.7 × 13.1 cm. Barcelona, Museu Picasso.

23 Pablo Picasso, *Yo*, 1900, ink and watercolour on paper, 9.5 × 8.6 cm. New York, Metropolitan Museum of Art.

24 Pablo Picasso, *Manuel Pallarès and Picasso*, *c.*1900, pen and ink on paper, 13.3 × 21 cm. Barcelona, Museu Picasso.

25 Pablo Picasso, *Picasso and Pallarès as 'Modernistes', Grecoesque Head and Other Sketches*, 1900, Conté crayon on paper, 16.9 × 22.7 cm. Barcelona, Museu Picasso.

26 Pablo Picasso, *Carles Casagemas and Picasso Following Two Girls*, 1900, pen and ink, watercolour, and gouache on paper pasted onto cardboard, 38 × 43 cm. Barcelona, Museu Picasso.

27 Pablo Picasso, *Picasso Presenting Casagemas to Rosita*, 1900, watercolour and Chinese ink on paper, 14 × 10 cm, Catalogue Zervos, vol. 21, image 143. Private collection.

28 Pablo Picasso, *Self-Portrait*, 1900, Conté crayon on paper, 10.5 × 5.8 cm. Barcelona, Museu Picasso.

29 Pablo Picasso, *Self-Portrait in a Wig*, 1900, oil on canvas, 55.8 × 45.8 cm. Barcelona, Museu Picasso.

30 Pablo Picasso, *Self-Portrait*, 1900, charcoal on paper, 22.5 × 16.5 cm. Barcelona, Museu Picasso.

31 Pablo Picasso, *Self-Portrait*, 1900, Conté crayon on paper, 33.8 × 23.4 cm. Barcelona, Museu Picasso.

32 Pablo Picasso, *Self-Portrait and Studies for a Poster for the Caja de Previsión y Socorro*, 1900, Barcelona, pen and ink and brushstrokes of watercolour on paper, 22.2 × 32 cm. Barcelona, Museu Picasso.

33 Pablo Picasso, *Picasso and Manuel Pallarès in Paris*, 1900, pen and ink on paper, 8.8 × 11.1 cm. Barcelona, Museu Picasso.

34 Pablo Picasso, *Self-Portrait*, before 1900, Conté crayon on paper, 31 × 16 cm, Catalogue Zervos, vol. 22, p. 38. Private collection.

35 Pablo Picasso, *Self Portrait*, published in *Arte Joven*, no. 1, 31 March 1901, Barcelona, Biblioteca de Catalunya.

36 Pablo Picasso, *Self-Portrait*, published in *Arte Joven*, no. 4, 1 June 1901, Barcelona, Biblioteca de Catalunya.

37 Pablo Picasso, *Bohemians from Madrid (Group of Artists)*, 1901, charcoal on paper, 24.5 × 32 cm. Barcelona, Museu Picasso.

38 Pablo Picasso, *Sketch for a Self-Portrait*, 1901, Chinese ink on paper, 31 × 20 cm. Private collection.

39 Pablo Picasso, *Profile*, 1901, ink on paper, 21 × 13 cm. Private collection.

40 Pablo Picasso, *Madrid: Notas de Arte*, 1901, charcoal, drawing for the announcement of the book *Madrid: Notas de Arte*, by Soler and Picasso, Catalogue Zervos, vol. 6, image 357. Private collection.

41 Pablo Picasso, *Picasso, Mañach, and Fuster in the Studio on Boulevard de Clichy*, 1901. On the left, a portrait of Iturrino; below the painting on the back wall, pages from *Arte Joven* and a sketch (now lost) for the Moulin de la Galette. Photograph Succession Picasso.

42 and 43 Pablo Picasso, letter to Miquel Utrillo, June 1901, ink and coloured pencil on paper, 18 × 11.5 cm. Private collection.

44 Pablo Picasso, *Self-Portrait outside the Moulin Rouge*, 1901, ink and coloured pencil on paper, 18 × 11.5 cm. Private collection.

45 Pablo Picasso, *Picasso and Jaume Andreu Bonsons Arriving in Paris*, 1901, ink and coloured pencil on paper, 33 × 38 cm. Berlin, Museum Berggruen.

46 Pablo Picasso, *Sketch for Yo Picasso*, 1901, pastel and charcoal on cardboard, 67.8 × 52 cm. Private collection.

47 Pablo Picasso, *Yo Picasso*, 1901, oil on canvas, 73.5 × 60.5 cm. Private collection.

48 *Pablo Picasso superimposed with canvases hung on the wall of the studio at 130 ter Boulevard de Clichy*, Paris, 1901 (anonymous photograph). Paris, Musée national Picasso.

49 Pablo Picasso, *Picasso with a Woman*, 1901, ink and watercolour on paper, 17.3 × 13 cm. Private collection.

50 Pablo Picasso, *Self-Portrait in Top Hat*, 1901, oil on canvas, 50 × 33 cm. Private collection.

51 Pablo Picasso, *Self-Portrait*, 1901, on cardboard mounted on wood, 51.4 × 31.8 cm. New York, Museum of Modern Art.

52 Pablo Picasso, *Self-Portrait*, 1901, pen and ink on cardboard, 12.8 × 9.8 cm. Barcelona, Museu Picasso.

53 Pablo Picasso, *Self-Portrait*, 1901, oil on canvas, 81 × 60 cm. Paris, Musée national Picasso.

54 Pablo Picasso, *Self-Portrait*, 1902, pen and ink on paper, 32.5 × 19 cm. Barcelona, Museu Picasso.

55 Pablo Picasso, *Brothel Scene with Self-Portrait*, 1901. Florence, shown in the exhibition *Picasso e dintorni*.

56 Pablo Picasso, *Hand of Picasso, Head of Max Jacob, and Cheiromantic Study with the Keys to Interpretation*, 1902, graphite pencil and pen and ink on paper, 29.6 × 19 cm. Barcelona, Museu Picasso.

57 Pablo Picasso, *Self-Portrait*, 1901/2, black chalk and watercolour on wove paper, 30.4 × 23.8 cm. Washington, National Gallery of Art.

58 Pablo Picasso, *Poster for Els Quatre Gats with self-portrait*, 1902, pen and ink on paper, 31 × 34 cm. In the foreground, the artist and Pere Romeu's dog; background, from left to right, Pere Romeu, Rocarol, Fontbona, Àngel F. de Soto, Sabartés. Private collection.

59 Pablo Picasso, *Picasso, Àngel Fernández de Soto, and Sebastià Junyer-Vidal in a Café*, c.1903, pen and ink on paper, 13.3 × .19 cm. Barcelona, Museu Picasso.

60 and 61 Pablo Picasso, letter to Max Jacob with two self-portraits (front and back), 1902. Private collection.

62 Pablo Picasso, *The Artist Nude by the Seaside*, 1902, coloured wax crayons and pen and brown ink on cardboard, 9 × 13.3 cm. Christie's Images.

63 Pablo Picasso, *Self-Portrait with Nude*, 1902, ink and coloured pencils on paper, 9 × 13.3 cm. Private collection.

64 Pablo Picasso, *Self-Portrait with Reclining Nude*, 1902–3, pen, wash, and coloured pencil on printed Bristol paper, 17.8 × 23.4 cm. Barcelona, Museu Picasso.

65 Pablo Picasso, *Self-Portrait and Woman*, *c.*1903, ink and coloured pencils on paper, 8 × 12 cm. Private collection.

66 Pablo Picasso, *Parody of Olympia*, 1902–3, 15.3 × 22 cm. Private collection.

67 Pablo Picasso, *Self-Portrait with Two Nudes*, 1903, pen and ink, Chinese white, and blue chalk on paper, 20 × 11.4 cm. Wadsworth Atheneum Museum of Art.

68 Pablo Picasso, *Self-Portrait with Arm Raised*, 1902–3, pencil on paper, 27.3 × 20.3 cm. Private collection.

69 Pablo Picasso, *Self-Portrait*, 1902–3, pen and ink on paper, 16 × 11 cm. Catalogue Zervos, vol. 6, image 556. Éditions Cahiers d'Art, Paris, 2021.

70 Pablo Picasso, *Self-Portrait with a Moustache*, 1903, ink on paper, 14 × 11 cm, Catalogue Zervos, vol. 22, image 38. Éditions Cahiers d'Art, Paris, 2021.

71 Pablo Picasso, *Self-Portrait*, 1903, ink on paper, 11 × 10.7 cm. Barcelona, Museu Picasso.

72 Pablo Picasso, *Self-Portrait with a Dog*, 1903. Catalogue Zervos, vol. 1, image 196. Éditions Cahiers d'Art, Paris, 2021.

73 Pablo Picasso, *Erotic Scene (La Douceur)*, 1903, oil on canvas, 70.2 × 55.6 cm. New York, Metropolitan Museum of Art.

74 Pablo Picasso, *Self-Portrait as a Pharaoh*, 1903–4, Chinese ink and coloured pencils on paper, 26 × 36 cm. Private collection.

75 Pablo Picasso, *Study for La Vie*, 1903, Chinese ink on paper, 26 × 19.7 cm, Catalogue Zervos, vol. 22, image 44. Collection Roland Penrose.

76 Pablo Picasso, *Study for La Vie*, 1903, fountain pen and ink on wove paper, 15.9 × 11.1 cm. Paris, Musée national Picasso.

77 Pablo Picasso, *Standing Self-Portrait*, 1903–4, ink on paper, 33.8 × 26.7 cm. Cambridge, Mass., Fogg Museum, Harvard Art Museums.

78 Pablo Picasso, *Picasso and Sebastià Junyer-Vidal Sitting Beside La Célestine*, 1903–4, wax crayon on paper, 25 × 32.9 cm. Private collection.

79 Pablo Picasso, *Picasso Painting La Célestine*, 1904, Conté crayon on paper, Catalogue Zervos, vol. 22, image 56.

80 Pablo Picasso, *Picasso and Sebastià Junyer-Vidal Set off on a Journey*, 1904, pen and ink and coloured pencils on paper, 22 × 16 cm. Barcelona, Museu Picasso.

81 Pablo Picasso, *Picasso and Sebastià Junyer-Vidal Arrive at the Border*, 1904, pen and ink and coloured pencils on paper, 22 × 16 cm. Barcelona, Museu Picasso.

82 Pablo Picasso, *Picasso and Sebastià Junyer-Vidal Reach Montauban*, 1904, pen and ink and coloured pencils on paper, 22 × 16 cm. Barcelona, Museu Picasso.

83 Pablo Picasso, *Picasso and Sebastià Junyer-Vidal Arrive in Paris*, 1904, pen and ink and coloured pencils on paper, 22 × 16 cm. Barcelona, Museu Picasso.

84 Pablo Picasso, *Sebastià Junyer-Vidal Calls on Durand-Ruel*, 1904, pen and ink and coloured pencils on paper, 22 × 16 cm. Barcelona, Museu Picasso.

85 Pablo Picasso, *Self-Portrait*, 1904, cutting from *El Liberal*, 24 March 1904. Barcelona City Archive.

86 Pablo Picasso, *Self-Portrait*, 1904, cutting from *La Tribuna*, 24 March 1904. Barcelona City Archive.

87 Pablo Picasso, *Picasso by Himself*, 1904, chalk and pastel on paper, 25.3 × 33 cm. Private collection.

88 Pablo Picasso, *Self-Portrait*, 1904, pen and ink on paper, dedicated to Max Jacob. Stockholm, Moderna Museet.

89 Pablo Picasso, *Portrait of Ricard Canals,* 1904, 15.3 × 17.7 cm. Paris, Musée national Picasso.

90 Pablo Picasso, *Meditation (Contemplation)*, 1904, watercolour and ink on paper, 36.9 × 26.7 cm. New York, Museum of Modern Art.

91 Pablo Picasso, *Picasso and Max Jacob*, 1904, ink on paper. Paris, Musée national Picasso.

92 Pablo Picasso, *Sketch: woman with Dutch hairstyle, other heads, inscriptions*, 1905, pen and ink on paper, 12 × 9.5 cm. Paris, Musée national Picasso.

93 and 94 Pablo Picasso, *Self-Portrait with Max Jacob*, 1904, pen and ink on paper, letter addressed to Suzanne Bloch. Location unknown.

95 Pablo Picasso, *Male Nude and Picasso in Profile*, 1904, Chinese ink on paper, 37 × 27 cm. Collection Maurice Aeschimann.

96 Pablo Picasso, *Self-Portrait with a Hat*, 1904–5, ink and watercolour on paper, 17 × 10.5 cm. Berlin, Museum Berggruen.

97 Pablo Picasso, *Au Lapin Agile*, 1905, oil on canvas, 100.3 × 99.1 cm. New York, Sotheby's.

98 Pablo Picasso, *Family of Saltimbanques*, 1905, oil on canvas, 212.8 × 229.6 cm. Washington, National Gallery of Art.

99 Pablo Picasso, *Self-Portrait*, 1906, charcoal on paper, 25 × 23 cm. Collection Maurice Aeschimann.

100 Pablo Picasso, *Studies for Self-Portraits*, 1906, lead pencil on paper, 31 × 47 cm. Paris, Musée national Picasso.

101 Pablo Picasso, *Studies for Self-Portraits*, 1906, pencil on paper, dimensions unknown (approximately 31 × 47 cm). Private collection.

102 Pablo Picasso, *Studies for Self-Portraits*, 1906, pencil on paper, dimensions unknown (approximately 31 × 47 cm). Private collection.

103 Pablo Picasso, *Studies for Self-Portraits*, 1906, graphite pencil on laid paper, 31.5 × 47.5 cm. Paris, Musée national Picasso.

104 Pablo Picasso, *Studies for Self-Portraits*, 1906, graphite pencil on laid paper, 32.5 × 48.2 cm. Paris, Musée national Picasso.

105 Pablo Picasso, *Studies for Self-Portraits*, 1906, graphite pencil on laid paper, 32.5 × 48.2 cm. Paris, Musée national Picasso.

106 Arlette Perrenoud, *Picasso's Studio at Notre-Dame-de-Vie*, 1971.

107 Pablo Picasso, *Self-Portrait*, 1906, oil on canvas, 6.5 × 5.4 cm, Paris, Musée national Picasso.

108 Pablo Picasso, *Study for Self-Portrait with Palette*, 1906, Paris, Musée national Picasso.

109 Pablo Picasso, *Self-Portrait with Palette*, 1906, oil on canvas, 91.9 × 73.3 cm. Philadelphia, Museum of Art.

110 Pablo Picasso, *Self-Portrait*, 1906, pen and ink on paper, 31.8 × 24.1 cm. Santa Barbara Museum of Art.

111 Pablo Picasso, *Self-Portrait*, 1906, oil on canvas, 39 × 30 cm. Private collection.

112 Pablo Picasso, *Self-Portrait*, 1906, oil on canvas mounted on honeycomb panel, 26.7 × 19.7 cm. New York, Metropolitan Museum of Art.

113 Pablo Picasso, *Self-Portraits*, on a cutting from *Le Matin*, 30 December 1906, charcoal and Conté crayon, 33.7 × 13.5 cm. Paris, Musée national Picasso.

114 Pablo Picasso, *Study of Hand for Les Demoiselles d'Avignon*, 1907, ink, pastel, pencil, and charcoal on Ingres paper, 19.5 × 24.3 cm. Paris, Musée national Picasso.

115 Pablo Picasso, *Study of Hand for Les Demoiselles d'Avignon*, 1907, ink, pastel, pencil, and charcoal on Ingres paper, 19.5 × 24.3 cm. Paris, Musée national Picasso.

116 Pablo Picasso, *Self-Portrait*, 1907, oil on canvas, 56 × 46 cm. Prague, National Gallery.

117 Pablo Picasso, sheet from notebook no. 15, 1908, pen and Chinese ink, coloured pencil, charcoal, and graphite pencil on laid paper, 21 × 13.5 cm, Paris, Musée national Picasso

118 Anonymous photograph, *Picasso, sitting in a bedroom at l'Auberge de la Trompette, in Horta de Sant Joan*, 1909, 11 × 8.6 cm. Paris, Musée national Picasso.

119 Anonymous photograph, *Picasso on a sofa in the studio at 11 Boulevard de Clichy, Paris*, December 1910, 14.7 × 11.6 cm. Paris, Musée national Picasso.

120 Anonymous photograph, *Picasso in the studio at 11 Boulevard de Clichy, Paris*, 1910, 6.5 × 9.8 cm. Paris, Musée national Picasso.

121 Anonymous photograph, *Picasso on a chaise longue, with the painting* L'Homme accoudé *in the studio at Rue Schœlcher, Paris, c.*1915–16. Paris, Musée national Picasso.

122 Anonymous photograph, *Picasso with brush and palette in front of the first state of the painting* Homme accoudé à une table, *painted in 1915, in the studio at Rue Schœlcher, Paris, c.*1915–16. Paris, Musée national Picasso.

123 Pablo Picasso, *Self-Portrait*, 1915, ink on envelope, 15 × 11 cm. Private collection.

124 Anonymous photograph, *Picasso in the studio at 5 bis Rue Schœlcher, Paris, c.*1915–16. On the left, *Guitare, clarinette et bouteille sur un guéridon*; in the background, *Homme accoudé à une table*. Collection Maurice Aeschimann.

125 Pablo Picasso, *Picasso in the studio at Rue Schœlcher, Paris, in shirt and patched work trousers, c.*1915–16. Private collection.

126 Pablo Picasso, *Picasso in the studio at Rue Schœlcher, Paris, in shorts and work shirt, c.*1915–16. In the background, *Homme assis au verre* in process. Paris, Musée national Picasso.

127 Pablo Picasso, *Picasso in the studio at Rue Schœlcher, Paris, in boxer's pose, c.*1915–16. Paris, Musée national Picasso.

128 Pablo Picasso, *Souvenir of our walk in Naples*, 20 April 1917, ink on paper, 19 × 14 cm. Paris, Musée national Picasso.

129 Pablo Picasso, *The Artists' Dining Room in Montrouge*, 9 December 1917, ink on paper, 27.7 × 22.6 cm. Paris, Musée national Picasso.

130 Pablo Picasso, *Self-Portrait, caricature*, 1917–18, ink on paper, 17.1 × 8.5 cm. Paris, Musée national Picasso.

131 Pablo Picasso, *Les Yeux de l'artiste*, 1917, pencil on wove paper, 9 × 5 cm. Private collection.

132 Pablo Picasso, *Self-Portrait*, 1917, graphite pencil on paper, 32 × 21.5 cm. Madrid, Fundación Almine y Bernard Ruiz-Picasso para el Arte.

133 Pablo Picasso, *Self-Portrait*, 1917, graphite pencil and charcoal on paper, 64 × 49.5 cm. Paris, Musée national Picasso.

134 Pablo Picasso, letter to Guillaume Apollinaire with a drawing of Picasso and Apollinaire toasting on the reverse, 16 August 1918, blue ink on paper, 2.7 × 2.12 cm. Paris, Musée national Picasso.

135 Pablo Picasso, *Self-Portrait*, letter to Jean Cocteau, 28 August 1918. Paris, Bibliothèque historique de la Ville de Paris.

136 Pablo Picasso, *Self-Portrait*, 1918, notebook page, lead pencil on paper, 14.2 × 9.5 cm. Madrid, Fundación Almine y Bernard Ruiz-Picasso para el Arte.

137 Pablo Picasso, *Self-Portrait*, 1918, pencil on paper, 34 × 26 cm. Private collection.

138 Pablo Picasso, *Hand*, 1919, notebook page, lead pencil on paper, 22.5 × 17.5 cm. Madrid, Fundación Almine y Bernard Ruiz- Picasso para el Arte.

139 Pablo Picasso, *Hand*, 1919, notebook page, lead pencil on paper, 22.5 × 17.5 cm. Madrid, Fundación Almine y Bernard Ruiz-Picasso para el Arte.

140 Pablo Picasso, *Hand*, 1919, notebook page, lead pencil on paper, 22.5 × 17.5 cm. Madrid, Fundación Almine y Bernard Ruiz-Picasso para el Arte.

141 Pablo Picasso, *Self-Portrait*, 1919, watercolour and graphite pencil on laid paper. Washington, National Gallery of Art.

142 Pablo Picasso, *Self-Portrait in the Mirror Cabinet*, 1921, 11.3 × 7.3 cm. Paris, Musée national Picasso.

143 Pablo Picasso, *Self-Portrait in Profile*, 1921, pencil on paper, 27 × 21 cm. Private collection.

144 Pablo Picasso, *Self-Portrait in Profile*, 1921, pencil on paper, 27 × 21 cm. Collection Catherine Hutin.

145 Pablo Picasso, *Nude in the Yellow Mirror*, 1927–8, oil on canvas, 65 × 28 cm. Collection Maurice Aeschimann.

146 Pablo Picasso, *Head of a Woman and Self-Portrait*, 1929, oil on canvas, 73 × 60 cm. Private collection, Courtesy McClain Gallery.

147 Pablo Picasso, *The Artist in Front of His Canvas*, 1938, charcoal on canvas, 130 × 94 cm. Paris, Musée national Picasso.

148 Pablo Picasso, *Maya in a Sailor Suit* (*The Sailor*), 1938, oil on canvas, 121.6 × 86.3 cm. New York, Museum of Modern Art.

149 Pablo Picasso, *In the Studio at Les Voiliers, Royan, the face of the artist reflected in the mirror, between sketches for portraits of Dora Maar*, 1940, 17.3 × 12.1 cm. Paris, Musée national Picasso.

150 Pablo Picasso, *Self-Portrait*, 11 August 1940, pencil on paper, 16 × 11 cm. Cologne, Museum Ludwig.

151 Pablo Picasso, *Self-Portrait*, 11 August 1940, pencil on paper, 16 × 11 cm, Catalogue Zervos, vol. 11, image 82. Éditions Cahiers d'Art, Paris, 2021.

152 Pablo Picasso, *Self-Portrait*, 1941, ink on paper, 31.5 × 23.8 cm, reproduced in *Le Désir attrapé par la queue* (Desire caught by the tail), published in *Message*, no. 3, 1944. Paris, Musée national Picasso.

153 Brassaï, *Impression of the right hand of Picasso*, 1942, 23.5 × 17.8 cm. Paris, Musée national Picasso.

154 Brassaï, *The Clenched Fist of Picasso*, 1943, 12.3 × 17.3 cm. Paris, Musée national Picasso.

155 Pablo Picasso, *Le Marin*, 28 October 1943, oil on canvas, 129.3 × 80.7 cm. Private collection.

156 Pablo Picasso, *The Dazzled Sun*, 29 July 1951, 28 × 39 cm. Private collection.

157 Pablo Picasso, *The Shadow*, 29 December 1953, charcoal on canvas, 129.5 × 96.5 cm. Paris, Musée national Picasso.

158 Pablo Picasso, *The Shadow on the Woman*, 29 December 1953, oil on canvas, 103.9 × 97.7 cm, Jerusalem, Israel Museum.

159 Pablo Picasso, *Self-Portrait*, 1955, ink on paper carton, 39.7 × 31.8 cm. Private collection.

160 Pablo Picasso, letter to Jean Cocteau, 8 November 1962. Private collection.

161 Pablo Picasso, *Seated Man*, 26 December 1966, bistre pencil on paper, 55 × 46 cm. Hakone, Japan, Hakone Open Air Museum.

162 Pablo Picasso, *Seated Man*, 3 April 1966, 100 × 81 cm. Private collection.

163 Pablo Picasso, *Self-Portrait with a cane, with actors in costume, Amour and women*, 25 March 1968, etching. Private collection.

164 Pablo Picasso, *Picasso, His Work, and His Public*, 22 March 1968, etching. New York, Museum of Modern Art.

165 Pablo Picasso, *The Young Painter*, 1972, oil on canvas, 91 × 72.5 cm. Paris, Musée national Picasso.

166 Pablo Picasso, *Self Portrait*, 30 June 1972, wax crayon on paper. Picasso Project, Sam Houston State University.

167 Pablo Picasso, *Self-Portrait*, 3 July 1972. Private collection.

168 Pablo Picasso, *Self-Portrait*, 28 June to 4 July 1972, 65.7 × 50.5 cm, coloured crayon, gouache, India ink and ink wash on paper. Éditions Cahiers d'Art, Paris, 2021.

169 Pablo Picasso, *Self-Portrait*, 3 July 1972, oil crayon white chalk on paper, 66 × 49 cm. Private collection.

Prologue by Cervantes

to a bibliography that cannot and does not wish to claim to be complete

To celebrate the 350th anniversary of the French translation of the first part of Miguel de Cervantes's *Don Quixote*, Louis Aragon asked Picasso to draw a picture for *Les Lettres françaises*. It appeared in the edition dated 18–24 August 1955. It shows Don Quixote de la Mancha riding Rocinante alongside Sancho Panza on his donkey, with windmills in the background. Above them is a sun with dancing rays of light.

Now that I dare to claim my book is finished, how can I not worry that it will prove to be 'devoid of artifice, diminished in style, poor in conceits, lacking in all erudition and doctrine, and without marginal citations and annotations at the end that I see in other books, even in the novelistic and secular ones, filled with maxims of Aristotle, Plato and the whole multitude of philosophers, that amaze the readers and make their authors appear well-read, erudite and eloquent?'

What is more, I must admit that 'I have no citations for the margins, nor any notes to put at the end, and I know even less which authors to put at the beginning in alphabetical order, like everyone else does, starting with Aristotle and ending with Xenophon and Zoilus or Zeuxis, although the former was a slanderer and the latter was a painter.'

Although I have refrained from adding footnotes or citations in the margins and I have often wondered which authors I should quote (or not), I have judged it appropriate to quote Cervantes's 'Prologue' here as a kind of warning.

The sheer number of books written about Picasso is comparable to the numbers written about Joan of Arc and Napoleon. Therefore the following bibliography includes only the works (biographies, essays, exhibition catalogues, etc.) that I consulted, read and reread. Although not all of them. Because sometimes, perhaps too often, I forgot to write down in my notebooks the names of authors and the titles of books that I read.

If it seems to you, my well-informed reader who is familiar with the work of Picasso, that such and such a title is missing, 'the cure is very simple – all you have to do is look for a book that lists references from A to Z'. A little piece of advice from Cervantes.

Sometimes, reading certain texts 'brought me back' to Picasso in the most unexpected ways. For example, *Goût du vrai* by Étienne Klein (Tracts Gallimard, no. 17, July 2020). On page 36, note 9, it says: 'As Paul La Porte writes in "Cubism and Relativity, with a letter of Albert Einstein" *Art Journal*, 25, no. 3, 1966, p. 246', a very precise citation that allowed me to quote Einstein. Another fortuitous example, which seemed at first to have nothing to do with Picasso, was Caroline Fourest's book *Génération offensée, de la police de la culture à la police de la pensée* (Grasset, Paris, 2020), in which she quoted Madonna on page 29, with a footnote giving the source: Matthew Jacobs, 'From 'Hell' And Back, Madonna Lives To Tell', *Huffpost*, 13 March 2015.

Bibliography

Alberti, Leon Battista, *On Painting* (1435), edited and introduction by Martin Kemp, translated by Cecil Grayson, London, Penguin Classics, 1991.

Anthologie bilingue de la poésie espagnole, edited and introduction by Nadine Ly, Paris, Gallimard, 'Bibliothèque de la Pléiade', 1995.

Apollinaire, Guillaume, *Œuvres en prose complètes II*, edited and annotated by Pierre Caizergues and Michel Décaudin, Paris, Gallimard, 'Bibliothèque de la Pléiade', 1991.

Apuleius, *Apologia. Florida. De Deo Socratis*, edited and translated by Christopher P. Jones, Cambridge, Mass., Harvard University Press, 2017.

Aragon, Louis, *Écrits sur l'art moderne*, edited by Jean Ristat, preface by Jacques Leenhardt, Paris, Flammarion, 1981.

Arasse, Daniel, *Léonard de Vinci*, Paris, Hazan, 1997.

Barthes, Roland, inaugural lesson delivered Friday, 7 January 1977, Paris, Collège de France, 1977.

Brassaï, *Conversations avec Picasso*, Paris, Gallimard, 'Idées', 1964; republished, 1997.

Breton, André, 'Écrits sur l'art et autres textes', in *Œuvres complètes IV*, Paris, Gallimard, 'Bibliothèque de la Pléiade', 2008.

Cabanne, Pierre, *Le Siècle de Picasso*, four volumes, Paris, Gallimard, 'Folio essais', 1992.

Camus, Albert, *Essais*, edited and annotated by Roger Quilliot and Louis Faucon, Paris, Gallimard, 'Bibliothèque de la Pléiade', 1965.

Cassou, Jean, *Panorama des arts plastiques contemporains*, Paris, Gallimard, 'Le Point du Jour', 1960.

Cervantes, Miguel de, *Don Quixote*, translated by John Rutherford, London, Penguin, 2003.

Char, René, *Œuvres complètes*, introduction by Jean Roudaut, Paris, Gallimard, 'Bibliothèque de la Pléiade', 1983.

Chauveau, Sophie, *Picasso, le Minotaure*, Paris, Gallimard, 'Folio', 2020.

Clair, Jean, *Cinq Repentirs de Pablo Picasso*, Paris, L'Échoppe, 2000.

Clair, Jean, *Picasso et le cirque: Parade et palingénésie*, Paris, L'Échoppe, 2014.

Claudel, Paul, *Œuvres en prose*, preface by Gaëtan Picon, edited and annotated by Jacques Petit and Charles Galpérine, Paris, Gallimard, 'Bibliothèque de la Pléiade', 1965.

Cocteau, Jean, *Picasso: Le Potomak – Le Grand Écart*, illustrations by Pablo Picasso, Jean Cocteau, and Leila Mikaeloff, Paris, Éditions Rombaldi, 1971.

Cocteau, Jean, *Œuvres poétiques complètes*, edited by Michel Décaudin, Paris, Gallimard, 'Bibliothèque de la Pléiade', 1999.

Cogniat, Raymond, *Picasso, Braque, Léger racontent leurs débuts*, Paris, L'Échoppe, 2019.

Daix, Pierre, *Picasso au Bateau-Lavoir*, Paris, Flammarion, 1994.

Daix, Pierre, *Dictionnaire Picasso*, Paris, Robert Laffont, 'Bouquins', 1995.

Desnos, Robert, *Écrits sur les peintres*, Paris, Flammarion, 1984.

Diderot, Denis, *Œuvres*, edited and annotated by André Billy, Paris, Gallimard, 'Bibliothèque de la Pléiade', 1951.

Éluard, Paul, *Œuvres complètes I et II*, edited and annotated by Marcelle Dumas and Lucien Scheler, Paris, Gallimard, 'Bibliothèque de la Pléiade', 1968.

Faure, Élie, *Œuvres complètes, Tome 3: Œuvres diverses, Essais et Correspondance*, Paris, Jean-Jacques Pauvert, 1964.

Garouste, Gérard (with Judith Perrignon), *L'Intranquille: Autoportrait d'un fils, d'un peintre, d'un fou*, Paris, L'Iconoclaste, 2009.

Gide, André, *Journal 1889–1939*, Paris, Gallimard, 'Bibliothèque de la Pléiade', 1939.

Gide, André, *Journal* (new edition), Volume I: 1887–1925, Paris, Gallimard, 'Bibliothèque de la Pléiade', 1996.

Gilot, Françoise and **Lake**, Carlton, *Vivre avec Picasso*, Paris, Calmann-Lévy, 1965, republished 1991.

Kahnweiler, Daniel-Henry, *Huit entretiens avec Picasso*, Paris, L'Échoppe, 1988.

Kahnweiler, Daniel-Henry, *Entretiens avec Picasso au sujet des femmes d'Alger*, Paris, L'Échoppe, 1991.

Kahnweiler, Daniel-Henry, *Six entretiens avec Picasso*, Paris, L'Échoppe, 1995.

Kahnweiler, Daniel-Henry and **Crémieux**, Francis, *Mes galeries et mes peintres, entretiens*, Paris, Gallimard, 1998.

Laërtius, Diogenes, *Lives of Eminent Philosophers*, edited by Tiziano Dorandi, Cambridge, Cambridge Univeristy Press, 2017.

Le Bon, Laurent et al, *Picasso bleu et rose*, exhibition catalogue, Paris, Hazan, 2018.

Leiris, Michel, 'Picasso and the Human Comedy, or the Avatars of Big Foot' (1954), in *Brisées: Broken Branches*, translated by Lydia Davis, San Francisco, North Point Press, 1989 (originally published in *Verve*, vol. 8, no. 29–30, 'Suite de 180 dessins de Picasso').

Leiris, Michel, *Journal, 1922–1989*, Paris, Gallimard, 1992.

Les Stoïciens, edited by Pierre-Maxime Schuhl, Paris, Gallimard, 'Bibliothèque de la Pléiade', 1962.

Leymarie, Jean, *Picasso: The Artist of the Century*, London, Macmillan, 1972.

Limbour, Georges, *Dans le secret des ateliers*, Paris, L'Élocoquent, 1986.

Lord, James, *Un portrait par Giacometti*, suivi d'*Où étaient les tableaux: Mémoire sur Gertrude Stein et Alice Toklas*, Paris, Gallimard, 'Art et Artistes', 1991.

Mailer, Norman, *Portrait of Picasso As a Young Man: An Interpretive Biography*, New York, Grove, 1995.

Malraux, André, *Œuvres complètes III*, edited by Marius-François Guyard, Paris, Gallimard, 'Bibliothèque de la Pléiade', 1996.

Palau i Fabre, Josep, *Picasso, 1881–1907: Life and Work of the Early Years*, Oxford: Phaidon, 1981.

Parmelin, Hélène, *Histoire de Madame H. P.: Portrait d'Hélène Parmelin par Picasso*, Paris, Éditions Marval, 1996.

Penrose, Roland, *Picasso: His Life and Work*, 3rd edition, Berkeley and Los Angeles, University of California Press, 1982.

Pessoa, Fernando, *The Book of Disquiet*, London, Serpent's Tail, 2018.

Pessoa, Fernando, *Selected Poems*, London, Penguin, 2000.

Picasso, Pablo, *Picasso: Documents iconographiques*, with a preface and notes by Jaime Sabartés, Geneva, Pierre Cailler, 1954.

Picasso/Apollinaire Correspondance, edited by Pierre Caizergues and Hélène Seckel, Paris, Gallimard and Réunion des musées nationaux-Grand Palais, 1992.

Picasso/Cocteau Correspondance 1915–1963, edited by Pierre Caizergues and Ioannis Kontaxopoulos, Paris, Gallimard and Musée national Picasso, 2018.

Picasso/Stein Correspondance, edited by Laurence Madeline, Paris, Gallimard, 2005.

Picon, Gaëtan and **Picasso**, Pablo, *La Chute d'Icare*, Geneva, Skira, 1971.

Pojarskaïa, Militsa and **Volodina**, Tatiana, *L'Art des Ballets russes: Projets de décors et de costumes, 1908–1929*, Paris, Gallimard, 1990.

Prévert, Jacques, *Œuvres complètes I et II*, edited and annotated by Danièle Gasiglia-Laster and Arnaud Laster, Paris, Gallimard, 'Bibliothèque de la Pléiade', 1992–1996.

Roy, Claude, *L'Amour de la peinture*, Paris, Gallimard, 'Folio essais', 1987.

Sabartés, Jaime, *Picasso: Portraits et souvenirs*, Paris, Louis Carré and Maximilien Vox, 1946.

St Augustine, *Confessions*, translated by R. S. Pine-Coffin, London, Penguin, 2003.

Starobinski, Jean, *Portrait de l'artiste en saltimbanque*, Paris, Gallimard, 2004.

Stein, Gertrude, *Dix Portraits* (1930), New York, David Zwirner Books, 2022.

Stein, Gertrude, *Picasso* (1938), New York, Dover Publications, 1984.

Stein, Gertrude, *Selected Writings of Gertrude Stein*, London, Vintage, 1990.

Tardieu, Jean, *Le Miroir ébloui: Poèmes traduits des arts*, Paris, Gallimard, 'Blanche', 1993.

Varnedoe, Kirk, 'Picasso's self-portraits', in **Rubin**, William (ed.), *Picasso and Portraiture: Representation and Transformation*, London, Thames & Hudson, 1996.

Vasari, Giorgio, *The Lives of the Artists*, translated by Julia Conaway Bondanella and Peter Bondanella, Oxford, Oxford University Press, 2008.

Vollard Ambroise, *De Cézanne à Picasso: Mes portraits*, Paris, Séguier, 'Carré d'art', 1996.

Postscript

Year after year, I trawled through the archives and managed to track down 181 self-portraits. Sketches, drawings, etchings and paintings. (And it is entirely possible that there are others I could not find.) The purpose of putting together a definitive catalogue is to ensure that nothing that is not Picasso's own work is attributed to him; and to ensure that everything he produced is recognized as part of his oeuvre. Many of the works have not been 'verified', recognized as authentic. Sometimes for what appear to be very arbitrary 'reasons'. Which leads us to wonder whether Picasso's work has been 'censored', reduced to what some people would like it to be.

Despite the tireless efforts of the publisher, and vital help from the Picasso Administration, it has not been possible to reproduce all of Picasso's authenticated self-portraits in this book, as some collectors refused permission to reproduce the self-portrait – or self portraits – that they owned, and we had to do without.

It is a sad state of affairs that current laws and regulations allow 'rights holders' to refuse permission to reproduce an artist's work for seventy years after their death if they wish, even when this goes against the wishes of the artist, who wanted his work to be shared and seen by the greatest possible number of people. As Picasso died on 8 April 1973, his work will not be 'in the public domain' until 2043. Only then will this book finally be able to become what it should be now. A frustrating situation; in the cultural sphere, Proudhon's claim that 'property is theft' seems applicable.

Finally, I must thank Jean Penicaut for providing valuable information about a self-portrait from Picasso's youth, and I am grateful to Christine Pinault, who was kind enough to apply to collectors in the name of the Picasso Administration for the rights to reproduce (almost) all his self-portraits in this work.

Picture credits

Numerals below refer to illustration numbers.
All artworks: © Succession Picasso, 2021.

On the jacket: (front) AKG Images; (back): Private collection, Bridgeman Images (Private collection), Bridgeman Images, Courtesy of McClain Gallery, Houston.

ADAGP, Paris, 2021 : © Dora Maar: 122, 149.
AKG-images: 45, 71, 97, 111, 137; Album / Kocinsky: 7, 18, 30, 33, 80, 81, 82, 83, 84; Album/ sfgp: 162; Bernard Bonnfon: 157, 163; André Held: 78, 112.
Biblioteca de Catalunya, Barcelona: 35, 36.
Bridgeman Images: 6, 8, 90, 107, 116, 165; A. E. Gallatin Collection, 1950: 109; Archives Charmet: 44; Christie's: 15, 62, 63, 155, 159; © Iberfoto: 98; © Israel Museum, Jerusalem, Loan of Ayala and Sam Zacks, Toronto: 158; Musée national Picasso, Paris. Photo Josse: 53, 100, 101; © Luisa Ricciarini: 17; © Peter Willi: 164; Private collection: 15, 46, 47, 50, 63.
Collection Maurice Aeschimann: 38, 95, 124, 145.
Collection Catherine Hutin: Photo Claude Germain: 9, 99, 144.
Collection Geneviève Laporte: 156.
Courtesy of McClain Gallery, Houston: Collection particulière: 146.
Courtesy of Sotheby's: 66
Éditions Cahiers d'Art, Paris 2021: 27, 34, 40, 69, 70, 72, 75, 79, 153, 169.
Fondation Almine et Bernard Ruiz-Picasso para el Arte: © FABA Photo: Hugard & Vanoverschelde Photography: 17, 132, 136, 138, 139, 140.
Hakon Open Air Museum, chokoku-no-mori Art Foundation, Hakone-Machi: 161.
Moderna Museet, Stockholm: 88.
Museu Picasso, Barcelona: Photo Gasull Fotografia: 2, 4, 5, 10, 14, 19, 22, 24, 25, 26, 28, 29, 31, 32, 37, 52, 54, 56, 59, 64.
Museum Ludwig/ Rheinisches Bildarchiv, Cologne: 150.
National Gallery of Art, Washington: 57, 141.
Parisienne de photographie: 135.
Picasso Project, Sam Houston State University: 166.
Photo © President and Fellows of Harvard College: 77.
Private collections: 1, 3, 11, 12, 16, 42, 43, 49, 58, 60, 61, 65, 68, 74, 85, 86, 93, 101, 102, 123, 125, 131, 143, 160, 164, 167, 168.
RMN-GP: © David Douglas Duncan/ image RMN-GP: 147; Musée national Picasso, Paris / Image RMN-GP: 89, 122, 126, 127, 128, 142, 149; Musée national Picasso, Paris / Daniel Arnaudet: 41, 48, 154; Musée national Picasso, Paris / Adrien Didierjean: 92, 94, 106, 107, 117, 121, 152, 153; Musée national Picasso, Paris / Béatrice Hatala: 76, 91; Musée national Picasso, Paris / Thierry Le Mage: 13, 103, 120, 130; Musée national Picasso, Paris / Mathieu Rabeau: 21, 104, 105, 113, 114, 115, 117, 129, 133, 134; Metropolitan Museum of Art, Dist. RMN-Grand Palais / image of the MMA: 23, 73; BPK, Berlin, Dist. RMN-Grand Palais / Jens Ziehe: 96.
Santa Barbara Museum of Art: 110
Scala: 55; MoMA, Mrs John Hay Bequest: 51; MoMA: 90, 148.
Wadsworth Atheneum Museum of Art: 67.